D0354214

The Kitchen of the Governor's Palace
at Williamsburg.

PLATE I.

E. JONES.

COPYRIGHT, Colonial Williamsburg, Incorporated, in December of the Year 1938, and in accordance with the Acts of Congress whereby all Rights are reserved. Tenth Printing. ❧ ❧ ❧ ❧ ❧ ❧

THE
WILLIAMSBURG
ART OF COOKERY

OR,

Accomplish'd Gentlewoman's
COMPANION:

Being a Collection of upwards of Five
Hundred of the moſt Ancient &
Approv'd Recipes in *Virginia*
COOKERY.

Soups & Sauces,	Preserving,
Flesh & Fish,	Confectionery,
Breads,	Cakes,
Garden Stuff,	Puddings,
Pastry,	Wines, Punches, &c.

AND ALSO

A Table of favorite *Williamſburg* Garden HERBS.

To which is Added,

An Account of *Virginia* Hoſpitality; Treatiſes on the
various Branches of Cookery; an Account of Health
Drinking; ſome Conſiderations on the Obſervation
of *Chriſtmas* in *Virginia*, with traditional Recipes for
this Seaſon; with the Author's Explanation of the
Method of Collecting & Adapting theſe choice
Recipes; and an alphabetical INDEX to the Whole.

By Mrs. *HELEN BULLOCK*

WILLIAMSBURG:

Publiſhed by *Colonial Williamſburg* and printed
by *The Dietz Press, Inc.*, at *Richmond, Virginia.*
Diſtributed by *Holt, Rinehart and Winſton, Inc.*,
New York.   MCM,LXV.

PREFACE.

*T*HE *first* American *Book on the Art of Cookery,* The Compleat House-wife, or Accomplish'd Gentle-woman's Companion, *was printed in the Year 1742, by* William Parks *in* Williamſburg *in* Virginia. *Mr.* Parks *in his Preface, begged leave to inform his Readers that he had collected the Volume from one much larger, by Mrs.* E. Smith, *printed in* England. *He omitted Recipes containing Ingredients or Materials not to be had in* Virginia, *printing only thoſe uſeful or practicable here and leaving out ſuch as would merely ſerve to* "ſwell out the Book and "increaſe its Price."

In a City which is attempting to recapture a Paſt that was enriched by ſuch able Craftſmen as Mr. Parks, *it ſeems fitting that any Attempt to produce a* Williamſburg *Art of* Cookery *ſhould be guided by Purpoſes ſimilar to his own. This cookery Book, then, is intended as a Compilation of favorite* Virginia *Recipes, collected from Books known to have been uſed in* Virginia *Houſeholds. Some of theſe Books were printed in* England *and ſold in the local Shops, while others were printed in* Virginia. *The beſt*
Source

PREFACE.

Source of Virginia *Recipes proved to be the little handwritten Books kept by early Housewives and cherished by their Descendants. Recipes on Scraps of Paper pinned into printed Books or tucked between Pages often gave Directions beyond mere Cookery.* Mrs. B's *Recipe for* Cocoanut Pudding *in* Mrs. Coalter's *cook Book concluded,* "Now the most im-"portant Recipe is to take care of yourself, not only "for your own Family's Sake but for that of my "whole Household." Mrs. Taylor *warned* Mrs. Bruce *of the Potency of General* Taylor's Fish House Punch —"Walter *says look out for swell* "Head next Morning."

An Effort has been made to select, as Mr. Parks *would have selected,* "only such Recipes as are useful "and practicable here" — *but the Author being inte-rested also in a History of Cookery has been tempted to include a few such Monuments of Cookery as* An Egg as big as Twenty, Solomon's Temple in Flummery, Snail Broth, Lisbon Cake *and* Plumb Porridge for Christmas. *It is hoped that these Curiosities will divert and amuse the Reader without confusing the Cook.*

Some present-day Recipes are included with their Prototypes, showing, for Example, how Veal Glue, *or* Cake Soop for the Pocket, *may find its Way to the modern Table as tasty, clear Broth or jellied Consommé.*

The Recipes have been tested carefully and all those which have been proved in the Kitchens of the Market Square Tavern, *the* Travis House *and* Blair House *have been marked thus* (❋). *The professed Cook may attempt some of the unproved Recipes or may*
                                                         choose

PREFACE.

*chooſe to adapt them in her own Way, while the leſs
Experienced may proceed with the proved Recipes.*

*Any Worth in the preſent Volume may be attrib-
uted to the Generoſity of the many Virginians who
contributed to it their moſt treaſured Recipes, cookery
Books and old Letters. Much Gratitude is due to thoſe
who ſkillfully aided in teſting and adapting the
Recipes — and ſtill Others who worked with great
Pains and Patience in the Preparation and Printing
of this Volume.*

*The Author would add only one Word more before
offering this Volume as the* Accompliſh'd Gentle-
woman's Companion — *leſt a Failure in Cookery
be attributed to any Lack of Management in the
Preparation of this Book:*

> "Heaven sends good Meat,
> but the Devil sends Cooks."

H. B.

Contents.

CONTENTS.

Favorite

CONTENTS.

ILLUSTRATIONS.

"The Inhabitants

THE
WILLIAMSBURG
Art of Cookery:
OR,
Accomplish'd Gentlewoman's
COMPANION.

OF *VIRGINIA* HOSPITALITY

"THE Inhabitants are very courteous to Travellers, who need no other Recommendation but the being human Creatures. A Stranger has no more to do, but to inquire upon the Road, where any Gentleman, or good Housekeeper lives, and there he may depend upon being received with Hospitality."

When *Robert Beverley*, Gent., a Native and Inhabitant of that Place, wrote these Words in 1705 in his *History of Virginia*, he was writing of a Tradition of Hospitality already firmly established on *Virginia's* Soil. It is little Cause for Wonder, then,

that

that there was a Law of the *Virginia* Colony called
"An Act concerning Entertainment of Strangers",
which was deſigned to protect Strangers from ava-
ricious Perſons by providing that "every one ſhall
"be reputed to entertayne thoſe of Curteſie with
"whome they make not a certaine Agreement."

And ſuch was the Courteſy of theſe early *Virginians* that ſcarce a Traveller's Account or a Hiſtory written in that Day may be found which fails
to mention in ſome Way their open-handed Liber-
ality. In the *London Magazine* printed in July,
1746, an obſerving Traveller in *Virginia* wrote:

> All over the Colony, an univerſal Hoſpitality
> reigns; full Tables and open Doors, the kind
> Salute, the generous Detention, ſpeak ſomewhat
> like the old Roaſt-beef Ages of our Fore-fathers,
> and would almoſt perſuade one to think their
> Shades were wafted into theſe Regions, to enjoy
> with greater Extent, the Reward of their Virtues.
> (What is ſaid here is moſt ſtrictly true, for their
> Manner of living is quite generous and open:
> Strangers are ſought after with Greedineſs, as
> they paſs the Country, to be invited. Their Break-
> faſt Tables have generally the cold Remains of
> the former Day, haſh'd or fricaſſeed; Coffee, Tea,
> Chocolate, Veniſon-paſty, Punch, and Beer, or
> Cyder, upon one Board; their Dinner, good Beef,
> Veal, Mutton, Veniſon, Turkies and Geeſe, wild
> and tame, Fowls, boil'd and roaſted; and perhaps
> ſomewhat more, as Pies, Puddings, &c., for
> Deſſert: Suppers the ſame, with ſome ſmall Addi-
> tion, and a good hearty Cup to precede a Bed of
> Down: And this is the conſtant Life they lead,
> and to this Fare every Comer is welcome.)

When *Williamſburg*, in 1699, became the Capital of the Colony and Dominion of *Virginia*, it
became

became alſo the Center of its official Hoſpitality. The Capital City was actually planned for the Accommodation of the great Concourſe of People who would naturally be called to the Place where the General Aſſembly and Courts were held. Pub-lick Houſes and Taverns flouriſhed in *Williamſburg* and the private Dwellings in Publick Times were open for the Entertainment of the Thouſands who poured into the City. Within the magnificent Palace, which had been built at publick Expence as a Houſe for the royal Governors, there was a fine Appearance of Ladies and Gentlemen, good Diverſion and ſplendid Entertainment.

It is not ſurpriſing that this Reſponſibility for official Hoſpitality occaſionally reſted heavily upon the royal Governor in his Palace. His Politeneſs was ſuch that no Intimation of its Burdenſomeneſs eſcaped him except in his moſt intimate Letters. The popular Governor *Gooch* wrote Home in 1727 to his Brother (later Biſhop of *Norwich*):

> My firſt Introduction is attended with a great Charge, for the very Moment I was ſworn and ſwore all the Council, we proclaimed His Majeſty after which I did according to Cuſtom entertain the Town and all the Neighbours around us, and tho' I can't as yet ſend over any Money, you may depend upon it the very firſt Opportunity I have.

Two Months later the Governor was ſtill apolo-gizing for his Delay in the Matter of Remittances, explaining it as owing to his conſtant great Expence of Houſekeeping, proclaiming His Majeſty at firſt and keeping very magnificently his Birthday ſince. His Maintenance of his Station, he affirmed, was

as

as expenſive and ſtately as any in this Part of the World—ſo much ſo, in Fact, that he wrote frequently to his Brother of his Apprehenſions that the Charge of his preſent Grandeur would prevent, in his old Age, his ſecuring a fair Retreat to keep him from conſtantly walking on Foot after riding ſo long in his Coach and Six.

That the Governor enjoyed this Burden muſt not be doubted. He told his Brother that the Gentlemen and Ladies of *Virginia* were perfectly well bred, and there was not an ill Dancer in his Government.

When News reached *Williamſburg* of the Battle of *Culloden*, Governor *Gooch*, though confined to the Palace ſuffering from an old Wound received in the *Carthagena* Campaign, ſaw ſuch an Occaſion for Rejoicing amongſt loyal Subjects of the King that he contributed handſomely to the Feſtivities. The *Virginia Gazette* of July 18, 1746, deſcribes the Celebration:

On receiving the News, in this City, of the glorious Victory gain'd over the Rebels, by his Royal Highneſs, the Duke of *Cumberland*, an univerſal Joy diffuſ'd among all Ranks of Perſons; the General Aſſembly being met, and much Company in Town, a grand Entertainment was made at the Capitol, on *Tueſday* Night, ſuitable to the extraordinary Occaſion, by the Honourable the Preſident and Council, Mr. Speaker, and the reſt of the Houſe of Burgeſſes; to which his Honour the Governor, who continues indiſpoſ'd, was pleaſ'd to contribute very largely. In the Evening a very numerous Company of Gentlemen and Ladies appear'd at the Capitol, where a Ball was open'd, and after dancing ſome Time, withdrew to
Supper,

Supper, there being a very handſome Collation
ſpread on three Tables, in three different Rooms,
conſiſting of near 100 Diſhes, after the moſt delicate Taſte. There was alſo provided a great Variety
of the choiceſt and beſt Liquors, in which the
Healths of the King, the Prince and Princeſs of
Wales, the Duke, and the reſt of the Royal Family, the Governor, Succeſs to his Majeſty's Arms,
Proſperity to this Colony, and many other loyal
Healths were cheerfully drank, and a Round of
Cannon, which were remov'd to the Capitol for
this Purpoſe, was diſcharg'd at each Health, to
the Number of 18 or 20 Rounds, which laſted 'til
near 2 o'Clock. The whole Affair was conducted
with great Decency and good Order, and an un-
affected Chearfullneſs appeared in the Counte-
nances of the Company. All the Houſes in the
City were illuminated, and a very large Bon-fire
was made in the Market-Place, 3 Hogſheads of
Punch given to the Populace; and the whole concluded with the greateſt Demonſtrations of Joy
and Loyalty.

Hoſpitality was not the excluſive Virtue of the
Gentry who attended the elegant Birthnight Balls
or other Entertainments at the Palace, or who
made ſuch a handſome Appearance at Dancing
Aſſemblies in the Capitol and the *Raleigh* Tavern—
it characteriſed all Ranks of People.

Lord *Adam Gordon* wrote in his *Journal* in 1765
of the extreme Civility of the People of *Williamſburg* toward Strangers; and many Years after the
Turmoil and Excitement of Publick Times had
ſubſided in the former Capital, *William Wirt*, in
1806, wrote affectionately of the old City, *"Wil-
"liamſburg* is juſt as beautiful and hoſpitable as
"ever."

Williamſburg,

Williamſburg, as a reſtored City, is ſo remindful of the City which ſerved as a Capital and Metropolis for *Virginia* from 1699 to 1779, that a modern Author can find no better Words with which to deſcribe it than thoſe firſt written more than a Century ago:

"*Williamſburg* is juſt as beautiful and hoſpitable "as ever."

❀❀❀❀❀❀❀❀❀❀❀❀❀❀❀❀❀❀❀

Obſervations upon SOUPS.

WHEN one reflects that two Centuries ago Soup was of ſuch Importance in the Diet that the Soup Tureen was upon practically every Table and the wiſe Traveller carried Soup in his Pocket on long Journeys, it ſeems ſtrange to find it of ſo little Conſequence Today.

The thoughtful Reader who is alſo an accompliſh'd Cook would find much Profit in ſtudying the Herbs, Seaſonings and Vegetables that gave theſe old Soups their Diſtinction. He may not find Pocket Soup as neceſſary as did that compleat Gentleman, *William Byrd* of *Weſtover* in *Virginia*, Eſquire, who, in 1729, recommended his favorite Recipe to Foreſters in his *Hiſtory of the Dividing Line*, ſaying:

". . . This Glue is ſo ſtrong, that two or three Drams, diſſolv'd in boiling Water, with a little Salt, will make half a Pint of good Broth, & if
you

you shou'd be faint with Fasting or Fatigue, let a small Piece of this Glue melt in your Mouth, and you will find yourself surprisingly refreshed.

One Pound of this Cookery wou'd keep a Man in good Heart above a Month, and is not only nourishing, but likewise very wholesome. Particularly it is good against Fluxes, which Woodsmen are very liable to, by lying too near the moist Ground, and guzzling too much cold Water. But as it will be only us'd now and then, in Times of Scarcity, when Game is wanting, two Pounds of it will be enough for a Journey of six Months.

But this Broth will be still more heartening if you thicken every Mess with half a Spoonful of Rockahominy, which is nothing but *Indian* Corn parched without burning, and reduced to Powder. . . . "

Soup had also its Place in the Literature of the Day and in 1760 when the Life and Opinions of *Tristram Shandy*, Gent., were on every Tongue, The *Gentleman's Magazine* appropriately published

A Recipe for a Soup for Tristram Shandy

TAKE a Knuckle of Veal,
   You may buy it, or steal;
In a few Pieces cut it,
   In a Stewing-pan put it;

Salt, Pepper, and Mace,
   Must season your Knuckle;
Then, what's join'd to a * Place,
   With other Herbs muckle.

That which † killed King *Will*,
And what ‡ never stands still:
Some § Sprigs of that Bed,
Whence Children are bred.
This much you will mend, it
Both Spinnage and Endive,

---
*Salary. †Sorrel ‡Thyme. §Parsley

And Lettice and Beet,
With Marygolds, meet.
Put no Water at all,
For it maketh things ſmall;
Which, leſt it ſhould happen,
A cloſe Cover clap on;
Put your Pot, of *Wood's* Metal,
In a boiling-hot Kettle.

And there let it be,
 (Mark the Doctrine I teach)
About (let me ſee)
 Thrice as long as you preach.

Then ſkimming the Fat off,
Say Grace with your Hat off;
Oh then with what Rapture,
Will it fill Dean and Chapter!

Soups & Sauces

Aſparagus Soup

TAKE four large Bunches of Aſparagus, ſcrape
it nicely, cut off one Inch of the Tops, and lay
them in Water, chop the Stalks and put them on
the Fire with a Piece of Bacon, a large Onion cut
up, Pepper and Salt, and two Quarts of Water; boil
them till the Stalks are quite ſoft, then pulp them
through a Sieve, and ſtrain the Water to it, which
muſt be put back in the Pot; put into it a Chicken
cut up, with the Tops of Aſparagus which had
been laid by, boil it until theſe laſt Articles are ſufficiently done, thicken with Flour, Butter, and
Milk, and ſerve it up.

(Mrs. *Mary Randolph's* Virginia Houſewife, 1831)

Another

Another Way *

WASH and remove the Tips from a Bunch of fresh green Asparagus, and simmer them until tender in a little Milk. Cut up the Stalks of the Asparagus, add one fourth Cupful of chopped Onion and one fourth Cupful of chopped Celery, and boil about half an Hour in six Cups of Meat Broth. Rub through a coarse Sieve, and place your Pan over boiling Water. Add a rich Cream-sauce made of three Tablespoonfuls of melted Butter, three of Flour and half a Cup of Cream. Add the Tips last.

(Mrs. *Randolph's* Recipe, 1831.
Adapted *Blair* Kitchen, 1938.)

To make Scotch *Barley-broth*

TAKE a Leg of Beef, chop it all to Pieces, boil it in three Gallons of Water with a Piece of Carrot and a Crust of Bread, till it is half boiled away; then strain it off, and put it into the Pot again with half a Pound of Barley, four or five Heads of Celery, washed clean and cut small, a large Onion, a Bundle of Sweet-herbs, a little Parsley, chopped small, and a few Marigolds. Let this boil an Hour. Take a Cock or large Fowl, clean picked and washed, and put into the Pot; boil it till the Broth is quite good, then season with Salt, and send it to Table, with the Fowl in the Middle. This Broth is very good without the Fowl. Take out the Onion and Sweet-herbs before you send it to Table.

Some make this Broth with a Sheep's-head instead of a Leg of Beef, and it is very good; but you must chop the Head all to Pieces. The thick Flank

(about

(about ſix Pounds to ſix Quarts of Water) makes
good Broth; then put the Barley in with the Meat,
firſt ſkim it well, boil it an Hour very ſoftly, then
put in the above Ingredients, with Turnips and
Carrots clean ſcraped and pared, and cut in little
Pieces. Boil all together ſoftly, till the Broth is very
good; then ſeaſon it with Salt, and ſend it to Table,
with the Beef in the Middle, Turnips and Carrots
round, and pour the Broth over all.

(Mrs. Glaſſe's Art of Cookery, London, 1774.)

Or do it thus ✻

TAKE three Pounds of Beef and one Pound of
Veal. Chop it all to Pieces and put it on to boil
ſoftly in one Gallon of cold Water with a Carrot
and a Cruſt of Bread till it is half boiled away;
then ſtrain it off and add two Cups of Celery
waſhed clean and chopped ſmall, a large Onion, a
Bundle of Sweet-herbs and a little Parſley chopped
ſmall. Let this cook an Hour then ſtrain again.
Then add one Tableſpoonful of Barley to each
Quart of the Broth and cook thirty or forty Minutes until the Barley is enough.

(Mrs. Glaſſe's Recipe, 1774, adapted
Market Square Tavern Kitchen, 1937.)

Barley Soup ✻

PUT on three Gills of Barley, three Quarts of
Water, few Onions cut up, ſix Carrots ſcraped
and cut into Dice, an equal Quantity of Turnips
cut ſmall; boil it gently two Hours, then put in
four or five Pounds of the Rack or Neck of Mutton

ton, a few Slices of lean Ham, with Pepper and Salt; boil it ſlowly two Hours longer and ſerve it up. Tomatoes are an excellent Addition to this Soup.

(Mrs. *Mary Randolph's* Virginia Houſewife, 1831.)

Beef Broth*

TAKE off the Fat and Skin of a Pound of lean Beef, and cut it into Pieces. Then put it into a Gallon of Water, with the Under-cruſt of a Penny-loaf, and a very little Salt. Let it boil till it be reduced to two Quarts, then ſtrain it off, and it will be very nouriſhing. In ſome Caſes, when the ſick Perſon be very weak, the Phyſician will order Beef-tea, which muſt be made thus: Take a Piece of lean Beef, cut it croſs and croſs, and then pour on it ſcalding Water. Cover it up cloſe, and let it ſtand till it be cold. Then pour it off as you want it, ſeaſon it moderately, and give it to the ſick Perſon, having firſt warmed it.

(Mr. *Farley's* Recipe, 1787, adapted *Market Square Tavern* Kitchen, 1937.)

Beef Soup*

PUT four pounds good Rump Steak in a Pot. Add five Quarts of cold Water and bring to boil. When boiling, add one Spoonful Salt, and boil for two Hours. Prepare and cut in large Pieces and add ſlowly three Onions, two Carrots, one Turnip, one Parſnip, one ſmall Cabbage, one ſmall Head of Celery, four Cloves, Bundle of Parſley, Bay-leaf, Thyme, Marjoram, and twenty Peppercorns. Cook another two Hours. Strain and cut up Vegetables into

into ſmall Cubes excepting the Cabbage. Cut two
Rolls in Slices and toaſt in Oven. Put all in a large
Tureen and heat thoroughly. Sprinkle over with
one Spoonful chopped Parſley and ſerve. Place
Meat and Cabbage on ſeparate Diſh and ſerve it up.

(A *Richmond* Family Recipe. Prov'd.)

Beef Soup *

TAKE the hind Shin of Beef, cut all the Fleſh
off the Leg-bone, which muſt be taken away
entirely, or the Soup will be greaſy. Waſh the
Meat clean and lay it in a Pot, ſprinkle over it one
ſmall Tableſpoonful of pounded black Pepper
and two of Salt; three Onions the Size of a Hen's
Egg, cut ſmall, ſix ſmall Carrots ſcraped and cut
up, two ſmall Turnips pared and cut into Dice;
pour on three Quarts of Water, cover the Pot cloſe,
and keep it gently and ſteadily boiling five Hours,
which will leave about three Pints of clear Soup;
do not let the Pot boil over, but take off the Scum
carefully, as it riſes. When it has boiled four Hours,
put in a ſmall Bundle of Thyme and Parſley, and a
Pint of Celery cut ſmall, or a Teaſpoonful of
Celery-ſeed pounded. Theſe latter Ingredients
would loſe their delicate Flavour if boiled too
much. Juſt before you take it up, brown it in the
following Manner: put a ſmall Tableſpoonful of
nice brown Sugar into an iron Skillet, ſet it on the
Fire and ſtir it till it melts and looks very dark,
pour into it a Ladlefull of the Soup, a little at a
Time, ſtirring it all the While. Strain this Browning
and mix it well with the Soup, take out the Bundle
of

of Thyme and Parſley, put the niceſt Pieces of
Meat in your Tureen, and pour on the Soup and
Vegetables; put in ſome toaſted Bread cut in Dice,
and ſerve it up.

(Recipe, 1831, Prov'd *Market
Square Tavern* Kitchen, 1937.)

Savoury Tomato Soup *

TO four Pounds of Beef Knuckles and Briſket,
add ſeveral Sprigs of Parſley, ſome Celery Tops,
four Stalks of Celery, one Onion, one Tableſpoon of
pickling Spices, Salt and Pepper. Cover with cold
Water and ſimmer gently for about five Hours.
Add one Tableſpoon each of Marjoram and Thyme
and one Blade of Mace. Cook about thirty Minutes. Settle with Egg Shells and ſtrain through a
Cloth. To this Stock add one Part of ſtrong Tomato
Juice to two Parts of Stock.

(Mrs. *Randolph*'s Recipe, 1831,
Adapted *Travis* Houſe, 1938.)

Calf's Head Soup *

WASH well and ſcald one Calf's Head. Put it to
boil in three Quarts of cold Water. Boil gently for five Hours, taking off Scum as it riſes; then
add one Onion, a Bunch of Parſley and Marjoram,
one Bay-leaf and Salt and boil one more Hour.
Strain and cool. Make ſmall Forc'd-meat Balls the
Size of a Walnut of Meat chopped from the Head,
grated Lemon Rind, chopped Parſley, one Egg, one
Tableſpoonful of Flour and Salt and Pepper. Fry
theſe well in Butter. Boil Soup and thicken with
three Tableſpoonfuls of Butter mixed with Flour.
Put

Put Forc'd-meat Balls into Tureen, pour boiling Soup over them, add one Glaſsful of Sherry or *Madeira* and ſerve it up.

(Old Recipe from *Kenbridge, Virginia.*)

Cheſtnut Soup

TAKE a Half Hundred of Cheſtnuts and notch them; put them in an earthen Pan, in a warm Oven for Half an Hour. Stew them one Hour in a Quart of Veal or Beef Broth; in the Meantime, take three or four Pieces of lean Ham or Bacon and put them at the Bottom of the Stew-pan, one Pound of Veal, one Pound of Beef, a Pigeon cut into Pieces, two Onions ſtuck with Cloves, two Blades of Mace, a Bundle of Sweet-herbs over the Ham, with half a Pint of Water; ſtew it gently till it ſticks, but muſt not burn; pour off boiling Water, and ſkim it well; ſtuff two Pigeons with Forc'd-meat, and ſtew them in the Soup till tender; then take the Pigeons out and ſtrain the Soup to the Cheſtnuts; ſeaſon it with Pepper and Salt to your Palate, and boil it up for five Minutes; put the Pigeons into the Tureen, the Cheſtnuts round them and pour the Soup, boiling hot, over them. Add two or three Pieces of criſp Bread at the Top; garniſh the Edge of the Diſh with ſome of the Cheſtnuts, ſplit in two.

N. B.—If you have a Partridge, you may uſe it inſtead of the Pigeons cut to Pieces.

(Recipe, 1797, from *Cheſter, Virginia.*)

Chowder,

Chowder, a Sea Dish *

TAKE any Kind of firm Fiſh, cut it in Pieces ſix Inches long, ſprinkle Salt and Pepper over each Piece, cover the Bottom of a ſmall *Dutch* Oven with Slices of Salt-pork about half boiled, lay in the Fiſh, ſtrewing a little chopped Onion between; cover with Crackers that have been ſoaked ſoft in Milk, pour over it two Gills of white Wine, and two of Water; put on the Top of the Oven, and ſtew it gently about an Hour; take it out carefully, and lay it in a deep Diſh; thicken the Gravy with a little Flour and a Spoonful of Butter, add ſome chopped Parſley, boil it a few Minutes, and pour it over the Fiſh—ſerve it up hot.

(Mrs. *Mary Randolph*'s Virginia Houſewife, 1831.)

Cat Fiſh Chowder *

WASH the Fiſh in warm Water, put it on in juſt Water enough to cover, boil until tender, or until the Bones will ſlip out; take out the largeſt Bones, chop up the Fiſh, put in a Stew-pan with a Pint of Water, a large Lump of Butter, one Cup of Cream, Pepper and not much Salt; one Onion, Teaſpoonful Muſtard, one-half Teaſpoonful of Walnut Catſup. Stew until quite thick, garniſh with sliced Lemon and ſerve hot.

(Old Recipe from *Toano*, *Virginia*.)

Clam Chowder *

CUT in fine Dice five medium Potatoes, one large Onion, two Slices of fried Bacon. Simmer this Mixture in the Clam Liquor with equal Amount

Amount of Water until Potatoes are ſoft but un-
broken. To this Mixture add one Pint thin Cream
and bring to a Boil. Seaſon with Salt and Pepper
and add finely chopped Parſley. Add twenty
finely-chopped Clams, five Minutes before ſerving.

(Adapted, 1937, from old Recipe.)

Cream Chicken Soup *

CUT up one Fowl, then ſimmer ſlowly in Water
to cover. Strain Broth and cool. Take off four
Tableſpoonfuls of the Fat and brown the Fowl in
it, then add the Broth, one chopped Onion, Salt,
and Pepper. Cook well one Cupful of Rice and add
it to the Broth and Fowl. Turn ſlowly over two
beaten Eggs, ſtrew with Parſley, chopped fine.

(Recipe from *Courtland, Virginia,* in uſe ſince 1780.)

Giblet Soup *

BOIL ſlowly one Pint of dried *Engliſh* Peaſe for
five Hours in nearly one Gallon of Water. Add
one Pound of Giblets, one Dozen of Cloves, one
ſmall Piece of red Pepper, and Salt. When Peaſe
are well cooked, ſtrain through a Sieve, cut Giblets
into ſmall Pieces, return to Soup, boil up and
ſerve.   (Old Recipe, *Toano, Virginia*)

Gumbo Soup *

TAKE a Fowl of good Size, cut it up, ſeaſon it
with Salt and Pepper, and dredge it with
Flour. Take the Soup-kettle, and put in it a
Tableſpoonful of Butter, one of Lard, and one of
Onions

Onions chopped fine. Next fry the Fowl till well-browned, and add four Quarts of boiling Water. The Pot ſhould now, being well covered, be allowed to ſimmer for a Couple of Hours. Then put in twenty or thirty Oyſters, a Handful of chopped Okra or Gumbo, and a very little Thyme, and let it ſimmer for a half an Hour longer. Juſt before ſerving it up, add about half a Tableſpoonful of curry Powder. This Soup is uſually eaten with the Addition of a little *Cayenne* Pepper, and is delicious.

(Old *Williamſburg* Recipe, c-1837, from Mrs. *Elizabeth Labbé Cole's* Collection.)

A Stock for an Herb-Soup

GET Chervil, Beets, Chards, Spinach, Sellery, Leeks, and ſuch like Herbs, with two or three large Cruſts of Bread, ſome Butter, a Bunch of Sweet-herbs, and a little Salt; put theſe, with a moderate Quantity of Water, into a Kettle, and boil them for an Hour and a half, and ſtrain out the Liquor through a Sieve, and it will be a good Stock for Soups, either of Aſparagus Buds, Lettuce, or any other Kind fit for Lent or Faſt-Days.

(The Lady's Companion, 1753; Cook Book owned by Miſs *Anna Maria Dandridge*, 1756.)

Mullagatawny Soup*

CUT up two Chickens as for Fricaſſee, place them in a Stew-pan, in which previouſly put Carrot, Onion, Celery, Parſley, Thyme, Bay-leaf, Cloves, and Mace; fill up with good Veal Broth, and when the Members of the Chicken are nearly done

done ſtrain them off into a Sieve, ſaving their Broth in a Baſin. Cool the Pieces of Chicken in Water, and then take them up on a clean Napkin, trim them neatly, and place them in a Soup-pot to put into the Soup afterward. Then cut four large Onions in Halves, taking out the Head or Root Part, and again cut theſe into Slices; place them in a Stew-pan with four Ounces of Butter, a cooked Carrot, and two Heads of cooked Celery cut ſmall, and fry theſe over a ſlow Fire until the Onion is nearly melted, and become of a fine light-brown Color, then throw in as much Flour as will ſuffice to thicken the Quantity of Soup you wiſh to make; ſtir this on the Fire two or three Minutes, and after adding a good Tableſpoonful of Curry Powder, and the ſame Quantity of Curry Paſte, proceed gradually to mix in with theſe firſt, the Broth the Chickens were boiled in, and afterward as much more Conſomme of Veal as may be found requiſite to produce the Quantity of Soup deſired. Place this on the Fire, ſtirring it the whole Time, and as ſoon as it boils, put it by the Side of the Stove to clarify itſelf in the uſual Way; then rub it through the Tammy, and pour it upon the Pieces of Chicken. Half an Hour before Dinner-time, place the Soup on the Stove, ſtir it till it boils, continue boiling gently for ten Minutes, by which Time the Chickens will be cooked; ſkim the Soup; ſee that the Seaſoning is right, and ſend to Table with two Plates of plain boiled Rice, to be paſſed with the Soup.

(Old *Williamſburg* Recipe, c-1837, from Mrs. *Elizabeth Labbé Cole's* Collection. Prov'd 1937.)

Ochra

Ochra Soup *

GET two double Handfuls of young Ochra, waſh and ſlice it thin, add two Onions chopped fine, put it into a Gallon of Water at a very early Hour in an earthen Pipkin, or very nice iron Pot; it muſt be kept ſteadily ſimmering, but not boiling: put in Pepper and Salt. At twelve o'Clock, put in a Handful of *Lima* Beans; at half-paſt one o'Clock, add three young Cimlins cleaned and cut in ſmall Pieces, a Fowl, or Knuckle of Veal, a Bit of Bacon or Pork that has been boiled, and ſix Tomatos, with the Skin taken off; when nearly done, thicken with a Spoonful of Butter, mixed with one of Flour. Have Rice boiled to eat with it.

.(Mrs. *Mary Randolph's* Virginia Houſewife, 1831)

An Onion Soup, call'd The King's Soup *

TAKE ſome Onions cut in very thin Slices, ſtew them till tender, in a ſmall Quantity of Water, then add Milk, let it all boil together, at leaſt half an Hour, with a pretty many Blades of Mace, and a quarter of a Pound of freſh Butter; a little before it is taken up, thicken it with the Yolks of two Eggs well beaten, and ſome Parſley, pick'd and chopp'd very ſmall; ſalt to your Taſte: Serve it up with Toaſt cut in Dice.

About four large Onions will do to two Quarts of Milk.

(The Lady's Companion, 1753; Cook Book owned by Miſs *Anna Maria Dandridge*, 1756.)

Another

Another Way*

SOME prefer to prepare this Soup as above directed, but add one Tablespoonful of Flour to Half of the Butter just before serving and use one whole Egg beaten well for thickening.

(*Market Square Tavern* Kitchen, 1937.)

Oyster Soup*

PUT one Pint of Oysters into a Sauce-pan with Pepper and Salt. Cover at once and cook until Gills of Oysters begin to curl. Heat one Pint of Milk and add one Tablespoonful of Flour and Butter which have been mixed together. Add to Oysters slowly and add Salt and Pepper. A beaten Egg added to the Soup before serving is a great Addition. Serve sprinkled with chopped Parsley.

(*Market Square Tavern* Kitchen, 1937.)

Black-eye Pea Soup*

WASH one Quart of Black-eye Peas well in cold Water and soak over-night. Put them to cook in four Quarts of cold Water with Salt, Pepper, one half Pound of Bacon or one Ham Bone until Peas are tender. Pass through a Sieve, rub together one Tablespoonful of Flour and one of Butter and thicken the Soup. Add one half Spoonful of Walnut Catsup Serve hot with toasted Bread cut in Dice.

(Old *Richmond* family Recipe.
Tested in *Williamsburg*, 1937.)

Dried

Dried Pea Soup *

TAKE one Quart of ſplit Peas, or *Lima* Beans,
which are better; put them in three Quarts of
very ſoft Water with three Onions chopped up,
Pepper and Salt; boil them two Hours; maſh them
well and paſs them through a Sieve; return the
Liquid into the Pot, thicken it with a large Piece
of Butter and Flour, put in ſome Slices of nice ſalt
Pork, and a large Teaſpoonful of Celery-ſeed
pounded; boil it till the Pork is done, and ſerve it
up; have ſome toaſted Bread cut into Dice and
fried in Butter, which muſt be put in the Tureen
before you pour in the Soup.

(Mrs. *Mary Randolph's* Virginia Houſewife, 1831.)

Williamſburg *Split Pea Soup* *

WASH and ſoak one Pound of dried ſplit Peas
for about three Hours. Put them on to cook
in three Quarts of cold Water, with one large
Onion, a Ham Bone, Pepper and Salt. Cook ſlowly
about three Hours until Soup is thick and Peas
very ſoft. Strain through a coarſe Sieve and ſerve
hot with toaſted Bread cut in Dice.

(Mrs. *Cole's* Recipe, c-1837, adapted
Market Square Tavern Kitchen, 1937.)

Green Pea Soup *

MAKE it exactly as you do the dried pea Soup,
only in Place of Celery-ſeed, put a Handful
of Mint chopped ſmall, and a Pint of young Peas,
which muſt be boiled in the Soup till tender;
thicken it with a quarter of a Pound of Butter,
and two Spoonfuls of Flour.

(Mrs. *Mary Randolph's* Virginia Houſewife, 1831.)

To

To make a Veal Glue, or Cake Soup to be carried in the Pocket

TAKE a Leg of Veal, strip it of the Skin and the Fat, then take all the muscular or fleshy Parts from the Bones; boil this Flesh gently in such a Quantity of Water, and so long a Time, till the Liquor will make a strong Jelly when it is cold: This you may try by taking out a small Spoonful now and then, and letting it cool. Here it is to be supposed, that though it will jelly presently in small Quantities, yet all the Juice of the Meat may not be extracted; however, when you find it very strong, strain the Liquor through a Sieve, and let it settle; then provide a large Stew-pan, with Water, and some *China* Cups, or glazed Earthenware; fill these Cups with Jelly taken clear from the Settling, and set them in a Stew-pan of Water, and let the Water boil gently till the Jelly becomes as thick as Glue; after which, let them stand to cool, and then turn out the Glue upon a Piece of new Flannel, which will draw out the Moisture; turn them once in six or eight Hours, and put them upon a fresh Flannel, and so continue to do till they are quite dry, and keep it in a dry warm Place: This will harden so much, that it will be stiff and hard as Glue in a little Time, and may be carried in the Pocket without Inconvenience. You are to use this by boiling about a Pint of Water, and pouring it upon a Piece of the Glue or Cake, about the Bigness of a small Walnut, and stirring it with a Spoon till the Cake dissolves, which will make very strong good Broth. As for the seasoning

Part,

Part, every one may add Pepper and Salt as they
like it, for there muſt be nothing of that Kind put
among the Veal when you make the Glue, for any
Thing of that Sort would make it mouldy. As we
have obſerved above, that there is nothing of
Seaſoning in this Soup, ſo there may be always
added what you deſire, either of Spices or Herbs,
to make it ſavoury to the Palate; but it muſt be
noted, that all the Herbs that are uſed on this
Occaſion, muſt be boiled tender in plain Water,
and that Water muſt be uſed to pour upon the
Cake Gravy inſtead of Simple Water: So may a
Diſh of good Soup be made without Trouble, only
allowing the Proportion of Cake Gravy anſwering
to the aboveſaid Direction: Or if Gravy be wanted
for Sauce, double the Quantity may be uſed that
is preſcribed for Broth or Soup.

(The Lady's Companion, 1753; Cook Book owned
by Miſs *Anna Maria Dandridge*, 1756.)

Pocket Soup on a new Plan*

CUT three Pounds of lean Veal from the Leg in
ſmall Pieces and cook ſlowly in three Quarts
of cold Water with a Bundle of Sweet-herbs, a
large Onion and ſome chopped Parſley about four
Hours. Strain well and add one Teaſpoonful of
Gelatin for each Pint of the Broth and ſet in a
very cold Place. Serve this as a cold jellied Broth.
If you omit your Gelatin you may ſerve your Soup
hot as a clear Broth.

(*Market Square Tavern* Kitchen, 1937.)

Snail

Snail Broth

WITH this, which is alſo a medicinal Broth, and very excellent in its Kind, we ſhall cloſe the preſent Chapter; it is one of thoſe Foods that may ſave much Money to the Phyſicians, and we ſhould do wiſely to copy the Practice of thoſe who find it ſo.

Pick twenty Garden Snails out of their Shells, and pound them in a marble Mortar; take the hinder Legs of thirty Frogs, pound them with the Snails, and put them into a Pot with three Quarts of Water and a little Salt; pare and ſlice very thin a Dozen fine Turnips, and ſlice alſo one large Leek, firſt ſtripping off the outer Skin; put theſe into the Pot, and add a double Handful of pearl Barley, and twenty Grains of Saffron.

Let all boil together till there is but a Quart left, run this through a Sieve without ſqueezing, and let it be taken at two Meſſes.

It is a very agreeably-flavoured Broth, though it taſtes weak. Many have recovered from the Beginning of Conſumptions by this Broth alone.

(Mrs. *Martha Bradley's* Britiſh Houſewife.)

Williamſburg *Savoury Jelly* ⁎

PUT three Pounds of lean Beaf and two Pounds of Fore-quarter of Veal with the Veal Bones into one Gallon of cold Water. Add three large Onions, three Carrots, three Turnips, some Sprigs of Parſley, Thyme, Marjoram, and Savoury with Salt & Pepper to taſte. Cook ſlowly until reduced by half. Strain through a Sieve. The next Day re-move

move Fat & bring to a Boil. Add one Cup of White-wine, three Slices of Lemon, the Whites of two Eggs beaten, and their Shells. Bring to a Boil again, and boil for two Minutes. Let ſtand twenty Minutes and ſtrain through doubled Cheeſe-cloth. This may be ſerved hot as a Broth, or by adding two Tableſpoonfuls of Gelatin at the laſt, may be chilled and ſerved as ſavoury Jelly.

(Mrs. *Randolph's* Recipe, 1831, adapted *Market Square Tavern* Kitchen, 1937.)

Celery Sauce*

WASH and pare a large Bunch of Celery very clean, cut it into little Bits, and boil it ſoftly till it is tender; add half a Pint of Cream, ſome Mace, Nutmeg, and a ſmall Piece of Butter rolled in Flour; then boil it gently. This is a good Sauce for roaſted or boiled Fowls, Turkeys, Partridges, or any other Game.

(Mrs. *Mary Randolph's* Virginia Houſewife, 1831.)

To fry Cucumbers for Mutton Sauce*

YOU muſt brown ſome Butter in a Pan and cut the Cucumbers in thin Slices; drain them from the Water, then fling them into the Pan, and when they are fried brown, put in a little Pepper and Salt, a Bit of an Onion and Gravy, and let them ſtew together, and ſqueeze in ſome Juice of Lemon; ſhake them well, and put them under your Mutton.

(*E. Smith's* Compleat Houſewife, *Williamſburg*, 1742.)

Common

Common Sauce *

PLAIN Butter melted thick, with a Spoonful of Walnut Pickle or Catsup, is a very good Sauce; but you may put as many Things as you choose into Sauces.

(Mrs. *Mary Randolph's* Virginia Housewife, 1831.)

Curry Powder *

ONE Ounce Turmeric, one do. Coriander Seed, one do. Cummin Seed, one do. white Ginger, one of Nutmeg, one of Mace, and one of *Cayenne* Pepper; pound all together, and pass them through a fine Sieve; bottle and cork it well—one Teaspoonful is sufficient to season any made Dish.

(Mrs. *Mary Randolph's* Virginia Housewife, 1831.)

To make Egg Sauce *

BOIL four Eggs for ten Minutes, chop half the Whites, put them with the Yelks, and chop them both together, but not very fine; put them into a quarter of a Pound of good melted Butter, and put it in a Boat.

(Mrs. *Mary Randolph's* Virginia Housewife, 1831.)

Horse-radish Sauce *

MIX together one Teacupful grated Horse-radish, one Tablespoonful ground Mustard, one Tablespoonful Sugar, four Tablespoonfuls Vinegar, (or Olive Oil if preferred), Pepper and Salt to Taste and one Teaspoonful Turmeric.

(Recipe from an old *Williamsburg* Cook Book.)

A

A Sauce for Fiſh in Lent, *or at any Time*

TAKE a little Thyme, Horſe-radiſh, a Bit of
Onion, Lemon-peel, and whole Pepper; boil
them a little in fair Water; then put in two Anchovies, and four Spoonfuls of White-wine, then
ſtrain them out, and put the Liquor into the
ſame Pan again, with a Pound of freſh Butter;
and when 'tis melted take it off the Fire, and ſtir
in the Yolks of two Eggs well beaten, with three
Spoonfuls of White-wine; ſet it on the Fire again,
and keep it ſtirring till 'tis the Thickneſs of
Cream, and pour it hot over your Fiſh. Garniſh
with Lemon and Horſe-radiſh.

(*E. Smith's* Compleat Houſewife, *Williamſburg*, 1742.)

To make a Sauce for a Gooſe *

PARE, core and ſlice ſome Apples; put them in
a Sauce-pan, with as much Water as will keep
them from burning, ſet them over a very ſlow
Fire, keep them cloſely covered till reduced to a
Pulp, then put in a Lump of Butter, and Sugar to
your Taſte, beat them well, and ſend them to the
Table in a *China* Bowl.

(Mrs. *Mary Randolph's* Virginia Houſewife, 1831.)

Minced Sauce *

CUT Onions, Muſhrooms, and Truffles, if you
have any, very ſmall, with Capers, and Anchovies, and keep them ſeparately; put into a
Stew-pan a little Butter with your Onions; put
your Stew-pan over a briſk Fire; give it two or
three

three Toſſes; then put in your Muſhrooms and
Truffles ſtrewing over them a Duſt of Flour, and
moiſten them with good Gravy, then put in it
your Capers and Anchovies, with a Glaſs of White-
wine; thicken your Sauce with a Spoonful of
Cullis. Let it be of a good Taſte, and you may uſe
it with all Diſhes with a minc'd Sauce.

(The Lady's Companion, 1753; Cook Book
owned by Miſs *Anna Maria Dandridge*, 1756.)

Muſhroom Sauce*

TAKE one Cup of Muſhrooms and cut them in
two, put them in a Pan with three Tableſpoonfuls of Butter and cook gently ſhaking your Pan.
Strew over this two Tableſpoonfuls of Flour, add
one Cup of Cream and cook ſlowly for eight Minutes. Add Salt and Pepper.

(Mrs. *Randolph's* Recipe, 1831. Adapted
Market Square Tavern Kitchen, 1937.)

Poor Man's Sauce with Oil*

CHOP a Handful of Leaves of Parſley picked
from the Stalks, make it very fine, and ſtrew
over it a little Salt; ſhred fine half a Dozen young
Onions, taking off two of the Skins; add theſe to
the Parſley, and put them into a Baſon with three
Spoonfuls of Oil; add to this ſome Vinegar to give
it a little Sharpneſs, and duſt in ſome Pepper; ſtir
all together, and ſend it up.

This eats extremely well with cold Lamb, cold
Veal, or cold Chicken; it may be eat with hot.

(Mrs. *Martha Bradley's* Britiſh Houſewife.)

Parſley

*Parsley and Butter Sauce**

SCALD a large Handful of Parsley in boiling Water that has some Salt in it. When tender, chop it fine and stir it into some rather thick melted Butter. There should be sufficient Parsley to make the Sauce green, and the Parsley should not be put to the melted Butter until about to be served, otherwise it will turn brown.

(Old Recipe from *Chase City, Virginia.* Adapted, 1937.)

*Sauce for Roast Venison**

JELLY of Currants melted and serv'd hot, with a Lemon squeez'd into it.

(*E. Smith's* Compleat Housewife, *London,* 1739.)

Sauce for Wild Fowl

TAKE a Gill of Claret, with as much Water, some grated Bread, three Heads of Shallots, a little whole Pepper, Mace, grated Nutmeg, and Salt; let them stew over the Fire, then beat it up with Butter, and put it under the wild Fowl, which, being a little roasted, will afford Gravy to mix with this Sauce.

(Mrs. *Mary Randolph's* Virginia Housewife, 1831.)

Of

Of FLESH & FISH

F ROM Rivers and Ocean, Field and Forest,
the *Virginia* Housewife had a varied and
abundant Supply of Meat and Fish, and the
Virginia Gentleman, good Hunting and Fishing.
In 1739, the Botanist, *John Clayton*, wrote to a
Friend in *England* of the Field Sports:

    ... To satisfie the Gentlemen you mention
who is so desirous of knowing the Diversion of
Hunting and Shooting here and the several Sorts
of Game pray give my Service to him and tell
him, that we have all the tame domestick Beasts
and Fowls that you have in *England*, and great
Variety of wild ones as Deer in great Pleanty,
Bears, Buffaloes, Wolves, Foxes, Panthers, Wild
Cats, Elks, Hares (smaller than any of y's which
run in Holes in the Earth and hollow Trees when
pressed by the Dogs, and are much like w't you
called in *England* Bush Rabbits), Squirrels 3 or 4
Sorts, Raccoons, Oppossums, Beavers, Otters,
Musk Rats, Pole Cats, Minks and there has been
two Porcupines killed here, but they are very
scarce.

    ... Then for Fowls, wild Turkey's very num-
erous, Partridges (the Size and Colour like y'r
Quails), wild Geese, Swans, Brants, Cormorants,
Teal Duck and Mallard, black Ducks, Plover 2
or 3 Sorts, Soris (a delicious eating Bird in Shape
and Way of Living like y'r Water Rails), Heath.
Fowls (called here improperly Pheasants) 2 Sorts,
wild Pidgeons in prodigious great Flocks, Field-
fares,

fares, Woodcocks (but what is very ftrange they
come here only in Summer) Snipes, Herons,
Bitterns, Eagles, Larks 2 Sorts one of w'ch are
here all the Year round, are as big as Quails, the
other are feen only in Winter and are much like
your Lark.

As for Fifh, frefh, falt Water and Shell-fifh,
Beverley contended "no Country can boaft of
"more Variety, greater Plenty or better of their
"feveral Kinds." He told of Rivers fo teeming with
Herring that Boats could hardly get through without treading on them, and of Sturgeon that would
leap into Boats.

> Thofe which I know of myfelf, [he faid,] I re-
> member by the Names. Of Herrings, Rocks,
> Sturgeons, Shads, Old-Wives, Sheep's-Heads,
> black and red Drums, Trouts, Taylors, Green-
> Fifh, Sun-Fifh, Bafs, Chub, Place, Flounders,
> Whitings, Fatbacks, Maids, Wives, Small-Turtle,
> Crabs, Oifters, Muffels, Cockles, Shrimps, Needle-
> Fifh, Breme, Carp, Pike, Jack, Mullets, Eels,
> Conger-Eels, Perch, and Cats, &c.

The Swine, Poultry and other domeftic Animals
brought from *England* augmented this abundant
natural Supply. The Hogs, one contemporary
Writer faid, fwarmed like Vermin upon the Earth
and were permitted to run as they lifted and find
their own Support in the Woods.

From thefe Hogs, the *Virginians* produced one
of their moft famous Foodftuffs and their moft
popular ftanding Difh. Whatever elfe appeared
upon the Table, Ham, Bacon, or Jowl were always
there. *Francis Louis Michel*, a *Swifs* who travelled
through *Virginia* in 1701-2, faid that all agreed
that the *Virginia* Pork was "the beft and the moft
"delicate."

"delicate." Another Traveller compared the Ham
to the beſt *Weſtphalian* Ham.

In the conſtant Exchange of genteel Preſents
which went on between *Virginia* and "Home",
Ham was one of the moſt appreciated Gifts. Sir
William Gooch (who was Lieutenant Governor of
Virginia, 1727-1749) ſent Hams to his Brother,
the Biſhop of *Norwich*, and to the Biſhops of
Saliſbury, *London* and *Bangor*.

Nor was the *Virginia* Ham leſs eſteemed in the
Colony, as the Fly-leaf of the Bible owned by the
firſt *William Byrd* of *Weſtover* can teſtify, for on it
was written:

> To eat ye Ham in Perfection ſteep it in half
> Milk and half Water for thirty-ſix Hours, and
> then having brought the Water to a Boil put ye
> Ham therein and let it ſimmer, not boil, for 4 or
> 5 Hours according to Size of ye Ham—for ſim-
> mering brings ye Salt out and boiling drives it
> in. [c-1674.]

In the Interchange of Letters between *Virginia*
and *England* and the other Colonies, Hams and
Bacon were frequently the Subject of much Diſ-
courſe. One ſuch Letter, written from *St. Croix* to
George Flowerdewe Norton of *Virginia* upon the
Occaſion of *Norton's* Marriage is ſtill preſerved in
Williamſburg.

> *St. Croix*
> July 11, 1785.

> . . . Mrs. *Reeve* & myſelf ſincerley congratu-
> late you & your amiable Lady (for amiable ſhe
> certainly muſt be if the Object of your Choice)
> on your Entrance into the matrimonial State—&
> wiſh you no more Love & Harmony, than we our-
> ſelves have enjoy'd therein—We have four
> >   Flitches

Flitches of Bacon now due—but fear we shall not very soon reach that Country* where they are demandable.

. . . Mrs. *Reeve* unites with me in sincere Wishes for your long Enjoyment of every terrestrial Bliss & believe me with great Sincerity

Yr Affect & Obed Servt
Thomas Reeve

* DUNMOW, there was an ancient Custom in the Priory, that if any Person from any Part of *England* would come thither, and humbly kneel at the Church Door before the Convent, and solemnly take the ensuing Oath, he might demand a Flitch or Gammon of Bacon, which should be freely given him.

> You shall swear by the Custom of our Confession
> That you never made any nuptial Transgression,
> Since you were married Man and Wife,
> By household Brawls or a contentious Strife;
> Or otherwise, in Bed or at Board,
> Offended each Other in Deed or in Word;
> Or since the Parish Clerk said Amen,
> Wished your selves unmarried again;
> Or in a Twelvemonth and a Day
> Repent not in Thought any Way;
> But continued True and in Desire
> As when you joined Hands in holy Quire.
> If to those Conditions, without all Fear,
> Of your own Accord you will freely swear;
> A Gammon of Bacon you shall receive,
> And bear it hence with Love and good Leave;
> For this is our Custom at *Dunmow* well known,
> Though the Sport be ours, the Bacon's your own.

(*Bailey's* Dictionary, *London,* 1730.)

Flesh

Fleſh & Fiſh

Beef A-la-mode

TAKE a good Buttock of Beef, interlarded with great Lard, roll'd up in ſavoury Spice, and Sweet-herbs; put it in a great Sauce-pan, and cover it cloſe and ſet in the Oven all Night. This is fit to eat cold.

(*E. Smith's* Compleat Houſewife, *Williamſburg*, 1742.)

Sirloin of Beef en Epigram

HAVING roaſted a Sirloin of Beef, take it off the Spit, and raiſe the Skin carefully off. Then cut out the lean Part of the Beef, but obſerve not to cut near the Ends nor Sides. Haſh the Meat in the following Manner: cut it into Pieces about the Size of a Crown Piece, put half a Pint of Gravy into a Toſs-pan, an Onion chopped fine, two Spoonfuls of Catchup, ſome Pepper and Salt, ſix ſmall pickled Cucumbers cut in thin Slices, and the Gravy that comes from the Beef, with a little Butter rolled in Flour. Put in the Meat, and toſs it up for five Minutes; put it on the Sirloin, and then put the Skin over, and ſend it to Table.

(*John Farley's* London Art of Cookery, 1787.)

Beef Steak Pye

BEAT ſome Rump Steaks with a Rolling-pin, and ſeaſon them with Pepper and Salt to your Palate. Make a good Cruſt, lay in your Steaks,
and

and then pour in as much Water as will half fill
the Diſh. Put on the Cruſt, and bake it well.

(*John Farley's* London Art of Cookery, 1787.
From *Brookbury, Cheſterfield* County, *Virginia.*)

Williamſburg *Beef Steak Pye* ❋

BEAT ſeveral Rump Steaks with a Rolling-pin,
cut them in Pieces and ſtrew with Flour. Fry
in Suet until brown, add ſome chopped Onion,
Salt, Pepper and a few Sprigs of Parſley. Add hot
Water to cover and ſimmer until thick. Put them
in a Baking-diſh with the Gravy, put on a top
Cruſt of rich Paſtry and bake about forty Minutes.

(Mrs. *Randolph's* Recipe, 1831. Adapted
Market Square Tavern Kitchen, 1937.)

Williamſburg *Beef Steak & Ham Pye* ❋

TAKE one Pound of nice Steaks and pound
well with Flour. Brown them in your Skillet
in a little Lard. Pour hot Water over them and
ſeaſon your Gravy well with Salt & Pepper. Arrange the Steaks in a Diſh with one half Pound of
ſliced boiled Ham, pour Gravy over, put on a Lid
of Paſtry and bake about forty Minutes.

(Mrs. *Randolph's* Recipe, 1831. Adapted
Market Square Tavern Kitchen, 1937.)

Roaſt Beef ❋

SELECT a five or ſix pound Piece of Beef fit for
roaſting. Rub over it a Piece of Suet, and in a
few ſmall Gaſhes inſert Slices of Onion or two ſmall
Cloves of Garlic. Place it on a Rack in a Dripping-
pan,

pan, put over it ſeveral Strips of Suet and place it
in a very hot Oven to ſear for about fifteen Minutes. Reduce the Heat and roaſt the Beef about
fifteen Minutes to the Pound or leſs if you prefer
it rare. When enough, lift out the Beef, remove
ſome of the Drippings to make your Gravy, pour
a *Yorkſhire* Pudding in the Pan and bake it
quickly. Serve it up with your thickened Gravy
in a ſeparate Diſh.

(Recipe from a *Williamſburg* Cook Book. Prov'd 1937.)

Yorkſhire *Pudding* *

BEAT three Eggs very light, add one and a half
Cups of ſweet Milk (or one Cup of Milk and
a half Cup of Chicken Stock) and three Tableſpoonfuls of melted Butter. Beat in one and a half
Cups of ſifted Flour. If you do not bake under the
Meat in a Dripping-pan, pour it into a well greaſed
ſhallow Baking-diſh and bake in a hot Oven.

(Mr. *Farley's* Recipe, 1787. Adapted *Travis* Houſe, 1938.)

Beef *Rolls* *

TAKE as many Beef Steaks as will fill a Diſh
—beat them tender then ſprinkle them with
the Crumbs of lite Bread. Pepper—Onions—
Parſley—Thyme—roll them up and tye them with
a String; fry them in Lard. The hind Quarter of
Shoat inſtead of Beef make nice Rolls.

(Manuſcript Cook Book, prior 1839.
Morton Family of *Charlotte* County, *Virginia.*)

English

Englifh *Steak & Kidney Pie* *

REMOVE the Skin from two fmall Beef Kidneys and wafh in falted Water. Cut in two-inch Squares and dredge with Flour. Have ready three fourths of a Pound of Beeffteak, pound it well in Flour and cut in fmall Pieces. Cook fome Bits of Suet or other Shortening in a large Frying-pan then brown the Steak with a finely-chopped Onion, add the Kidneys and cook flowly until browned. Add hot Water to cover and fimmer gently. Seafon with a fmall Bay-leaf, Parfley, Celery-tops, Salt and Pepper. Simmer gently in a covered Pan for about an Hour. The beft Cooks then add one Cupful of raw Mufhrooms, and one half Cup of finely diced cooked Carrots. If your Gravy needs Thickening add Flour mixed in cold Water. Pour all into a deep Baking-difh and cover with a Cruft of Paftry or of thinly-rolled Bifcuit Dough. Bake until the Cruft is done and ferve it up. This old *Englifh* Favorite was alfo popular in the Colonies.

(Old *Virginia* Recipe. Prov'd *Blair* Kitchen, 1938.)

Brunfwick *Stew* *

CUT up two Squirrels (or a three Pound Chicken) and put in a large Pan with three Quarts of Water, one large fliced Onion, one half Pound of lean Ham cut in fmall Pieces and fimmer gently for two Hours. Add three Pints of Tomatoes, one Pint of *Lima* Beans, four large *Irifh* Potatoes diced, one Pint grated Corn, one Tablefpoon Salt, one fourth Teafpoon Pepper, a fmall Pod of red Pepper. Cover and fimmer gently for one more
Hour

Hour ſtirring frequently to prevent Scorching. Add three Ounces of Butter and ſerve hot.

(Old Recipe from *Richmond, Virginia.*)

Or make it thus: *

CUT one large Chicken in eight Pieces. Cook ſlowly in one Gallon of cold Water two and a quarter Hours, being careful not to boil rapidly at any Time. To the Chicken and Broth add two Cups of freſh ſliced Okra, two Cups of *Lima* Beans, four Cups of chopped, peeled Tomatoes and two ſliced Onions. Then ſlowly cook for ſix Hours adding hot Water occaſionally ſo that there will be between five and ſix Quarts of this Mixture. Then add four diced white Potatoes and four Cups of Corn. Cook one Hour. Stir to prevent Scorching. Seaſon with two Teaſpoonfuls of Salt, one-half Spoonful of Pepper and a little Sugar.

(*Market Square Tavern* Kitchen, 1937.)

Brunſwick *Stew to ſerve Twenty* *

IN a heavy *Dutch* Oven put two Pounds of diced Beef, two Veal Shanks cut up, a four-pound Chicken jointed, one half Pound of diced ſmoked Bacon, and one Squirrel if obtainable. Cover with cold Water, ſeaſon with Salt and a Pod of red Pepper and ſimmer until Meat falls from Bones. Add a Quart and a half of diced *Iriſh* Potatoes, one and a half Pounds of *Lima* Beans, two Pounds of peeled, ſliced Tomatoes. Cook until Potatoes maſh up to thicken Stew. One half Hour before ſerving add Corn cut from one dozen Ears, one half

half Pound of Butter, one Teaſpoon black Pepper.
This requires at leaſt ſix Hours ſlow cooking. It
may be made the Day before ſerving.

(Traditional *Virginia* Recipe. Prov'd 1937.)

Smothered Chicken*

SINGE a young Fowl and ſplit it down the
Back. Draw it, then lay the Chicken, with
Inſide downward, in a Baking-pan, breaking the
Breaſt Bone to make it lie flat. Spread the Breaſt
with Butter, dredge with Pepper. Put Salt and
about one half Cup of Water in the Bottom of the
Baking-pan, place in a hot Oven, cover with
another Pan, let bake for half an Hour, baſting
every ten Minutes. Remove upper Pan, turn Fowl,
baſte well on Inſide, cover again and bake for
another half Hour. When done place it on a hot
Diſh; put Pan in which it was cooked on Top of
Fire to brown, add Flour and ſtir until ſmooth
and brown, then add a half Pint of Milk and ſtir
until it boils. Add Salt and Pepper and ſend up
your Gravy in a Boat.

(Old Recipe from *Kenbridge, Virginia.* Prov'd 1937.)

A Pilau

PUT on a good Piece of Middling of Bacon and
two Fowls to boil. When done take them out
and cover them over the Fire. Put into the Water
in which they were boiled as much Rice as will fill
yʳ Diſh with ſome Grains of black Pepper and
Allſpice if you like it—when the Rice is ſoft pour
off all the Water, return the Fowls and Bacon to
the

the Pot firſt ſkinning the Bacon and let them ſtand
over the Fire till you diſh them. Then lay yʳ Fowls
and Bacon firſt in, and cover them with the Rice.

(Manuſcript Cook Book, c-1801, of Mrs. *Frances
Bland Tucker Coalter.* Owned by Dr. *St.
George Tucker Grinnan, Richmond.*)

India *Pilau*

WASH and pick clean two Pounds Rice put in
a Colander and drain very dry—put one
Pound Butter and one half a Pint of Water into a
Stew-pan—put in the Rice. Seaſon it with beaten
Cloves, Mace, grated Nutmeg, Pepper and Salt.
Cover cloſe and keep in the Steam. Stir it gently
and ſtir it often to keep it from burning till it is
tender. In the Meantime boil two Fowls and two
Pounds of Bacon. Put the Fowls into a Diſh cut
the Bacon in two and lay it on each Side put the
Rice over and garniſh with hard Egg and a Dozen
Onions, fried whole and brown.

This is the true *India* Pilau.

(Manuſcript Cook Book, c-1801, of Mrs. *Frances
Bland Tucker Coalter.* Owned by Dr. *St.
George Tucker Grinnan, Richmond.*)

Chicken Pilau ✳

BROWN two large chopped Onions in a large
Frying-pan in three Tableſpoonfuls of Butter,
add three Cups of ſtewed Tomatoes, four Stalks
of Celery chopped fine, a finely chopped green
Pepper, three Teaſpoons Salt, ſome Pepper, three
Cups of cold chopped Chicken and two Cups of
boiled

boiled Rice. Cook for fifteen Minutes ſtirring to prevent Scorching. Pour into buttered Baking-diſh, cover with one Cup of well buttered Bread-crumbs and bake in moderate Oven an Hour and a quarter.

(Prov'd *Travis* Houſe, 1938.)

Chicken & Dumplins *

CUT and joint a large Chicken. Cover with Water and let boil gently until tender. Seaſon with Salt and Pepper and thicken the Gravy with two Tableſpoonfuls of Flour mixed ſmooth in a Piece of Butter the Size of an Egg. Have ready nice light Bread Dough about an Inch thick; cut with a Biſcuit-cutter. Drop into the boiling Gravy, having previouſly removed the Chicken to a hot Platter; cover and let theſe boil from one half to three quarters of an Hour.

To aſcertain whether they are done ſtick them with a Fork; if it comes out clean they are done. Lay them on the Platter with the Chicken; pour the Gravy over and serve.

(Old Recipe from *Highland Springs, Virginia.* Prov'd 1937.)

Croquettes *

CHOP one Pound of cold Turkey or Chicken very fine; mix with Salt and Pepper one Teaſpoon chopped Onion, three Teaſpoons chopped Parſley. Seaſon delicately with Mace and grated Nutmeg. Moiſten with three Tableſpoons of ſweet Cream, ſhape into Pear-ſhaped Balls. For the Stems inſert Cloves. Dip this in beaten Egg and then

then in grated Bread-crumbs. Cook in boiling
Lard until nice and brown.

(Recipe, c-1855, from *Wicomico Church, Virginia.*
Prov'd *Market Square Tavern* Kitchen, 1937.)

Chicken Gumbo*

JOINT a young four-pound Chicken. Roll in
Flour and fry till light brown in three Tableſpoons Butter and three Tableſpoons Lard. Put
Chicken and a Ham Bone in large Soup-kettle.
Into the Skillet in which the Chicken was fried
ſlice three medium ſized Onions and fry golden
brown. Put into the Soup-pot with three Cups
ſtewed Tomatoes, three Pints of young Okra ſliced,
three Cups ſliced Celery and two Quarts cold
Water. Simmer for four or five Hours adding one
Tableſpoon Salt and one half Teaſpoon Pepper
toward the End. The Chicken muſt drop from
Bones. Take out the Bones. Have boiled Rice
ready. Preſs Portions into ſmall buttered Cups to
mold and turn out onto Soup-plates. Pour the hot
Gumbo around it.

(Old Recipe from *Richmond, Virginia.* Prov'd 1937.)

Chicken Terrapin*

TAKE one Quart of cold diced Chicken and put
it in a Sauce-pan with one fourth of a Pound
of melted Butter, ſift over it two Tableſpoonfuls of
Flour then ſtir in one half Cup of Cream. Seaſon
with one fourth Teaſpoon of powdered Mace, one
eighth Teaſpoon of pounded Cloves, and Salt and
Pepper to your Taſte and beat thoroughly on a ſlow
Fire.

Fire. Chop the Whites of three hard-boiled Eggs very fine and add. Mix the Yolks of the Eggs with a few Spoonfuls of Cream and add. Add one half Cup of Sherry and ſerve at once. Calf's Liver may be parboiled for fifteen Minutes and is delicious dreſſed in the ſame Manner.

(Old Recipe from *Richmond, Virginia.* Prov'd 1937.)

Chicken Pudding, a Favourite Virginia *Diſh*

BEAT ten Eggs very light, add to them a Quart of rich Milk, with a quarter of a Pound of Butter melted, and ſome Pepper and Salt; ſtir in as much Flour as will make a thin good Batter; take four young Chickens, and after cleaning them nicely, cut off the Legs, Wings, &c. put them all in a Sauce-pan, with ſome Salt and Water, and a Bundle of Thyme and Parſley, boil them till nearly done, then take the Chickens from the Water and put it in the Batter, pour it in a deep Diſh, and bake it; ſend nice white Gravy in a Boat.

(Mrs. *Mary Randolph's* Virginia Houſewife, 1831.)

Williamſburg *Chicken Pudding* *

CUT up a four or five Pound Fowl as for Frica-ſee, put it in your Kettle with Water to cover, with one Onion, a few Celery Tops, ſome Sprigs of Parſley, a Teaſpoonful of Thyme, Salt and Pepper. Simmer gently until Fowl is tender. Take from Broth, remove Skin and place in a ſhallow Baking-diſh. Pour over it one Cup of ſtrained Broth. Make a Batter of one Pint of Milk, three well-beaten Eggs, one-fourth Cup of Flour, one-fourth
Cup

Cup melted Butter and one Teafpoon of Salt.
Pour this over your Chicken and bake in a moderate Oven about thirty-five Minutes. Serve immediately with a Gravy made of thickened Broth
in a feparate Difh.

(Mrs. *Randolph's* Recipe, 1831. Adapted
Market Square Tavern Kitchen, 1937.)

Chicken Pye

PUT yʳ Pafte in the Difh (in the Winter make it
with full Weight of Butter, and in the Summer
with as much Butter as the Flour will take in).
Lay in two large or three fmall Chickens cut up,
ftrew between the Layers and at Top, a double
Handful of Bits of lean Bacon boiled or raw (if
raw yʳ Pye will require lefs Salt—Lay at Top
feveral large Lumps of Butter, about one fourth
of a Pound. Strew over a heaped Tablefpoon of
Salt and an even one of fine Pepper *black*). Fill
laft of all with cold Water—Put into a *Dutch* Oven
firft laying in the Bottom a little warm Afhes and
let it bake gradually with the Top of very moderate Heat and put Coals under from Time to
Time, when nearly done increafe the Fire on the
Top to brown the Pafte. It will take near two
Hours baking.

(Manufcript Cook Book, c-1801, of Mrs. *Frances Bland
Tucker Coalter.* Owned by Dr. *St. George
Tucker Grinnan, Richmond.*)

Chicken Corn Pye *

BOIL up one Cup of Rice and butter it well
while it is hot. Put a Layer of Rice in the
Bottom of a buttered Baking-difh, add one
Chicken

Chicken which has been cooked in a well-seasoned Broth, and the Corn scraped from three large Ears. Pour over this one Cup of Broth, add three Tablespoons of Butter, Salt and Pepper. Cover with the Rice, glaze it with a beaten Egg and bake to a delicate brown.

(Old Recipe, *Henrico* County, *Virginia*. Prov'd 1937.)

Fricassee of Small Chickens *

TAKE off the Legs and Wings of four Chickens, separate the Breasts from the Backs, cut off the Necks and divide the Backs across, clean the Gizzards nicely, put them with the Livers and other Parts of the Chicken, after being washed clean, into a Sauce-pan, add Pepper, Salt, and a little Mace, cover them with Water, and stew them till tender—then take them out, thicken half a Pint of the Water with two Tablespoonfuls of Flour rubbed into four Ounces of Butter, add half a Pint of new Milk, boil all together a few Minutes, then add a Gill of White-wine, stirring it in carefully that it may not curdle; put the Chickens in, and continue to shake the Pan until they are sufficiently hot, and serve them up.

(Mrs. *Mary Randolph's* Virginia Housewife, 1831. Prov'd 1937.)

Fried Chickens *

CUT them up as for the Fricassee, dredge them well with Flour, sprinkle them with Salt, put them into a good Quantity of boiling Lard, and fry them a light brown; fry small Pieces of Mush and a Quantity of Parsley nicely picked, to be
served

ſerved in the Diſh with the Chickens; take half a
Pint of rich Milk, add to it a ſmall Bit of Butter,
with Pepper, Salt, and chopped Parſley; ſtew it a
little, and pour it over the Chickens, and then
garniſh with the fried Parſley.

(Mrs. Mary Randolph's Virginia Houſewife, 1831.)

Williamſburg *Fried Chicken* ❊

JOINT the Chickens neatly, waſh and drain.
Soak in cold Milk for half an Hour. Dredge
them well with Flour to which Salt and Pepper
have been added. Fry in an iron Skillet in boiling
Fat almoſt deep enough to cover the Pieces of
Chicken. Turn each Piece at leaſt three Times.
Fry to a nice brown, drain on brown Paper and
ſerve with Gravy ſent up in a ſeparate Boat.

GRAVY: Brown ſome Flour in ſome of the Fat
in which the Chicken was fried. Seaſon and add
chicken Stock. Stir until thick and ready to ſerve.

(Prov'd Travis Houſe, 1938.)

Pullet, or Chicken Surprize

ROAST them off; if a ſmall Diſh, two Chickens,
or one Pullet, will be enough. Take the Lean
of your Pullet, or Chickens, from the Bone, cut it
in thin Slices an Inch long, and toſs it up in ſix or
ſeven Spoonfuls of Milk or Cream, with the Bigneſs of half an Egg of Butter, grated Nutmeg,
Pepper, and Salt; thicken it with a little Duſt of
Flour, to the Thickneſs of a good Cream, then boil
it up, and ſet it to cool; then cut ſix or ſeven thin
round Slices of Bacon, place them in a Patty-pan,

and

and put on each Slice ſome Forc'd-meat, then
work them up in Form of a *French* Roll, with raw
Egg in your Hand, leaving a hollow Place in the
Middle; then put in your Fowl, and cover them
with ſome of the ſame Forc'd-meat, rubbing it
ſmooth over with your Hand, and an Egg, make
them of the Height and Bigneſs of a *French* Roll;
throw a little fine grated Bread over them, bake
them three quarters of an Hour in a gentle Oven,
or under a Baking-cover, till they come to a yellow
brown, place them on your Mazarine, that they
may not touch one another, but ſo that they may
not fall flat in the Baking: But you may form
them on your Kitchen Table, with your Slices of
Bacon under them; then lift them up with your
broad Kitchen Knife, and place them on that
which you intend to bake them on. Let your
Sauce be Butter and Gravy, and ſqueez'd Lemon,
and your Garniſhing fry'd Parſley, and cut Orange.
You may put the Legs of one of your Chickens into
the Sides of one of your Loaves that you intend to
put in the Middle of your Diſh. This is proper for
a Side-diſh, for a firſt Courſe, either in Summer or
Winter, where you can have the Ingredients above
mention'd.

(The Lady's Companion, 1753; Cook Book
owned by Miſs *Anna Maria Dandridge*, 1756.)

Williamſburg *Chicken Surprize* *

TAKE the Meat of a three or four pound
Chicken which has been cooked in a Broth
ſeaſoned with Salt, Pepper, Parſley, Onion and
Celery, and cut it in ſmall Pieces. Melt two Tableſpoons

ſpoons of Butter, ſtir in one of Flour and add a
Pint of thin Cream and pour over Chicken and
ſet it aſide to cool. Make a Force-meat of two
Cups of dry Bread-crumbs, one minc'd Onion,
two Tableſpoons chopped Parſley, one half Teaſpoonful each of Sage & Savory, ſeaſon with Salt
and Pepper and moiſten with Broth. Have ready
ſix Slices of Ham, or wide Strips of Bacon and put
your Force-meat on theſe and roll them up and
hold together with wooden Tooth-picks. Lay theſe
Rolls around the Sides of your Baking-diſh, and
put your Chicken in the Center. Sprinkle the
Whole with buttered Crumbs and bake in a moderate Oven about forty-five Minutes.

(*Market Square Tavern* Kitchen, 1937.)

Ducks to ſtew—Mrs. Walker＊

TRUSS the Ducks and ſtuff them with Bread
and Butter and Onion. Flour them and brown
them in Lard in a Frying-pan. Have prepared in
an Iron Pot Slips of Bacon, Giblets, Onion, Water,
Pepper, Salt and a little Clove or Mace if you like
it—Put in yʳ Ducks and let them ſtew gently but
conſtantly two Hours then add the Juice of green
Grapes preſſed between two pewter Plates, or
Lemon-juice or Lemon-pickle. Flour yʳ Ducks
each time that you turn them in the Pot. Thicken
with Butter rolled in Flour—This Receipt for
large Ducks. Thoſe not grown will require leſs
Time.

(Manuſcript Cook Book, c-1801, of Mrs. *Frances
Bland Tucker Coalter.* Owned by Dr. *St.
George Tucker Grinnan, Richmond.*)

Nice

Nice brown Gravy for Ducks—Roaſt &c.*

MAKE a Spider quite hot. Keep it on the Fire and put into it a Tableſpoonful of Butter. Let it boil up, throw in a deſert Spoon of Sugar, ſtir them together as they boil till brown, dredge in Flour ſufficient to thicken and continue to ſtir. Add yʳ Dripping and as much boiling Water in which you may firſt have boiled Sweet-herbs, Onion and Celery as will make a proper Quantity of Gravy, with Pepper and Salt. If for Ducks ſtew yʳ Giblets with Onion and a Bunch of Herbs and add them with the Water they were ſtewed inſtead of the plain Water. Keep it gently ſtewing till ready to diſh.

(Manuſcript Cook Book, c-1801, of Mrs. *Frances Bland Tucker Coalter.* Owned by Dr. *St. George Tucker Grinnan, Richmond.*)

Salmi of Wild Duck*

PREPARE a Pair of Ducks as for roaſting; put a thin Slice of Bacon over the Breaſt of each; place them in a Pan with one-half Pint of Water, and bake in a hot Oven until nearly done, baſting frequently with Water; take from the Oven and carve the Ducks into as many Pieces as convenient; ſtir two Tableſpoons Butter and two of Flour together until perfectly ſmooth; put it into a Stew-pan and ſtir until a dark Brown; add the Broth; let it come to a Boil, ſtirring conſtantly; then add the Bundle of Sweet-herbs, one Tableſpoonful Onion-juice, and one of Lemon-juice, one Tableſpoon Muſhroom Catſup, Salt, and Pepper; let all ſimmer together twenty Minutes; take out the

the Herbs; add the Ducks and all the Gravy from
the Dish on which you carve them; cover and
simmer twenty Minutes longer; add one half Cup
Sherry, and serve on a hot Dish. It is pretty served
on a flat Dish garnished with sliced Bread cut into
Triangles before frying; arrange with the Points
up; scatter stoned Olives over the Top of the Dish.

(Old Recipe, *Richmond, Virginia.*)

Another Way*

CUT cold wild Duck into neat Pieces. Place
Bones and Trimmings in Stew-pan with one
small Onion, two Sprigs Thyme, one Bay-leaf,
Salt and Pepper to Taste. Melt two Tablespoons
Butter with one Tablespoon Flour. Add strained
Broth and stir until it boils and thickens. Add the
Duck, one Glass Claret (or any red Wine), one
Teaspoon each of Orange and Lemon Juice. Serve
very hot on Toast or Puff-paste. Garnish with
Olives, Mushrooms or Truffles. Decorate with
Slices of Orange and Lemon.

(Old Recipe from *Richmond, Virginia,* prov'd.)

To roast Wild Ducks or Teal*

WHEN the Ducks are ready dressed, put in
them a small Onion, Pepper, Salt, and a
Spoonful of red Wine; if the Fire be good, they
will roast in twenty Minutes; make Gravy of the
Necks and Gizzards, a Spoonful of red Wine, half
an Anchovy, a Blade or two of Mace, one Onion,
and a little *Cayenne* Pepper; boil it till it is wasted
to half a Pint, strain it through a hair Sieve, and
pour

pour it on the Ducks—ſerve them up with Onion
Sauce in a Boat; garniſh the Diſh with Raſpings
of Bread.

(Mrs. *Mary Randolph's* Virginia Houſewife, 1831.)

A Fowl in Haſh

GET ſome Fowls ready dreſſ'd, then take the
Fleſh, and cut it very ſmall; take the Car-
caſſes, put them in a Stew-pan with good Broth,
an Onion cut into Slices, Parſley, and Sweet-herbs;
when it is boil'd enough, ſtrain it off; then put in
it a Bit of Butter roll'd in Flour, and let it ſtew a
Moment again; then put in it your Haſh of Fowls;
let your Haſh be reliſhing, thicken it with three
Yolks of Eggs, or more according to the Quantity
of Haſh you make; it being thick, put in it the
Juice of a Lemon, and ſerve them up hot for
Hors d'Oeuvre.

(The Lady's Companion, 1753; Cook Book owned
by Miſs *Anna Maria Dandridge*, 1756.)

Chicken Haſh *

CUT in ſmall Pieces the Meat from a boiled or
roaſted Chicken. Take the Carcaſs and put it
in a Stew-pan with a good Broth, an Onion cut in
Slices, ſome Parſley and Sweet-herbs. Simmer
ſlowly then ſtrain. Melt four Spoonfuls of Butter
and thicken with Flour, add ſeveral Cups of
Broth, and the Chicken and beat well. This may
be ſerved on Waffles as a Supper Diſh.

(Miſs *Dandridge's* Recipe, 1753. Adapted
Market Square Tavern Kitchen, 1937.)

A

A Goose, Turkey, or Leg of Mutton, A-la-daube

LARD it with Bacon, and half roaſt it; then take it off the Spit, and put it in as ſmall a Pot as will boil it, put to it a Quart of White-wine, ſtrong Broth, a Pint of Vinegar, whole Spice, Bay-leaves, ſweet Marjoram, Winter-ſavoury, and green Onions. When it is ready lay it in the Diſh, make Sauce with ſome of the Liquor, Muſhrooms, dic'd Lemon, two or three Anchovies; thicken it with brown Butter, and garniſh it with ſliced Lemon.

(*E. Smith's* Compleat Houſewife, *Williamſburg,* 1742.)

Wild Goose*

PUT a ſmall Onion, a Slice of Pork, Pepper, Salt, and a Spoonful of red Wine inſide the Gooſe. Lay it in a Pan with Water enough to make Gravy. Dredge with Flour and baſte with Butter frequently. Cook quickly and ſerve with Gravy made from the thickened Stock.

(Old Recipe from *Toano, Virginia.*)

Baked Ham*

MOST Perſons boil Ham. It is much better baked, if baked right. Soak it overnight in clear Water, and wipe it dry. Next ſpread it all over with a thin Batter and then put it into a deep Diſh with a Rack under it to keep it out of the Gravy. When it is fully cruſted upon the Fleſh Side ſet it aſide to cool. It ſhould bake from four to ſix Hours.

After

After removing the Skin ſprinkle over with two Tableſpoons of Sugar, ſome black Pepper and powdered Crackers. Put in a Pan and return to the Oven to brown; then take up and ſtick Cloves through the Fat and duſt with powdered Cinnamon.

(Old Recipe, c-1851, *Wicomico Church, Virginia.*)

Spiced Ham*

WASH a ten-pound Ham in cold Water, put in a large Boiler nearly filled with cold Water. Add two Blades of Mace, a dozen Cloves, half a Dozen Peppercorns and a Bay-leaf. Set over a ſlow Fire. Let heat gradually. Let ſimmer for one and a half Hours then boil gently fifteen Minutes to every Pound. When done let cool in Water in which it was cooked. Then take up and ſkin. Bruſh the Fat over with dried Bread-crumbs in which is mixed four Spoonfuls of brown Sugar. Set in a moderate Oven to brown. Baſte with a Pint of White-wine to which has been added a Tableſpoonful each of Celery-ſeed, Cloves, and Ginger. When browned, take up, ſtick whole Cloves over thickly. Set away twenty-four Hours before uſing. (Old Recipe, *Chaſe City, Virginia.*)

Baked Spiced Ham*

SELECT a nicely cured Ham. Soak overnight in cold Water. Wipe off and put on in enough Water to cover. Simmer for three Hours. Let cool in the Water it was cooked in. Take out and trim. Put into Baking-pan, ſtick with Cloves and cover with

with brown Sugar. Bake in a moderate Oven for
two Hours. Baſte with white Wine. Serve with a
ſavoury Salad.

(Old Recipe from *Charlotte Court Houſe.* Said to have
been uſed by *Jefferſon's* Family at *Monticello.*)

How to cook an old Virginia *Ham**

SELECT a three to five Year old Ham weighing
twelve to eighteen Pounds. Trim and waſh
carefully and ſoak Overnight. Change Water and
add one Cup of Apple Vinegar and one Cup of
brown Sugar. Cover with Water. Boil very ſlowly
five or ſix Hours, or until end Bone is looſe. Leave
the Ham in the Water in which it was cooked until
the Water is cold then ſkin. Stuff and bake in the
following Manner; gaſh Fat on Top of Ham in
Gaſhes one Inch apart, ſtuff with Bread-crumbs
mixed with Chow-chow Pickle, a little of the Ham
Stock, and Butter. Pat ſmooth and put on Top
Cucumber Pickle cut in Rings. Put Ham in Baking-
pan and bake to a nice Brown.

(*Eggleſton* Family Recipe, 1840.)

*Boiled Ham**

THE Day before you wiſh to boil a Ham, ſcrape,
waſh and wipe dry and put in the Sun. At
Night put it into Water and ſoak until next
Morning. Then lay it with the Skin down in a
Boiler of cold Water, and boil ſlowly for five
Hours. If the Ham is large, boil for ſix Hours.
When tender, ſet the Boiler aſide, with the Ham
and Liquor untouched, until cold. Then take off
Skin,

Skin, sprinkle black Pepper over thickly, and sift over it Crackers first browned and pounded. For special Occasions, place at equal Distances over the Ham scraped Horse-radish in Lozenge Shape and edge with curled Parsley. This Mode keeps the Ham juicy.

(Old Recipe, *Toano, Virginia*.)

Ham and Egg Pudding (*A Spring Dish*)*

TAKE some Slices of boiled Ham (both Fat and Lean) and sprinkle with Pepper, lay them across a deep Dish that has been buttered. Make a Pudding Batter of six Eggs beaten very light, a light Pint of Flour, a Pint of Milk, a small Piece of Butter, and Salt and Pepper to the Taste. Pour this Pudding Batter over the Ham and bake quickly.

(Recipe from an old *Williamsburg* Cook Book.)

Jugged Hare or Rabbit*

CUT into Joints one Hare or two Rabbits. Dust with Flour and fry until brown. Put into Stew-pan and add—one Onion, one Turnip, two Celery Stalks, small Bunch of Parsley, small Slice of Lemon-rind, two Cloves, two Bay-leaves, one Blade of Mace, three Peppercorns, one half Teaspoon Salt. Fill Stew-pan with boiling Broth and simmer for three Hours. When cooked, take out Pieces of Meat and keep hot. Make Force-meat Balls of the following—four Tablespoons Bread-crumbs, one and a half Tablespoons ground Suet, one Teaspoon Parsley, one half Teaspoon each of Thyme and Marjoram, pinch of powdered Mace, one

one half Teaſpoon grated Lemon, Salt and Pepper
to Taſte, four Tableſpoons chopped Ham or Veal.
Mix well, moiſten with Broth and add one Egg,
well beaten. Roll in Flour and cook in boiling
Broth for fifteen Minutes. Skim out and set aſide
with Meat to keep hot. Thicken Gravy with Flour,
pounded Livers and one Tableſpoon red Currant
Jelly, Juice of one half Lemon, two wine Glaſſes of
red Wine (preferably Port). Parboil and ſkin one
Cup of Cheſtnuts. Heat all together very thoroughly with Meat, Force-meat and ſerve.

(Old Recipe, c-1780, *Richmond, Virginia.*)

Kidney Stew *

SOAK overnight in cold, ſalted Water ſix Lamb
Kidneys. Drain—parboil in Water to cover,
three Times. Waſh in cold Water, remove all Fat,
cut in Cubes, add three Potatoes and one Onion
which have been cubed, cover with Water and
cook thirty Minutes. Add Cream, Butter and
chopped Parſley, Salt and Pepper to Taſte. Serve
on Waffles.

(Traditional *Virginia* Recipe. Adapted 1937.)

A Fricaſy of Lamb

CUT an hind Quarter of Lamb into thin Slices,
ſeaſon it with ſavoury Spices, Sweet-herbs,
and a Shalot; then fry them, and toſs them up in
ſtrong Broth, White-wine, Oyſters, Balls, and
Palates, a little brown Butter to thicken it, or a
Bit of Butter roll'd up in Flour.

(*E. Smith's* Compleat Houſewife, *Williamſburg*, 1742.)

Loin

Loin or Neck of Lamb *

HAVING cut your Lamb into Chops, rub both Sides of them with the Yolk of an Egg, and sprinkle some Crumbs of Bread over them, mixed with a little Parsley, Thyme, Marjoram, Winter Savory, and a little Lemon-peel, all chopped very fine. Fry them in Butter till they are of a nice light Brown, and garnish with fried Parsley.

(*John Farley's* London Art of Cookery, 1787.
Prov'd *Market Square Tavern* Kitchen, 1937.)

Calf's Liver *

LARD it with Bacon, (spit it first) and roast it. Serve it up with good Gravy.

(*John Farley's* London Art of Cookery, 1787.
Prov'd *Market Square Tavern* Kitchen, 1937.)

Mutton *

WHEN you intend to hash your Mutton, you must cut it in Slices, and put a Pint of Gravy or Broth into a Tossing-pan, with a Spoonful of Mushroom Catchup, and one of Browning. Add to it a sliced Onion, and a little Pepper and Salt. Put it over the Fire, and thicken it with Butter and Flour. When it boils, put in your Mutton; keep shaking it till it be perfectly hot, and then serve it up in a Soup-dish.

Another Method to hash Mutton, is cut it as thin as you can, strew a little Flour over it, have ready some Gravy, in which have been boiled Sweet-herbs, with some Onions, Pepper, and Salt.

Put

Put in your Meat, and with it a ſmall Piece of Butter rolled in Flour, a little Salt, a Shalot cut fine, and a few Capers cut fine. Toſs all together for a Minute or two, and have ready ſome Bread toaſted, and cut into thin Sippets. Lay them round the Diſh, pour in your Haſh, and garniſh with Pickles and Horſe-radiſh. To toaſt the Sippets may be conſidered as an Improvement.

(*John Farley's* London Art of Cookery, 1787.)

A Leg of Mutton A-la-royal

LARD your Mutton and Slices of Veal with Bacon roll'd in Spice and Sweet-herbs, then, bringing them to a Brown with melted Lard, boil the Leg of Mutton in ſtrong Broth, with all Sort of Sweet-herbs, and an Onion ſtuck with Cloves; when it is ready, lay it on the Diſh, lay round the Collops; then pour on it a Ragoo and garniſh with Lemon and Orange.

(*E. Smith's* Compleat Houſewife, *Williamſburg*, 1742.)

To fry Mutton Cutlets

CUT a Neck of Mutton Bone by Bone, and beat it flat with your Cleaver; have ready Sea-ſoning, with grated Bread, a little Thyme rubb'd to Powder, ſhred Parſley, with grated Nutmeg, and ſome Lemon-peel minc'd; then beat up two Eggs with Salt, flour your Cutlets on both Sides, and dip them in the Eggs, ſprinkle them with Seaſoning on both Sides; put ſome Butter in a Frying-pan, and when it is hot lay in your Cutlets,

and

and fry them brown on both Sides; for Sauce take
Gravy, or ftrong Broth, an Onion, fome Spice, a
Bit of Bacon, and a Bay-leaf, and boil them well
together; then beat it up with Anchovy, or fome
Oyfters, and a quarter of a Pint of red Wine, and
pour over your Cutlets, garnifh with pickled
Walnuts cut in Quarters, Barberries, Samphire,
pickled Cucumbers, and flic'd Lemon.

(The Lady's Companion, 1753; Cook Book owned
by Mifs *Anna Maria Dandridge*, 1756.)

Mutton Chops dreffed with Tomatoes ※

PLACE in a Pan Tomatoes peeled and chopped;
feafon with Butter, Pepper, Sugar and Salt.
Take from your Gridirons fome nicely broiled
Mutton Chops; put in a Pan, cover clofe and
fimmer for fifteen Minutes. Lay the Chops on a
hot Difh, put on a little Butter, Pepper and Salt.
With a Spoon cover each Chop with Tomatoes.
Sift pounded Crackers over and ferve.

(Old Recipe, *Toano, Virginia.*)

Oxford John ※

CUT a ftale Leg of Mutton into as thin Collops
as you can, and take out all the fat Sinews.
Seafon them with a little Salt, Pepper, and Mace,
and ftrew among them a little fhred Parfley,
Thyme, and two or three Shalots. Put a good
Lump of Butter into a Stew-pan, and as foon as
it be hot, put in all your Collops. Keep ftirring
them with a wooden Spoon till they be three Parts
done, and then add half a Pint of Gravy, a little
Juice

Juice of Lemon, and thicken it with Flour and Butter. Let them simmer four or five Minutes, and they will be quite enough; but if you let them boil, or have them ready before you want them, they will grow hard. Throw fried Pieces of Bread, cut in Dices, over and round them, and serve them up hot.

(John Farley's London Art of Cookery, 1787. Prov'd *Market Square Tavern* Kitchen, 1937.)

To roast Partridges or any small Birds *

LARD them with Slips of Bacon, put them on a Skewer, tie it to the Spit at both Ends, dredge and baste them, let them roast ten Minutes, take the grated Crumb of half a Loaf of Bread, with a Piece of Butter the Size of a Walnut, put it in a Stew-pan, and shake it over a gentle Fire till it is of a light brown, lay it between your Birds, and pour over them a little melted Butter.

(Mrs. *Mary Randolph's* Virginia Housewife, 1831.)

Pigeon Pye *

TAKE four Pigeons nicely cleaned and simmer gently until done in Water with an Onion, some Parsley and a few Celery-seeds. Season with Pepper and Salt and put inside of every one a large Piece of Butter and the Yolk of a hard-boiled Egg. Have ready a Paste, allowing one Pound of Butter to two Pounds of Flour. Roll it out rather thick and line with it the Bottom and Sides of a large deep Dish. Put in the Pigeons and lay on the Top some Bits of Butter rolled in Flour. Pour in nearly enough Water to fill the Dish. Cover the Pye with

a

a Lid of Paste rolled out thick and neatly notched. Ornament with Paste Leaves and Flowers, and bake until Crust is enough.

(Old Recipe, c-1848, from *Atlee, Virginia*.)

Squab Pie *

AFTER the Squabs are picked as for roasting, put them in a Sauce-pan with a close Cover. Cover with boiling Water and boil slowly till tender, with a little Salt and an Onion and Cloves. Then take them out, drain and dry, and put in each Squab a Teaspoonful of Butter, a little Pepper, Salt, minced Parsley and Thyme. Then put into the Cavity of each Squab, a hard-boiled Egg. Lay them in a large, round, earthen Baking-dish, three or four Inches deep. Strain over them the Liquor in which they were simmered. Add a Tablespoonful of Butter and a Teacup of Milk or Cream. Sift in two Tablespoonfuls of Cracker-crumbs not browned, a Tablespoonful of minced Parsley and Thyme, and a little Salt. Put in a few Slips of Pastry. Cover with a rich Crust and bake.

The same Recipe will answer for Robins, except that the Eggs must be chopped, instead of being placed whole in the Bird.

(Recipe from *Lynchburg, Virginia*.)

Leg of Pork with Pease Pudding

BOIL a small Leg of Pork that has been sufficiently salted, score the Top and serve it up; the Pudding must be in a separate Dish, get small delicate Pease, wash them well, and tie them in a

Cloth,

Cloth, allowing a little Room for swelling, boil them with the Pork, then mash and season them, tie them up again and finish boiling it; take care not to break the Pudding in turning it out.

(Mrs. *Mary Randolph's* Virginia Housewife, 1831.)

To roast Quails*

GET Quails, truss them, stuff their Bellies with Beef-sewet and Sweet-herbs, chopp'd well together; spit them on a small Spit, and when they grow warm, baste first with Water and Salt, but afterwards with Butter, and drudge them with Flour. For Sauce, dissolve an Anchovy in Gravy, into which put two or three Shalots, slic'd and boil'd; add the Juice of two or three *Seville* Oranges and one Lemon; dish them in this Sauce, and garnish with Lemon-peel and grated Manchet: Be sure to serve them up hot.

(The Lady's Companion, 1753; Cook Book owned by Miss *Anna Maria Dandridge*, 1756.)

Roasted Quail*

TAKE as many Quail as you have Guests, remove Feathers and Entrails without splitting as you would a Fowl for roasting. Fill Cavity with a large Oyster or two small ones. Sprinkle the Oysters with Pepper and Salt and a few Breadcrumbs. Put Birds in a Baking-pan with some Water and Butter, bake in a moderate Oven, basting frequently, until well brown and done. Serve on Toast with the Gravy poured over each one.   (Old Recipe, 1863, *Phenix, Virginia*.)

Roast

Roast Quail*

PLUCK and draw the Birds, rub a little Butter over them, tie a Strip of Bacon over the Breasts, set them in the Oven for twenty or twenty-five Minutes.

(Old Recipe from *Wicomico Church, Virginia.*)

Stewed Rabbit*

CUT up the Rabbit and wash it. Put it in a Stew-pan and season with Salt and Pepper. Pour in half a Pint of Water, and when this has nearly stewed away, add half a Pint of *Port* Wine, two or three Blades of Mace, and a Tablespoonful of Flour mixed with a quarter of a Pound of Butter. Let it stew gently till quite tender, and then serve hot. (Old Recipe, *Toano, Virginia.*)

Excellent Recipe for Sausage*

GRIND twelve Pounds of the Lean of the Chine of Pork and six Pounds of the Fat. Add to it five Tablespoonfuls of Salt, six of Sage, two of Thyme, five of black Pepper, three of sweet Marjoram and mix all together well.

(Traditional *Virginia* Recipe. Prov'd *Brookbury*, 1938.)

Sausages*

TAKE six Apples, and slice four of them as thick as a Crown-piece; cut the other two in Quarters, and fry them with the Sausages till they be brown.

brown. Lay the Sauſages in the Middle of the Diſh, and the Apples round them. Garniſh with the quartered Apples. Sauſages fried, and ſtewed Cabbage, make a good Diſh. Heat cold Peaſe-pudding in the Pan, lay it in the Diſh, and the Sauſages round; heap the Pudding in the Middle and lay the Sauſages all round up edge-ways, except one in the Middle at length.

(*John Farley's* London Art of Cookery, 1787, from *Brookbury, Cheſterfield* County, *Virginia.*)

Sauſage and Fried Apples *

SHAPE the Sauſage Meat in ſmall Cakes and cook ſlowly in an iron Frying-pan until the Middle is well done. Do not cook too faſt, nor let the Outſide get too hard. Pour off moſt of the Fat. Have ready good cooking Apples which have been cored and ſliced (without peeling) in Slices about one fourth Inch thick. Put theſe in the Pan and cover your Pan for a While. Turn the Apples carefully to avoid breaking. Sprinkle well with brown Sugar and cook ſlowly, well-covered, until the Apples are almoſt tender. Remove the Cover and cook until the Apples are well glazed. Theſe may be ſeaſoned with powdered Cinnamon and Cloves if deſired. Place the Apples in the Center of a hot Platter and arrange the Sauſage around the Edge.

(Old *Williamſburg* Recipe. Prov'd *Blair* Kitchen, 1938.)

To

To Cook Sora, Ortolans, and Other Small Birds *

AFTER they are split open in the Back and dressed, lay them in weak Salt and Water for a short Time. Then lay them on a Board and roll with a Rolling-pin to flatten the Breast-bone. Put Butter, Pepper, and Salt on them. Lay them on a Gridiron and broil slowly. When just done, add more Butter and Pepper, lay in a flat tin Bucket, which set over a Vessel of boiling Water to keep the Birds hot, juicy, and tender till wanted.— Mrs. *T.*

(Old Recipe from a *Williamsburg* Cook Book.)

Another Way to Cook Small Birds *

THEY should be carefully cleaned, buttered, sprinkled with Pepper and Salt, and broiled. When they are served, butter them again. If you like, serve each Bird on a Piece of Toast, and pour over them a Sauce of red Wine, Mushroom Catsup, Salt, *Cayenne* Pepper, and Celery.

(Old Recipe from a *Williamsburg* Cook Book.)

Barbecued Squirrel *

PUT some Slices of fat Bacon in an Oven. Lay the Squirrels on them and lay two Slices of Bacon on the Top. Put them in the Oven and let them cook until done. Lay them on a Dish and set near a Fire. Take out the Bacon, sprinkle one Spoonful of Flour in the Gravy and let it brown.
Then

Then pour in one Teacup of Water, one Tablespoonful of Butter and some Tomato or Walnut
Catsup. Let it cool and pour over the Squirrel.

(Old Recipe from *Toano, Virginia.*)

To broil Steaks*

FIRST have a very clear brisk Fire: let your
Gridiron be very clean; put it on the Fire,
and take a Chaffing-dish with a few hot Coals out
of the Fire. Put the Dish on it which is to lay your
Steaks on, then take fine Rump Steaks about half
an Inch thick; put a little Pepper and Salt on
them, lay them on the Gridiron, and (if you like
it) take a Shalot or two, or a fine Onion and cut it
fine; put it into your Dish. Don't turn your Steaks
till one Side is done, then when you turn the other
Side there will soon be fine Gravy lie on the Top
of the Steak, which you must be careful not to
lose. When the Steaks are enough, take them carefully off into your Dish, that none of the Gravy be
lost; then have ready a hot Dish and Cover, and
carry them hot to Table, with the Cover on.

(Mrs. *Hannah Glasse's* Art of Cookery, 1774.)

Fried Sweetbreads—Mushroom Sauce*

SOAK Sweetbreads for one half Hour in cold,
salted Water to cover. Remove from Water
and boil gently in fresh Water for twenty-five
Minutes. When thoroughly cooled cut in Slices
one half Inch thick. Dip in beaten Egg which has
been

been seasoned with Salt and Pepper. Roll in Bread-crumbs, fry in deep Fat until a golden brown. Serve on Toast with Mushroom Sauce. (See Recipe on Page 28).

(*Market Square Tavern* Kitchen, 1937.)

To make a Pie of Sweetbreads and Oysters

BOIL the Sweetbreads tender, stew the Oysters, season them with Pepper and Salt, and thicken with Cream, Butter, the Yelks of Eggs, and Flour, put a Puff-paste at the Bottom and around the Sides of a deep Dish, take the Oysters up with an Egg-spoon, lay them in the Bottom, and cover them with the Sweetbreads, fill the Dish with Gravy, put a Paste on the Top, and bake it. This is the most delicate Pie that can be made. The Sweetbread of Veal is the most delicious Part, and may be broiled, fried, or dressed in any Way, and is always good.

(Mrs. *Mary Randolph's* Virginia Housewife, 1831.)

Williamsburg *Oyster and Sweetbread Pie* ⁂

PREPARE one Pint of Sweetbreads as for fried Sweetbreads then cut them in Cubes. Heat one Pint of Oysters through and drain off all Liquor. Add well seasoned Cream Sauce to Oysters and Sweetbreads, cover with rich Pie Crust (not too thin). Brush Top with Cream and bake for forty Minutes.

(*Market Square Tavern* Kitchen, 1937.)

Or

Or do it thus *

BAKE your creamed Sweetbreads and Oyſters in a covered Baking-diſh and ſerve them up with a Paſtry Lid which has been cut round with a large Cutter, well-pricked and baked on a Tin Sheet.

(Prov'd at *Travis* Houſe, 1938.)

Tongue a la Terrapin *

TAKE a freſhly boiled Tongue, ſplit it and ſtick ſome Cloves in; cut up a ſmall Onion, put in ſome Blades of Mace and a little browned Flour in Butter. Have Water enough in a Stew-pan to cover the Tongue; mix in the Ingredients before putting in the Tongue. Add three hard-boiled Eggs chopped up fine. Send to Table hot, gar-niſhed with hard-boiled Eggs cut in Rings.

(Old Recipe, *Toano, Virginia.*)

Roaſt Turkey *

PUT the Gizzard, Heart and Liver in cold Water and boil till tender. When done, chop fine and add ſtale Bread, grated, Salt and Pepper, Sweet-herbs, two Eggs well beaten.

Fill the Turkey with this Dreſſing, ſew the Openings, drawing the Skin tightly together. Put a little Butter over the Turkey and lay it upon the Grate of your Meat-pan. Cover the Bottom of the Pan well with boiling Water. In half an Hour, baſte the Turkey by pouring over it the Gravy that has begun to form in the Pan. Repeat this

this Basting every fifteen Minutes. In an Oven of
average Temperature, a twelve-Pound Turkey will
require at least three Hours' cooking.—Mrs. *A. D.*
(Old Recipe from a *Williamsburg* Cook Book.)

Oyster Stuffing for Turkey *

TO a Pint of Cracker-crumbs add a Pint of
solid Oyster-meats, moisten the Whole with
new Milk or sweet Cream, adding Butter, Salt,
and Pepper to Taste; the Stuffing ought to be prepared some Time before needed.

(Old *Williamsburg* Recipe, c-1837, from
Mrs. *Elizabeth Labbé Cole's* Collection.)

Sausage Stuffing for a Turkey *

SOAK one large Loaf of stale Bread in Milk
enough to moisten, add Salt, Pepper, one half
Teaspoon of Thyme, the Same of Marjoram, three
large Sprigs of chopped Parsley, one finely chopped
Onion, two Stalks of Celery cut fine, twelve Olives
stoned and cut small, and one Pound of Sausage
which has been slightly cooked in a Skillet. Knead
this all very well together then add one Pound of
roasted Chestnuts cut in two. Stuff your Turkey,
sew it and truss it well. Cook in a moderate Oven
and baste frequently. This will fill a ten or twelve
pound Turkey. (Old *Morgan* Family Recipe.)

Wild Turkey *

IF the Turkey is old, after it is dressed wash it
inside thoroughly with Soda and Water. Rinse
it and plunge it into a Pot of boiling Water for five
Minutes.

Minutes. Make a Stuffing of Bits of Pork, Beef, or any other cold Meat, plenty of chopped Celery, ſtewed Giblets, hard-boiled Eggs, pounded Cracker, Pepper, and Salt, and a heaping Spoonful of Butter. Work this well and fill the Turkey. With another large Spoonful of Butter greaſe the Bird, and then ſprinkle Salt and Pepper over it. Lay in a Pan, with a Pint of Broth in which Meat has been boiled. Place in a hot Oven. When it begins to brown, dredge with Flour and baſte, turning often, ſo that each Part may be equally browned. Put a buttered Sheet of Paper over the Breaſt, to prevent Dryneſs. When thoroughly done, lay on a Diſh, brown ſome Crackers, pound and ſift over it, and ſerve with Celery or Oyſter Sauce.

(Recipe from an old *Williamſburg* Cook Book.)

Turkey Haſh *

CUT up the Meat very fine. Stew the Bones in a little Water, ſtrain, then ſtir into this Water the Meat, adding a large Tableſpoonful Butter mixed with Flour, a Cup of Cream, Salt and Pepper, a little chopped Parſley, Thyme or Celery (or elſe a very few Celery-ſeeds). Stew all together.

(Recipe from an old *Williamſburg* Cook Book.)

Veal Rolls *

TAKE ten or twelve little thin Slices of Veal, lay on them ſome Force-meat according to your Fancy, roll them up, and tie them just acroſs the Middle with coarſe Thread, put them on a Bird-ſpit, rub them over with the Yolks of Eggs,
flour

flour them, and baste them with Butter. Half an Hour will do them. Lay them into a Dish, and have ready some good Gravy, with a few Truffles and Morels, and some Mushrooms. Garnish with Lemon.

(Mrs. *Hannah Glasse's* Art of Cookery, 1774.)

Williamsburg *Veal Partridges* *

TAKE twelve very thin Slices of Veal Cutlet and have ready two Cups of Force-meat made of stale Bread-crumbs, a small Onion chopped fine and browned in Butter, Salt, Pepper, one half Teaspoon each of Thyme, Marjoram, and Basil, moistened with Milk. Lay your Force-meat on a Piece of Veal and roll it up and skewer together with two wooden Tooth-picks stuck through diagonally to cross each other. Roll in Flour and brown in Fat. As they brown place them in a Baking-dish. Thicken the Fat in the Pan with Flour, add hot Water. Pour over the Veal, cover your Baking-dish and bake in a slow Oven forty Minutes. Serve with steamed wild Rice.

(*Market Square Tavern* Kitchen, 1937.)

Venison Pastey *

CUT the Venison into small Pieces; place them in a Sauce-pan with one Ounce of Butter, and brown them well; then one Ounce of Flour, which should be browned; stir until perfectly smooth; add one Quart of Broth, one large Onion, a Bundle of Sweet-herbs, Salt, Pepper, and a little Nutmeg; place on the Stove where it will simmer for one Hour;

Hour; when done, add two Teaspoons of Walnut
Catsup, one half Cup of *Madeira* Wine. By this
Time the Gravy will be thick. Butter a deep
Baking-dish and put the Stew in it, first taking out
the Onion and Herbs; cover it with a Top of Puff-
pastry; make Slits in the Top of the Pastry. Serve
hot. If preferred, this Stew may be served over
Toast or Waffles instead of being baked in a Dish
as above directed.

(Recipe from an old *Williamsburg* Cook Book.)

Scotch *Collops* ✱

TAKE Veal, cut it thin, beat it well with a
Rolling-pin and grate some Nutmeg over them,
dip them in the Yolk of an Egg, and fry them in a
little Butter till they are of a fine brown then pour
the Butter from them, and have ready half a Pint
of Gravy, a little Piece of Butter rolled in Flour,
a Glass of White-wine, the Yolk of an Egg and a
little Cream mixed together. Stir it all together
and when it is of a fine Thickness dish it up. It does
very well without Cream if you have none and
very well without Gravy, only put in just as much
warm Water and either red or white Wine.

(Manuscript Cook Book, c-1825, of Miss *Margaret
Prentis* of *Williamsburg.* Owned by *Robert
H. Webb*, Esq., *Charlottesville.*)

To fry cold Veal

CUT it in Pieces and dip them into the Yolk of
an Egg and then in Crumbs of Bread with a
few Sweet-herbs, and spread Lemon Peel in it. Grate
a little Nutmeg over them and fry them in fresh
Butter.
                                                      The

The Butter muſt be hot, juſt enough to fry them in. In the meantime make a little Gravy of the Bone of the Veal, when the Meat is fried take it out with a Fork and lay it in a Diſh before the Fire then ſhake a little Flour into the Pan and ſtir it round, then put in the Gravy, ſqueeze in a little Lemon and pour it over the Veal.—Garniſh with Lemon.

(Manuſcript Cook Book, c-1825, of Miſs *Margaret Prentis* of *Williamſburg.* Owned by *Robert H. Webb*, Eſq., *Charlotteſville.*)

To make an Egg as big as Twenty

PART the Yolks from the Whites of twenty Eggs, ſtrain the Yolks by themſelves, and the Whites by themſelves, boil the Yolks in a Bladder, in the Form either of an Egg or Ball; when they are boiled hard, put the Ball of Yolks into another Bladder, and the Whites round about it, and bind it up oval or round, and boil it. Theſe Eggs are uſed in grand Sallads.

If you pleaſe you may add to the Yolks of the Eggs, Ambergreeſe, Muſk, grated Biſcuits, candy'd Piſtachoes and Sugar; and to the Whites, Muſk, Almond-paſte, beaten Ginger, and the Juice of Oranges, and ſerve them up with Butter, Almond-milk, Sugar, and Juice of Orange.

(The Lady's Companion, 1753; Cook Book. owned by Miſs *Anna Maria Dandridge*, 1756.)

Williamſburg *Stuffed Eggs* ☀

TAKE a Dozen hard-boiled Eggs, ſplit them in two and maſh up the Yolks. Saute three large Muſhrooms and one Tableſpoon of minced Onion in in Butter. Add to the Yolks one Tableſpoon chopped Parſley, one Tableſpoon fine Bread-crumbs, a Pinch of Savory, a Teaſpoon of prepared Muſtard, one Tableſpoon Lemon-juice, Salt, Pep-per and the Muſhroom and Onion. Fill the Whites of the Eggs with it and lay them in a Baking-diſh in which you have placed a Layer of Force-meat made with Chicken or Veal. Bake them in a ſlow Oven until they are brown and ſerve them hot with a Muſhroom Sauce, or a Cream-ſauce ſeaſoned with White-wine.

(Miſs *Dandridge's* Recipe, 1756. Adapted
Market Square Tavern Kitchen, 1937.)

To make a Welch *Rabbit*＊

TOAST the Bread on both Sides, then toaſt the Cheeſe on one Side, lay it on the Toaſt, and with a hot Iron brown the other Side. You may rub it over with Muſtard.

(Mrs. *Hannah Glaſſe's* Art of Cookery, 1774.)

To make an Engliſh *Rabbit*＊

TOAST a Slice of Bread brown on both Sides, then lay it in a Plate before the Fire, pour a Glaſs of red Wine over it, and let it ſoak the Wine up; then cut ſome Cheeſe very thin, and lay it very thick over the Bread, and put it in a Tin Oven before the Fire, and it will be toaſted and browned preſently. Serve it away hot.

(Mrs. *Hannah Glaſſe's* Art of Cookery, 1774.)

Devilled

Devilled Crabs *

BLEND together two Tablespoons Flour with two Tablespoons Butter. Add one Cup Cream, stirring constantly. Mix with Yolks of four hard-boiled Eggs chopped fine, two Teaspoons chopped Parsley and one Teaspoon Walnut Catsup. Add one Pound Crab-flakes, season to Taste. Put them back in the well-cleaned Shells, sprinkle with buttered Bread-crumbs and bake in a moderate Oven until brown.

(Recipe from *Richmond, Virginia*.)

Another Way *

TO the Meat of one Dozen Crabs, boiled fifteen Minutes and picked free from Shell, add three Tablespoonfuls stale Bread-crumbs, two Tablespoonfuls Cream, Yolks of three Eggs, a little chopped Parsley, one Tablespoonful Butter, Salt and Pepper to Taste. Put in Shells and bake in a quick Oven.

(Old Recipe, *Toano, Virginia*.)

Scalloped Crabs *

TO one Pound of well-cleaned Crab-meat add a Sauce made as follows:

Blend four Tablespoons of Flour and Butter and add one Pint of rich Milk. Cook over a slow Fire, stirring constantly, until thick. Remove. Add one Teaspoonful of *Worcestershire* Sauce, one half Teaspoonful of Salt, a few Dashes of Pepper Sauce and one third of a Cup of dry Sherry. Beat in two Egg Yolks.

Mix lightly with Crab and place in buttered
Scallop

Scallop Shells, ſprinkle with Crumbs, dot with Butter, and bake in moderate Oven until light brown. Serve with a ſmall, thin Slice of Lemon on each.

(Williamſburg Recipe, c-1830.
Prov'd Blair Kitchen, 1938.)

Soft Shell Crabs *

WASH and dry thoroughly. Remove the Eyes and Sandbag. After removing Subſtance under Flaps on each Side and the Piece called the Apron, waſh and dry thoroughly. Dip in Eggs which have been beaten well and ſeaſoned with Salt and Pepper. Roll in Bread-crumbs. Fry in hot Fat until well browned on both Sides. Serve with a good Sauce.

(Market Square Tavern Kitchen, 1937.)

To boil Flounders or Plaice *

PUT Salt, whole Spice, White-wine, and a Bunch of Sweet-herbs into your Water; when it boils put in a little Vinegar, for that will make the Fiſh criſp; let it boil apace before you put in your Fiſh; let them boil till they ſwim, then take them up, and drain them; take a little of the Liquor, put it into ſome Butter, two or three Anchovies, and ſome Capers; ſet it over the Fire, and beat it up thick, then pour it over the Fiſh, with Parſley, Capers, Orange and Lemon.

(The Lady's Companion, 1753; Cook Book
owned by Miſs Anna Maria Dandridge, 1756.)

To

To pickle Herring or Mackerel

CUT off the Heads and Tails of your Fiſh, gut them, waſh them, and dry them well; then take two Ounces and a Half of Salt-petre, three quarters of an Ounce of *Jamaica* Pepper, and a quarter and half quarter of white Pepper, and pound them ſmall; an Ounce of ſweet Marjoram and Thyme chopp'd ſmall; mix all together, and put ſome within and without the Fiſh; lay them in an earthen Pan, the Roes at Top, and cover them with White-wine Vinegar, then ſet them into an Oven, not too hot, for two Hours. This is for Fifteen; and after this Rule do as many as you pleaſe.

(The Lady's Companion, 1753; Cook Book owned by Miſs *Anna Maria Dandridge*, 1756.)

To fry Oyſters *

BEAT Eggs, with a little Salt, grated Nutmeg, and thicken it like thick Batter, with grated white Bread and fine Flour; then dip the Oyſters in it, and fry them brown with Beef-dripping.

(*E. Smith's* Compleat Houſewife, *Williamſburg*, 1742.)

Batter to fry Oyſters in *

SIX Eggs beaten very light; add to them ſix Tableſpoonfuls ſifted Flour, and one and a half Pint rich Milk, and one-fourth Teaſpoonful grated Nutmeg; beat all together to a ſmooth Paſte.

(Old *Williamſburg* Recipe, c-1837, from Mrs. *Elizabeth Labbé Cole's* Collection)

Fried

Fried Oysters *

DRAIN Liquor from one Quart of large Oysters.
Prepare three Eggs, well-beaten, to which
has been added two Tablespoons Milk, one half
Teaspoon Salt, one fourth Teaspoon Pepper. First
dip Oyster in beaten Egg, then in Bread-crumbs.
Fry in deep Fat until golden brown. Serve immediately.

(Prov'd *Market Square Tavern* Kitchen, 1937)

Oyster Loaves

TAKE a Quart of middling Oysters, and wash
them in their own Liquor; then strain them
through a Flannel, and put them on the Fire to
warm; then take three quarters of a Pint of Gravy
and put to the Oysters, with a Blade of Mace, a
little white Pepper, a little Horse-raddish and a
Piece of lean Bacon, and half a Lemon; then stew
them leisurely. Take three Penny Loaves, and pick
out the Crumb clean; then take a Pound of Butter,
and set on the Fire in a Sauce-pan that will hold
the Loaves, and when it is melted, take it off the
Fire, and let it settle; then pour off the Clear, and
set it on the Fire again with the Loaves in it, and
turn them about till you find them crisp; then put
a Pound of Butter in a Frying-pan, and with a
dredging Box dust in Flower till you find it of a
reasonable Thickness, then mix that and the
Oysters together; and when stewed enough take
out the Bacon, and put the Oysters into the
Loaves; then put them into a Dish, and garnish
the Loaves with the Oysters you cannot get in,
and

and with Slices of Lemon; and when you have
thickened the Liquor, ſqueeze in Lemon to your
Taſte; or you may fry the Oyſters with Batter to
garniſh the Loaves.

(*E. Smith's* Compleat Houſewife, *London*, 1739.)

Panned Oyſters *

PUT in a Sauce-pan, over the Fire, enough
Butter to cover the Bottom when melted. When
hot, pour in one Quart of nice Oyſters, ſhake the
Pan until the Oyſters curl. Serve hot on Toaſt.
Some of the Liquor may be added to the Oyſters
in the Pan.

(Old *Maryland* Recipe from a *Virginia* Cook Book.)

Pickled Oyſters *

TAKE one Gallon Oyſters and cook them in
their own Liquor till nearly done. Then ſkim
out the Oyſters and add to the Liquor one Teaſpoonful whole black Pepper, one Teaſpoonful
Allſpice, one Teaſpoonful Mace, a little red
Pepper and half a Pint of ſtrong Vinegar. Let it
boil a few Minutes and then pour over the Oyſters.
When nearly cool, ſlice in them a large freſh Lemon.

(Old Recipe from *Lynchburg, Virginia,*
in a *Williamſburg* Cook Book.)

Oyſters Pickled *

COOK Oyſters with a little Salt. Then ſtrain
through a Sifter, throw the Oyſters in Ice-
water, ſtrain the Liquor. To every two Cups of
Liquor

Liquor add one Cup of good Vinegar, some whole Peppercorns and a little Mace; boil until seasoned. Let it be very cold before adding the Oysters. Add sliced Lemon before serving.

(Old *Nelson* Family Recipe.)

Scalloped Oysters *

HAVING opened your Oysters into a Bason, and washed them out of their own Liquor, put some into your Scollop-shells, and strew over them a few Crumbs of Bread. Lay a Slice of Butter on them, then more Oysters, Bread, and Butter successively, till your Shell be as full as you intend it. Put them into a *Dutch* Oven to brown, and serve them up in the Shells in which they are scolloped.

(*John Farley's* London Art of Cookery, 1787, from *Brookbury, Chesterfield* County, *Virginia.* Prov'd 1937.)

Oyster Soup

TAKE two Quarts of fine Oysters, strain the Liquor and if there is not Liquor sufficient to make your Soup, put as much Water—one Onion, two Blades of Mace, boil these well together, throw in your Oysters and give them a Boil, have ready a Piece of Butter say from a quarter to half a Pound, with Flour sufficient to thicken, rub them up together. Season with Pepper and Salt to your Taste. When just ready to dish throw in at least half a Pint of rich Cream, then give one more Boil,

Boil, ſend up to Table. The Oyſters will be plump and the Soup very nice.

[Note: This Recipe is on a Slip of Paper pinned to a Page of the Cook Book and is ſigned

"with much love
Mrs. *B.* recipes"]

(Manuſcript Cook Book, c-1801, of Mrs. *Frances Bland Tucker Coalter.* Owned by Dr. *St. George Tucker-Grinnan, Richmond.*)

Stewed Oyſters *

HAVE the Veſſel hot, then take the Oyſters out of their own Liquor with a Fork, and put them in the Veſſel, ſtirring them ſo as to prevent Burning or Scorching. Cook quickly, when half done add to each Quart of Oyſters, a Piece of freſh Butter the Size of a large Egg, half Pint of Cream or rich Milk, the Yolks of two Eggs well beaten up, Pepper and Salt to Taſte and ſerve hot.

(Old Recipe from *Matthews Court Houſe, Virginia.*)

Stuffed Oyſters *

PUT together in a Pan two Dozen Oyſters, drained and chopped fine; two Slices of Bread, crumbled; half an Onion, ſome chopped Celery, one Tableſpoon Parſley chopped, a little *Cayenne* Pepper, one Teaſpoonful Walnut Catchup, Butter the Size of an Egg, Juice and grated Rind of one Lemon. Cook on Top of Stove ſtirring conſtantly for thirty Minutes. Add two beaten Eggs. Put Mixture in Oyſter Shells. Cover with buttered Crumbs, and brown in Oven. Serve with thin Slices of Lemon. (Old Recipe, adapted 1937.)

To

To bake Shad

THE Shad is a very indifferent Fiſh unleſs it be large and fat; when you get a good One, prepare it nicely, put ſome Force-meat inſide, and lay it at full length in a Pan with a Pint of Water, a Gill of red Wine, one of Muſhroom Catſup, a little Pepper, Vinegar, Salt, a few Cloves of Garlic, and ſix Cloves: ſtew it gently till the Gravy is ſufficiently reduced; there ſhould always be a Fiſh-ſlice with Holes to lay the Fiſh on, for the Convenience of diſhing without breaking it; when the Fiſh is taken up, ſlip it carefully into the Diſh; thicken the Gravy with Butter and brown Flour, and pour over it.

(Mrs. *Mary Randolph's* Virginia Houſewife, 1831.)

Baked Shad*

CLEAN Shad, being careful not to break Roe, if there is any. Make a plain Stuffing of Bread-crumbs, Butter, Salt and Pepper as for Fowls, and ſtuff the Body of the Fiſh with it, ſewing it up with a ſoft Thread; lard one Side of the Fiſh and ſcore it with a ſharp Knife, making the Scores about one Inch apart, and put a Strip of ſalt Pork in each Gaſh. Butter a Tin Sheet, dredge with Salt, Pepper and Flour, cover the Bottom of the Pan with boiling Water and put into a hot Oven. Bake fifteen Minutes for every Pound of Fiſh, baſting each ten Minutes with the Gravy in the Pan. When done lift out carefully and

and slide in Center of the Dish to be served. Garnish with sliced Lemon, fried Potato Balls and Parsley. (Old Recipe, *Richmond, Virginia.*)

Another Way*

OPEN the Shad down the Back, wash well and salt it; wipe dry and rub inside and out with a little *Cayenne* Pepper. Prepare a Stuffing of Bread, seasoned with Pepper, Salt, Thyme or Parsley, Celery-feed, a little chopped Onion, Piece of Butter the Size of a Walnut. Tie up the Fish and put in a Baking-pan with one Pint Water and Butter the Size of an Egg. Sprinkle with Flour, baste well and bake slowly an Hour and a half.

(Old Recipe from *Toano, Virginia.*)

To butter Shrimps*

STEW a Quart of Shrimps in Half a Pint of White-wine, a Nutmeg grated, and a good Piece of Butter; when the Butter is melted, and they are not through, beat the Yolks of four Eggs with a little White-wine, and pour it in, and shake it well, till it is of the Thickness you like; then dish it on Sippets, and garnish with sliced Lemon.

(Mrs. *E. Smith's* Compleat Housewife, *London*, 1739. Prov'd 1937.)

To bake Sturgeon*

GET a Piece of Sturgeon with the Skin on, the Piece next to the Tail, scrape it well, cut out the Gristle, and boil it about twenty Minutes to take

take out the Oil; take it up, pull off the large
Scales, and when cold, ſtuff it with Force-meat
made of Bread-crumbs, Butter, chopped Parſley,
Pepper and Salt, put it in a *Dutch* Oven juſt large
enough to hold it, with a Pint and a half of Water,
a Gill of red Wine, one of Muſhroom Catſup, ſome
Salt and Pepper, ſtew it gently till the Gravy is
reduced to the Quantity neceſſary to pour over it;
take up your Sturgeon carefully, thicken the Gravy
with a Spoonful of Butter rubbed into a large One
of brown Flour, ſee that it is perfectly ſmooth
when you put it in the Diſh.

(Mrs. *Mary Randolph's* Virginia Houſewife, 1831.)

To fry Trouts *

YOU muſt, with a Knife, gently ſcrape off all the
Slime from your Fiſh, waſh them in Salt and
Water, gut them, and wipe them very clean with
a Linnen Cloth; that done, ſtrew Flour over them,
and fry them in ſweet Butter, till they are brown
and criſp; then take them out of the Frying-pan,
and lay them on a Pewter Diſh, well-heated before
the Fire; pour off the Butter they were fry'd in,
into the Greaſe Pot, and not over the Trouts:
Afterwards, good Store of Parſley and young Sage
being fry'd criſp in other ſweet Butter, take out
the Herbs, and lay them on your Fiſh. In the mean-
while, ſome Butter being beaten up with three or
four Spoonfuls of ſcalding hot Spring-water, in
which an Anchovy has been diſſolved, pour it on
the Trouts, and let them be ſerved up. Garniſh
with the Leaves of Strawberries, Parſley, &c.

After this Manner, Grailings, Perches, ſmall
Pikes

Pikes or Jacks, Roaches and Gudgeons may be fry'd, their Scales being firſt ſcraped off: And you may thus fry ſmall Eels, when they are flea'd, gutted, wiped clean, and cut into Pieces of four or five Inches long; ſeveral Pieces of Salmon, or a Chine of it, may likewiſe be dreſſed in the ſame Manner.

(The Lady's Companion, 1753; Cook Book owned by Miſs *Anna Maria Dandridge*, 1756. Recipe prov'd 1937.)

Turtle Soup *

KILL the Turtle at Daylight in Summer, the Night before in Winter, and hang it up to bleed. After Breakfaſt, ſcald it well and ſcrape the outer Skin off the Shell; open it carefully, ſo as not to break the Gall. Break both Shells to Pieces and put them into the Pot. Lay the Fins, the Eggs and ſome of the more delicate Parts by— put the Reſt into the Pot with a Quantity of Water to ſuit the Size of your Family. Add two Onions, Parſley, Thyme, Salt, Pepper, Cloves and Allſpice to ſuit your Taſte.

About half an Hour before Dinner thicken the Soup with brown Flour and Butter rubbed together. An Hour before Dinner, take the Parts laid by, roll them in brown Flour, fry them in Butter, put them and the Eggs in the Soup; juſt before Dinner add a Glaſs of Claret or *Madeira* Wine.

(Recipe from an old *Williamſburg* Cook Book.)

Turtle

Turtle or Terrapin Stew

AFTER they are well cleaned, parboil the Meat, then pick it to Pieces. Seaſon highly with Pepper, Salt, *Cayenne* Pepper, hard-boiled Egg, Spices, Lemon, and Champagne or other Wine. Stew until well done.

(Old Recipe, *Cheſterfield* County, *Virginia*.)

Of BREAD

"AND as they brew, ſo do they bake daily, "Bread or Cakes, eating too much hot and "new Bread, which cannot be wholſom, tho' it be "pleaſanter than what has been baked a Day or "two."

Theſe Words, written by the Reverend *Hugh Jones* in 1724, in *The Preſent State of Virginia* reflected an early Apprehenſion for the good Digeſtion of the *Virginians*, who, then as now would ſcorn to eat any Bread ſo old it had even grown cool. And it may be remarked, by one who has had Opportunity for cloſe Obſervation, that the Digeſtion of thoſe addicted to this and ſimilar Apprehenſions, cannot compare in Soundneſs with that of the *Virginians* who have been for Generations eſtabliſhed in this Habit.

The moſt characteriſtic hot Breads are thoſe which

which are made from *Indian* Corn. As early as the Year 1608, the Colonists had gathered *Indian* Corn of their own planting and had learned to make Bread of it in the *Indian* Manner, by mixing Corn Meal and Water, shaping it into Cakes, or Pones, which were baked in hot Ashes, or on Hoes. Of Corn Pone, the Historian, *Beverley*, wrote in 1705:

> The Bread in Gentlemen's Houses is generally made of Wheat, but some rather choose the Pone, which is the Bread made of *Indian* Meal. Many of the poorer Sort of People so little regard the *English* Grain, that though they might have it with the least Trouble in the World, yet they don't mind to sow the Ground, because they won't be at the Trouble of making a Fence particularly for it. And therefore their constant Bread is Pone, not so called from the *Latin*, *Panis*, but from the *Indian* Name *Oppone*.

Although Pone (or Hoe Cakes and Ash Cakes as they were also called) became the "constant Bread" of the Slaves and the poorer People, excellent Breads were developed from *Indian* Meal during the seventeenth and eighteenth Centuries, which remain in staunch Favour today among all Classes of *Virginians*. There are the Batter Breads (by some, especially those in the more southern Colonies, called Spoon Breads) Egg Breads, and Corn Breads for which proper Recipes are given in this Chapter.

Of prime Importance in the Making of these Breads is the Selection of a proper Meal. Only the native Corn, ground slowly in a Water Grist Mill may be used and under no Circumstances should a Cook so far depart from the good Judgment of
Generations

Generations of *Virginia* Housewives as to permit
Sugar in any Variety of Corn Bread.

Biscuits, Muffins, *Sally Lunn*, Rolls, Waffles,
and other Breads made of Wheat Flour are also
served "hot and new"; and to those who enjoy
Virginia Hospitality for the first Time they are
usually served with the Instruction "Take two,
"and butter them while they're hot". So seductive is
the Custom, that it may be observed that it is a rare
Visitor to whom the Instruction must be repeated.

All Sorts of BREADS

Apoquiniminics—*Mrs.* Skipwith

INTO one Quart of Flour rub one Spoonful Butter and two Eggs, Whites and Yolks. Put in as
much sweet Milk as will make it the Consistence of
Paste—Roll them [thin, and cut into round Cakes]
and bake on a Gridiron.—Dip them in Butter
melted in a Plate.   (Manuscript Cook Book, c-1801,
of Mrs. *Frances Bland Tucker Coalter*.
Owned by Dr. *St. George Tucker Grinnan, Richmond*.)

Beaten Biscuits *

TAKE one Quart of Flour, Lard the Size of a
Hen's Egg, one Teaspoonful of Salt. Make into
a moderately stiff Dough with sweet Milk. Beat for
half an Hour. Make out with the Hand or cut with
the

the Biſcuit Cutter. Stick with a Fork and bake in
a hot Oven, yet not ſufficiently hot to bliſter the
Biſcuit.

(Recipe from *Lynchburg, Virginia.*
From an old *Williamſburg* Cook Book.)

Beaten Biſcuit *

ONE Quart of Flour, one Teacup of Lard (if you
prefer it uſe Lard and Butter mixed), one Teaſpoon of Salt, one Cup of ſweet Milk. Make a ſtiff
Dough, then beat it fifteen or twenty Minutes
until it bliſters. Roll and cut in ſmall round Biſcuits. Bake in a moderately hot Oven.

(*Read* Family Recipe.)

Cheeſe Biſcuit *

SIFT one Cup of Flour with one fourth Teaſpoon
of Salt, cut in one third of a Cup of Butter. Add
one Cup of grated Cheeſe. Work lightly into a ſtiff
Paſte. Roll out one half Inch thick and cut with
very ſmall Cutter and prick Tops with Fork. Bake
in a moderate Oven about twelve Minutes, but do
not brown. Theſe burn very eaſily.

(Old *Williamſburg* Recipe. Prov'd *Blair* Kitchen, 1938.)

Breakfaſt Puffs *

HEAT greaſed iron or other heavy Muffin Pans
in the Oven until very hot. Fill two-thirds full
with a Batter made as follows: Sift one Cup of
Flour with one fourth Teaſpoon of Salt. Mix together two well-beaten Eggs, ſeven-eighths of a
Cup of Milk and one Tableſpoonful of melted Butter.

ter. Stir ſlowly into Flour but do not overmix.
Bake in a hot Oven for about twenty Minutes and
dry them in a moderate Oven for about fifteen.
Serve at once.

(Old Recipe, *Toano, Virginia*.
Prov'd *Blair* Kitchen, 1938.)

To Make Bread*

SCALD three Cups of Milk and pour them in a
large Bowl in which you have three fourths of
a Cup of Sugar, two Teaſpoons of Salt and one
Tableſpoonful of Butter. Cool and add one Yeaſt
Cake diſſolved in one half Cup lukewarm Water,
and ſift in three Quarts of Flour (enough to make a
ſtiff Dough). Knead ſmooth, ſet to riſe in a warm
Place, when it has doubled in Bulk turn onto
floured Board and knead lightly. Shape into
Loaves. Place in Pans and ſet to riſe again. Bake
in moderate Oven about one Hour.

(Mrs. *Cole's* Recipe, c-1837. Adapted
Market Square Tavern Kitchen, 1937.)

Buns—*Miſs* Bowdoin

TAKE eight Eggs, one Pound Sugar, two
Pounds Flour, one half Pound freſh Butter.
Work half the Flour with the Butter till very light.
Beat the Eggs light with the Sugar and the Bal-
ance of the Flour. Mix all together with a Glaſs of
Wine, half a Nutmeg, and a Teaſpoonful of beaten
Mace. Bake them in a quick Oven, either in
Shapes or (which I like beſt) by dropping the Bat-
ter in Spoonfuls on the Bottom of the *Dutch* Oven.

(Manuſcript Cook Book, c-1801,
of Mrs. *Frances Bland Tucker Coalter*.
Owned by Dr. *St. George Tucker Grinnan, Richmond*.)

Williamſburg

Williamſburg *Buns* ⁂

SCALD one Cup of Milk, add one half Cup of melted Butter, two Teaſpoonfuls of Salt and one half Cup of Sugar. Cool to lukewarm. Add two Yeaſt Cakes which have been diſſolved in one fourth Cup of warm Water. Add three beaten Eggs to Liquids, then beat in well four and a half Cups of Flour. (One Teaſpoonful each of Nutmeg and Mace and a Wine-glaſſ of Sherry may be added.) Let the Dough riſe until double in Bulk, turn it out and knead lightly. Fill Muffin Pans two-thirds full and let riſe until light (about twenty Minutes). Bruſh with melted Butter and bake in a moderately hot Oven about twenty Minutes. Makes about three Dozen ſmall Buns which are very nice for Tea.

(Miſs *Bowdoin's* Recipe, c-1801. Adapted *Blair* Kitchen, 1938.)

Coach Wheels ⁂

ROLL out your Dough in a long narrow Strip. Rub with ſoft Butter, ſprinkle with brown Sugar and Cinnamon. Roll up into a Roll as round as your Buns are to be. Slice three quarters Inch thick with a floured Knife, and place almoſt touching in a well-buttered Pan. Let them riſe until light and bake in a moderate Oven.

(*Richmond* Recipe. Prov'd *Blair* Kitchen, 1938.)

Madiſon *Cakes* ⁂

COOK two medium-ſized *Iriſh* Potatoes in one and one fourth Cups of boiling Water, ſtrain off the Water into a Cup. Maſh the Potatoes well, and meaſure

meaſure one Cupful of Potato Water (adding cold
Water if not enough). When lukewarm, diſſolve one
Yeaſt Cake in it. To maſhed Potatoes add four
Tableſpoonfuls of Butter, twoTeaſpoonfuls of Salt,
two Tableſpoons of Sugar, and two beaten Eggs.
Add Yeaſt Mixture then one and one half Quarts of
ſifted Flour. Knead until ſmooth and ſpongy. Put
in a greaſed Crock and let riſe four or five Hours
until light. Roll one Inch thick and cut up into
Rolls. Set them far apart on your buttered Sheet,
let riſe until light and bake twenty Minutes in a
moderate Oven.

(Old *Virginia* Recipe. Prov'd 1937.)

Crumpets *

TAKE a Quart of Dough from your Bread at a
very early Hour in the Morning; break three
freſh Eggs, ſeparating the Yelks from the Whites—
whip them both to a Froth, mix them with the
Dough, and add gradually milk-warm Water, till
you make a Batter the Thickneſs of Buckwheat
Cakes: beat it well, and ſet it to riſe till near Breakfaſt Time; have the Griddle ready, pour on the
Batter to look quite round: they do not require
turning.

(Mrs. *Mary Randolph's* Virginia Houſewife, 1831.)

Huckleberry Muffins *

SIFT together two Cups of Flour, four Tableſpoonfuls of Sugar, four Teaſpoons of baking
Powder, one half Teaſpoon of Salt. Add one Cup
of well-cleaned Huckleberries. Beat an Egg and
add

add to it one Cup of Milk and pour into Flour. Then add four Tablespoons of melted Butter. Half fill buttered Muffin Tins and bake in a moderate Oven. (*Williamsburg* Family Recipe, Adapted 1938.)

Rice Muffins *

SIFT together three Cups of Flour, two Tablespoons of Sugar, three Teaspoons of baking Powder and one Teaspoon of Salt. Stir in three fourths of a Cup of Milk, then add one and a half Cups of cooked Rice which is mixed with one Cup of Milk. Add three beaten Eggs, and one fourth of a Cup of melted Butter. Bake in well-greased Tins in a hot Oven. This will make twenty-four Muffins.

(Old Recipe from *Disputanta, Virginia*. Prov'd *Williamsburg*, 1937.)

Martha Washington's *Potato Light Rolls* *

BOIL and mash two good sized *Irish* Potatoes and while still hot add two Tablespoons of Butter, one Tablespoon of Lard, two Tablespoons of Sugar, one Teaspoon Salt, and one and a half Cupfuls of Water in which the Potatoes were boiled, and one Cupful of tepid Milk. Beat all well, adding gradually four Cups sifted Flour and when lukewarm stir in a Yeast Cake dissolved in one fourth Cup of tepid Water. Beat very hard, then turn out on a Board, adding more Flour as required and knead well. Set away in a warm sheltered Place for six Hours. Do not knead again. Roll, cut into Rounds, let stand until very light, and bake in a hot Oven. (Old Recipe, *Chase City, Virginia*.)

Sour

Sour Milk Griddle Cakes *

DISSOLVE one and a half Teaſpoons of Soda in
ſour Milk. Add one and one half Cups of
Flour, one Tableſpoonful of Sugar and one half
Teaſpoon of Salt which have been ſifted together.
Add two unbeaten Eggs and beat well. Add one
Tableſpoon of melted Butter. Drop on hot Griddle.
Brown on both Sides. This Recipe may be varied
by uſing half Corn Meal and half Flour or half
Hominy Grits and half Flour.

(*Virginia* Recipe, adapted and prov'd 1937.)

Sally Lunn *

BEAT four Eggs well; then melt a large Tableſpoonful of Butter, put it in a Teacup of warm
Water, and pour it to the Eggs with a Teaſpoon of Salt and a Teacup of Yeaſt (this means
Potato Yeaſt); beat in a Quart of Flour making the
Batter ſtiff enough for a Spoon to ſtand in. Put it
to riſe before the Fire the Night before. Beat it over
in the Morning, greaſe your Cake-mould and put
it in Time enough to riſe before baking. Should you
want it for Supper, make it up at 10:00 o'Clock in
the Morning in the Winter and 12: o'Clock in the
Summer.

(Recipe, c-1770, of Governor *Spotſwood's* Grand-daughter.
From *Charlotte Court Houſe, Virginia*.)

Williamſburg Sally Lunn *

PUT one Yeaſt Cake in one Cup of warm Milk.
Cream together one half Cup of Butter and one
third of a Cup of Sugar, add three beaten Eggs and
mix

mix well. Sift in one Quart of Flour, alternately
with the Milk and Yeaft. Let rife in a warm Place
then beat well. Pour into one well-buttered *Sally
Lunn* Mold or two fmaller Molds. Let rife again
before baking in a moderate Oven.

(*Barlow* Family Recipe, *Williamfburg.*
Prov'd *Market Square Tavern* Kitchen, 1937.)

Sally Lunn Muffins *

SCALD one and one fourth Cups Milk and let
cool until luke-warm. Add two heaping Teaspoons Sugar and two Yeaft Cakes to diffolve.
Then add two Eggs, well beaten, two Tablefpoons
Cream, four Tablefpoons melted Butter, three and
one third Cups of Flour, one Teafpoon Salt. Beat
hard and let rife again, about two Hours in all.
Put in greafed Muffin Tins and let rife again for an
Hour. Bake in moderate Oven.

(Traditional *Virginia* Recipe.
Prov'd *Market Square Tavern* Kitchen, 1937.)

Williamfburg *Sweet Potato Buns* *

MASH two boiled fweet Potatoes while hot
with three Tablefpoons of Butter. When
cool add one well-beaten Egg, one Teafpoon of
Salt, three Tablefpoons of Sugar, then one half of
a Yeaft Cake diffoved in half a Cup of warm Water.
Then fift in four Cups of Flour alternately with
about one Cup of warm Water (or enough to make
a foft Dough). Knead until fmooth, let it rife in a
warm Place until double in Bulk. Put in well-
buttered

buttered Muffin Pans, let rife again and bake in a moderate Oven. Juft before removing from Oven rub the Tops with melted Butter.

(Mrs. *Randolph's* Recipe, 1831.
Adapted *Market Square Tavern* Kitchen, 1937.)

Sweet Potato Bifcuits *

SIFT together two Cups of Flour, one half Teafpoon of Soda, and one Teafpoon of Salt. Work in four level Tablefpoons of Lard. Mix one Cup of mafhed fweet Potatoes with one half Cup of four Milk and mix to a foft Dough. Roll thin, cut and bake in a hot Oven.

(Old Recipe from *Difputanta, Virginia.*
Adapted *Market Square Tavern* Kitchen, 1937.)

Waffles *

TAKE one and a half Cups Buttermilk, two Eggs, one-half Teafpoon Salt, one-half Teafpoon Sugar, one Tablefpoon of Butter, one Teafpoon Baking-powder, one half Teafpoon Soda, one Pint of Flour. Melt Butter, beat Eggs, add Salt and Sugar, then Buttermilk. Sift Flour, Soda, and Powder into the Milk and Egg Mixture. Laftly add melted Butter. If Batter is too ftiff, add a Bit of cold Water. Have Waffle Iron well greafed and fmoking hot.

(Old Recipe from *Phenix, Virginia.*)

Old

The Market Square Tavern Kitchen
at Williamsburg.

PLATE II.

Old Virginia *Ash Cake* ✵

A DD a Teaspoonful of Salt to a Quart of sifted
Corn Meal. Make up with boiling Water and
knead well. Make into round, flat Cakes. Sweep a
clean Place on the hottest Part of the Hearth. Put
the Cake on it and cover it with hot Wood Ashes.

Wash and wipe it dry before eating it. Sometimes
a Cabbage Leaf is placed under it, and one over it,
before baking, in which Case it need not be washed.

(*Shepperson* Family Recipe, *Charlotte* County.
Prov'd *Highland* County, *Virginia*, 1938.)

Batter Bread ✵

T AKE six Spoonfuls of Flour and three of Corn
Meal, with a little Salt—sift them, and make a
thin Batter with four Eggs, and a sufficient Quantity of rich Milk; bake it in little Tin Moulds in a
quick Oven.

(Mrs. *Mary Randolph's* Virginia Housewife, 1831.)

Another Batter Bread ✵

A DD two well-beaten Eggs to one and three
fourths Cups of cooked Rice or fine Hominy.
Add two and one half Cups of sweet Milk then sift
in one Cup of Meal, one Teaspoon of Salt and add
one Tablespoon of melted Butter. Beat very thoroughly and bake in hot well-buttered Baking-dish
for forty Minutes in a very hot Oven.

(Old Recipe, *Richmond, Virginia.*
Prov'd *Market Square Tavern* Kitchen, 1937.)

Batter

Batter Cakes*

BOIL two Cups of ſmall Hominy very ſoft; add an equal Quantity of Corn Meal with a little Salt, and a large Spoonful of Butter; make it in a thin Batter with three Eggs, and a ſufficient Quantity of Milk—beat all together ſome Time, and bake them on a Griddle, or in Waffle Irons. When Eggs cannot be procured, Yeaſt makes a good Subſtitute; put a Spoonful in the Batter, and let it ſtand an Hour to riſe.

(Mrs. *Mary Randolph's* Virginia Houſewife, 1831.)

Old Virginia *Batter Cakes**

BEAT two Eggs very light in a Bowl. Add one Teacup of Clabber, one of Water, one of Corn Meal, a Teacup of Flour, one-half Teaſpoonful of Salt. Juſt before baking, ſift in half a Teaſpoonful of Soda and ſtir well. It is better to greaſe the Griddle with fat Bacon than with Lard.

The above Proportions will make enough Batter Cakes for two or three Perſons.

(Recipe from a *Williamſburg* Family Cook Book.)

Williamſburg *Corn Meal Bread**

POUR one Cup of boiling Water over one Cup of Meal, add one Cup of ſweet Milk, one Teaſpoon of Salt, one beaten Egg, and two Tableſpoons of melted Butter, one half Cake of Yeaſt diſſolved in one fourth Cup of warm Water. Let riſe one Hour, bake in buttered Muffin Tins in quick Oven about twenty Minutes.

(Mrs. *Randolph's* Recipe, 1831.
Adapted *Market Square Tavern* Kitchen, 1937.)

Spoon

Spoon Bread *

STIR one Cup of Corn Meal into one Pint of boiling Water, which contains one half Teaspoon of Salt. Stir one Minute, remove from Fire and add two Tablespoons of Butter. Beat well, add four beaten Eggs and beat in one Cup of cold Milk. Beat again and pour into hot buttered Baking-dish. Bake twenty-five Minutes in hot Oven and serve from Baking-dish.

(Traditional *Virginia* Recipe. Prov'd *Market Square Tavern* Kitchen, 1937.)

Another Way *

PUT one Pint of Milk on the Fire and when it comes to a Boil stir in two Tablespoons of Corn Meal. Let cook until very thick stirring constantly. Cool, add three beaten Eggs, two Tablespoons of Flour, one half Teaspoon of Salt, one Tablespoon melted Butter. Bake in a buttered Dish for thirty-five Minutes in a moderate Oven.

(Old Recipe, *Petersburg, Virginia.* From a *Williamsburg* Family Cook Book.)

Hoe Cakes *

SCALD one Pint of *Indian* Meal with enough boiling Water to make a stiff Batter (about three Cups). Add one Teaspoon of Salt. Drop on hot greased Tin and bake in hot Oven thirty Minutes. (Some Cooks prefer to spread their Batter one half Inch thick in their Dripping-pan and serve the Cake up hot by cutting it in Squares.)

(*Virginia* Recipe, c-1776.)

Corn

Corn Sticks *

BEAT together three Cups of Meal, three Cups of Milk, two Eggs, two Tablespoons of melted Lard, one and a half Teaspoons of Salt and three Teaspoons of baking Powder. Bake in hot greased Bread-stick Pans in hot Oven for twenty Minutes.

(*King's Arms* Recipe, *Williamsburg.*)

Cracklin Bread *

TAKE one Quart sifted Corn Meal and a Teacup of Cracklins. Rub the latter in the Meal as fine as you can. Add a Teaspoonful of Salt and make up with warm Water into a stiff Dough. Make into Pones, and eat hot.

(Old Recipe, *Lynchburg, Virginia.*
From a *Williamsburg* Family Cook Book.)

Soft Egg Bread *

MIX one Cup of Meal with one Quart of Buttermilk or Clabber. Add three beaten Eggs and one half Teaspoon of Salt. Bake in slow Oven in well-buttered Pudding-dish until a Silver Knife thrust into it comes out clean.

(Old Recipe, *Toano, Virginia.*)

Of

Of GARDEN STUFF

CAPTAIN *Newport*, in 1607, said that *Virginia* was Nature's Nurse to all Vegetables—a Land where *West Indies* Plants would thrive and all *English* Garden-seeds prosper well. After the Lapse of a Century, a native Inhabitant reported of the *Virginians:*

> They live in so happy a Climate, and have so fertile a Soil, that no Body is poor enough to beg, or want Food, though they have Abundance of People that are lazy enough to deserve it.

The Kitchen Gardens of the Town Houses in *Williamsburg*, and of the great Plantation Houses were not Products of Nature's Nurse and Laziness. It required constant and careful Effort from the Householder to get a proper Supply of Seeds and to superintend the Planting, Cultivating and Harvesting of the Kitchen Garden.

Seeds could be propagated by the Gardener, bought in the Shops in *Williamsburg*, or ordered from *London* Seedsmen. Again and again, the Letters from *Virginia* carried Complaints and Injunctions like the following, found in the Papers of the Counting House of *John Norton & Sons*, Merchants of *London* and *Virginia:*

> The Seedsmen I can't but complain of for sending such a Parcel of Trumpery, several of the
> Articles

Articles are Weeds in this Country & many of the Seeds are not good.

I did not receive your Letter of the *1st* of Decr. pr. Capt. *Grieg* 'till Yesterday, with the Physick, Garden-seeds & Biscuit; which however are not yet landed, so that by the Length of the Passage, the Seeds are but of little Use for this Year's Crop.

The few Bushels of Eggshell Wheat imported last Spring proved good for Nothing; I suppose not one Grain in a Hundred vegitated; so that my Friend is greatly disappointed. If you can prevail with the Captain to bring my Seeds in his Cabbin, it will be the most likely Means of preserving them.

In a Letter dated September 7th, 1771, *Robert Carter Nicholas* of *Williamsburg* (Treasurer of the Colony of *Virginia*) sent the following List to *John Norton & Sons:*

Garden Seeds to be sent as early as possible in the Cabbin if it can be done.

2 Galls. earliest Pease
4 do midling
2 do of the latest Sort
1 Gal *Windsor* Beans
2 qts best *French* Beans
8 oz. orange Carrot
4 oz. swelling Parsnip
1 lb. earliest Turnip
4 lb. hardiest Winter do.
4 oz. Turnip Radish. 1 pt. Salmon do.
1 oz. white Cass Lettuce 1 oz. *Silecia* do.
1 oz. *Dutch* Cabbage do.
1 qt. round Spinage—1 qt. prickly do.
1 oz. best Endive. 1 oz. best Cellery 1 oz. *Roman* Mellon 1 oz. Cantaloupes
1 oz. Celleriack. 1 oz. sollid Cellery

1 pt.

1 pt. water Creſſes. 1 pt. white Muſtard—1 do. corn Sallad—2 qts Rape Seed

2 oz. early Colliflower—Seed—2 oz. latter do.

2 oz. earlieſt ſugar Loaf Cabbage 1 oz. red Cabbage. 2 oz. green Savoy—2 oz. yellow do.

1 oz. green Brocoli—1 oz. red do. 1 oz. purple do. 1 oz. white do. 1 oz. prickly Cucumber—1 oz. earlieſt do.—1 oz. green & white Turkey Cucumber.

N. B. if theſe Seeds are not quite freſh & good it will not be worth while to ſend them; many of thoſe laſt ſent faild to my great Diſappointment.

It was a Citizen of *Williamſburg*, *John Randolph*, the Attorney General of the Colony, who wrote the earlieſt *American* Book on Kitchen Gardening, baſing his Obſervations upon his own Garden in the City.

It was firſt publiſhed about 1766, and was republiſhed ſeveral Times, becauſe of its Uſe in adapting *Engliſh* Agriculture to Conditions in *Virginia*. One of the later Publiſhers wrote of Mr. *Randolph's* Work:

The annexed little TREATISE was written many Years ago, by a learned and eminent CITIZEN OF VIRGINIA, who delighted in directing under his own Eye the Cultivation of his Garden, and who printed it for the Uſe of Friends, by whom it has been long and highly prized for the useful Information it conveys in a ſmall Compaſs, and without the Introduction of a uſeleſs Word.

The Reſidence of the Author, and his Garden, from which he drew his Obſervations, were in *Williamſburg*, *Virginia*.

Thoſe who conſult the Treatiſe, will know from this Hint, how to make a proper Allowance according to Variance in Climate, for the Seaſons and Times of ſowing, planting, &c.   Garden

Garden Stuff & Salads

To make a Sallad of Anchovies *

WASH them in Water or Wine till the Liquor be clear; then dry them with a Linnen Cloth; take off the Tails and Fins, ſlip them from the Bones, and having laid them in a Plate, garniſh them with young Onions, Parſley, Slices of Lemon and Beet-roots; then beat up ſome ſweet Oil with Lemon-juice, and pour it on the Anchovies.

(The Lady's Companion, 1753; Cook Book owned by *Miſs Anna Maria Dandridge* 1756.)

Aſparagus forced in French *Rolls*

CUT a Piece out of the Cruſt of the Tops of three *French* Rolls, and take out all their Crumb; but be careful that the Cruſts fit again in the Places from whence they were taken. Fry the Rolls brown in freſh Butter. Then take a Pint of Cream, the Yolks of ſix Eggs beat fine, and a little Salt and Nutmeg. Stir them well together over a ſlow Fire till it begins to be thick. Have ready an Hundred of ſmall Graſs boiled, and ſave Tops enough to ſtick the Rolls with. Cut the Reſt of the Tops ſmall, put them into the Cream and fill the Loaves with them. Before you fry the Rolls, make Holes thick in the Top-cruſts, to ſtick the Graſs in.
Then

Then lay on the Pieces of Cruſt, and ſtick the Graſs in, that it may look as if it were growing. At a ſecond Courſe, this makes a pretty ſide Diſh.

(*John Farley's*, London Art of Cookery, 1787. From *Brookbury, Cheſterfield* County, *Virginia*.)

French *Beans* ✻

STRING your Beans, cut them in Two, and then acroſs; but if you wiſh to do them in a nice Manner, cut them into Four, and then acroſs, so that each Bean will then be in eight Pieces. Put them into Salt and Water, and when the Pan boils, put them in with a little Salt. They will be ſoon done, which may be known by their becoming tender; but take Care that you do not ſuffer them to loſe their fine green Colour. Lay them in a Plate, and ſend them up with Butter in a Boat.

(*John Farley's*, London Art of Cookery, 1787. Prov'd *Market Square Tavern* Kitchen, 1937.)

To dreſs Brockala ✻

STRIP all the little Branches off til you come to the top One, then with a Knife peel off all the hard outſide Skin, which is on the Stalks and little Branches, and throw them into Water. Have a Stew-pan of Water with ſome Salt in it: when it boils put in the Brockala, and when the Stalks are tender it is enough, then ſend it to Table with Butter in a Cup. The *French* eat Oil and Vinegar with it.

(Mrs. *Hannah Glaſſe's* Art of Cookery, 1774. Prov'd *Market Square Tavern* Kitchen, 1937.)

Brocoli

Brocoli*

THE Kind which bears Flowers around the Joints of the Stalks muſt be cut into convenient Lengths for the Diſh; ſcrape the Skin from the Stalk, and pick out any Leaves or Flowers that require to be removed; tie it up in Bunches and boil it as Aſparagus; ſerve it up hot, with melted Butter poured over it. The Brocoli that heads at the Top like Cauliflowers muſt be dreſſed in the ſame Manner as the Cauliflower.

(Mrs. *Mary Randolph's* Virginia Houſewife, 1831.)

Lima *Beans and Sweet Corn**

FOR a Change I cook theſe together, cutting the Corn from the Cob and cooking with the Beans until tender and about dry. Seaſon with Butter, Cream and Pepper, Salt being added when they are put on to boil.

(*Williamſburg* Recipe, c-1837. From Manuſcript of Mrs. *Elizabeth Labbé Cole.*)

Cabbage*

PICK Cabbages very clean, and waſh them thoroughly; then look them carefully over again; quarter them if they are very large; put them into a Sauce-pan with plenty of boiling Water; if any Skum riſes, take it off, put a large Spoonful of Salt into the Sauce-pan, and boil them till the Stalks feel tender. A young Cabbage will take about twenty Minutes, or half an Hour; when full grown, nearly an Hour; ſee that they are well covered with Water all the Time, and that no Dirt or Smoke ariſes from ſtirring the Fire. With careful Management,

ment, they will look as beautiful when dreſſed as they did when growing. It will much ameliorate the Flavour of ſtrong old Cabbages, to boil them in two Waters, i.e. when they are half done, to take them out, and put them into another Sauce-Pan of boiling Water.

(Mrs. *Mary Randolph's* Virginia Houſewife, 1831.)

Williamſburg *Stuffed Cabbage*✸

TAKE the Inſide of the Cabbage and chop it fine, if you have any freſh Meat chop it up with ſome chopped fat Bacon, Crumbs of Bread. Mix it all up together with one or two Eggs, Butter, Pepper, Salt, then put it all in the outſide Part of the Cabbage. Put in a Cloth and boil it until done, ſerve it up with melted Butter.

(*Williamſburg* Recipe, c-1837. From Manuſcript Collection of Mrs. *Elizabeth Labbé Cole.*)

Purple Cabbage✸

SPLIT the Cabbage, and ſprinkle them well with Salt, pack them in a Jar one Night then drain them, pack them in a Puter Baſon, add Pepper, Allſpice, Gingir, Cloves, Horſe-raddiſh, Mace, Muſtard-ſeed. Cover them with Winegar and ſimmer them over hot Embers untill they are tender.

(Manuſcript Cook Book, prior to 1839. *Morton* Family of *Charlotte* County, *Virginia.*)

To Stew Cucumbers

PARE your Cucumbers and ſlice them thick and put them to drain, then lay them on a coarſe Cloth till they are dry, flour them and fry them
brown

brown in Butter, then put to them some Gravy, a
little Claret, ſome Pepper, Cloves, and Mace and
let them ſtew a little then roll a bit of Butter in
Flour and toſs them up.

(Manuſcript Cook Book, c-1825, of Miſs *Margaret
Prentis* of *Williamſburg.* Owned by *Robert H.
Webb,* Eſq., *Charlotteſville.*)

Chicken Salad and Dreſſing ⁎

CUT one well boiled Hen into Dice, add an
equal Quantity of Celery cut into ſmall Pieces
the Whites of four boiled Eggs chopped rather fine.
Mix theſe Ingredients well together, juſt before the
Salad is to be made, then ſerve the Dreſſing with
it.

DRESSING*: Yolks of four Eggs, one Gill of
good Vinegar (or Juice of Lemon if that is preferred),
one Gill of Olive Oil, one and one-half Teaſpoonfuls
of Salt, one-quarter Teaſpoonful of *Cayenne* Pepper,
one large Tableſpoon of mixed Muſtard, a little
Sugar to give a piquant Zeſt to the Vinegar. Beat
the Yolks of four Eggs to a light Cream, then ſtir
the Vinegar gradually into them, beating hard all
the Time. Stir the Mixture over the Fire until it
thickens, then remove, and beat gradually into it
the Sugar, Salt and Pepper and Oil. Do not fail to
beat it well. When very ſmooth ſet it upon Ice to
become well chilled.

(Recipe from *Cape Charles, Virginia.*
Manuſcript in *Barlow* Family Cook Book, *Williamſburg.*)

Cold

Cold Slaw *

CUT up a Quantity of Cabbage, and ſprinkle upon it a Teaſpoonful Salt. For a large Diſh uſe two Eggs, a Piece of Butter the Size of an Egg, one-half Cupful Water, one-half Teacupful Vinegar; beat the Eggs very light; add the Water, Vinegar, and Butter, with a little Pepper and Muſtard, and pour while hot over the Cabbage.

(Mrs. *Cole's* Recipe, c-1837. Prov'd
Market Square Tavern Kitchen, 1937.)

To dreſs Parſnips *

BOIL them tender, ſcrape them clean, then ſcrape all the ſoft Part into a Sauce-pan; leave out the Strings, and put as much Milk or Cream as may be neceſſary, ſtir them over the Fire till they are thick, add a good Piece of Butter and a little Salt and when the Butter is melted ſend them to Table.

(Manuſcript Cook Book, c-1825, of Miſs *Margaret
Prentis* of *Williamſburg.* Owned by
Robert H. Webb, Eſq., *Charlotteſville.*)

Corn Fritters *

GRATE the Corn from three Dozen Ears, add to it three Tableſpoonfuls of Flour, and gradually mix with ſix Eggs, beaten well. Beat all hard together, and add Salt to the Taſte. Drop in oval Shapes, three Inches long, into a Pan, in which fry them brown, in equal Parts of Lard and Butter.

(Old Recipe, *Bedford* County, *Virginia.* From a
Williamſburg Family Cook Book, Prov'd, 1937.)

Williamſburg *Corn Fritters* ⁂

TAKE two Cups of Corn. Make a Batter by
ſifting one and two thirds Cups of Flour with
three fourths of a Teaſpoon Salt, and two and one
half Teaſpoons baking Powder. Beat two Eggs, add
one third Cup of Milk and beat into the dry Ingredients. Add Corn and ſtir into the Batter. Drop by
Spoonfuls into hot Fat.

(Old *Williamſburg* Family Recipe. Prov'd.)

Corn Pudding ⁂

TAKE ſix large, tender, milky Ears of Corn.
Split the Corn down the Center of each Row;
cut off the Top and then ſcrape the Cob well. Beat
two Eggs and ſtir them into the Corn. Add one
fourth Cup of Flour, one Teaſpoon of Salt and one
half Teaſpoon of black Pepper. Stir in one Pint of
freſh Milk and mix all together thoroughly. Put in
a cold buttered Pan about four Inches deep. Cover
the Top with two heaping Tableſpoonfuls of Butter
cut in ſmall Pieces. Bake in a moderately hot Oven
about one Hour. Serve hot.

(Traditional *Virginia* Recipe.
From *Morgan* Family. Prov'd 1937.)

Squaſh or Cimlin ⁂

GATHER young Squaſhes, peel, and cut them
in Two; take out the Seeds, and boil them till
tender; put them into a Colander, drain off the
Water, and rub them with a wooden Spoon
through the Colander; then put them into a Stew-
pan,

pan, with a Cup full of Cream, a ſmall Piece of Butter, ſome Pepper and Salt—ſtew them, ſtirring very frequently until dry. This is the most delicate Way of preparing Squaſhes.

(Mrs. *Mary Randolph's* Virginia Houſewife, 1831. Prov'd *Market Square Tavern* Kitchen, 1937.)

Cymlings Fried with Bacon *

FRY some Slices of fat Bacon in a Pan. Remove the Bacon and keep hot. Fry in the Drippings ſome Cymlings that have been boiled tender and cut in Slices. While frying, maſh fine with a large Spoon and add Pepper and Salt. Fry brown and ſerve with the Bacon.

(Old Recipe, *Toano, Virginia.*)

Oyſter Salad *

DRAIN the Liquor from one-half Gallon freſh Oyſters and throw them into ſome hot Vinegar on the Fire; let them remain until they are plump, not cooked. Then put them at once into clear, cold Water. Drain the Water from them and ſet them away in a cool Place, and prepare your

DRESSING: Maſh the Yolks of four hard-boiled Eggs as fine as you can and rub into it two Teaſpoonfuls Salt, two Teaſpoonfuls black Pepper and two Teaſpoonfuls made Muſtard, then rub two large Spoonfuls Salad Oil or melted Butter in, a few Drops at a Time. When it is all ſmooth, add one raw Egg, well beaten, and then one Teacup good Vinegar, a Spoonful at a time. Set aſide. Mix Oyſters, Celery (nearly as much Celery as Oyſters) cut

cut up into ſmall Dice, and two good ſized pickled Cucumbers, cut up fine, toſſing up well with a Silver Fork. Sprinkle in Salt to your Taſte. Then pour Dreſſing over all.

(Old Recipe, *Lynchburg, Virginia.*
From a *Williamſburg* Family Cook Book.)

Green Peas *

TO have them in Perfection, they muſt be quite young, gathered early in the Morning, kept in a cool Place, and not ſhelled until they are to be dreſſed; put Salt in the Water, and when it boils, put in the Peas; boil them quick, twenty or thirty Minutes, according to their Age; juſt before they are taken up, add a little Mint chopped very fine; drain all the Water from the Peas, put in a Bit of Butter, and ſerve them up quite hot.

(Mrs. *Mary Randolph's* Virginia Houſewife, 1831.
Recipe prov'd 1937.)

Black-eye Peas *

SHELL early in the Morning, keep in Water until an Hour before Dinner, then put into boiling Water, covering cloſe while cooking. Add a little Salt juſt before taking from Fire. Drain and ſerve with a large Spoonful freſh Butter.

(Old Recipe, *Toano, Virginia.*)

Mrs. B's *Pumpkin Fritters* *

THE Pumpkin muſt be well boiled, left from Dinner. Take four Spoonfuls Pumpkin, two Eggs, one half Pint to more of Milk (or Cream if you wiſh) one or more Tableſpoonfuls of brown Sugar.

Sugar. Thicken with Wheat Flour about the Thick-neſs of Batter for Waffles well beaten and light. Fry in boiling Lard two or three Spoonfuls for each Fritter. Tried and found good.

(Manuſcript Cook Book, c-1801, of Mrs. *Frances Bland Tucker Coalter.* Owned by Dr. *St. George Tucker Grinnan, Richmond.*)

Spinach *

HAVING picked your Spinach very clean, and waſhed it in five or ſix Waters, put it into a Sauce-pan that will juſt hold it, throw a little Salt over it, and cover it cloſe. Put in no Water, but take Care to ſhake the Pan often. Put your Sauce-pan on a clear and quick Fire, and as ſoon as you find your Greens are ſhrunk and fallen to the Bot-tom, and the Liquor that comes out of them boils up, it is a Proof your Spinach is enough. Throw them into a clean Sieve to drain, and juſt give them a gentle Squeeze. Lay them in a Plate, and ſend them up with Butter in a Boat, but never pour any over them. (*John Farley's* London Art of Cookery, 1787. From *Brookbury, Cheſterfield* County, *Virginia.*)

Baked Tomatoes *

PEEL the Tomatoes. Cut in ſmall Pieces, ſeaſon with a little Sugar, Salt, Pepper, and finely minced Onion. Greaſe a Baking-diſh and line it with thin Slices of buttered Bread. Pour the Toma-toes in the Diſh, crumbing up a little Bread on them. Dot the Top with Butter and bake.

(Recipe from a *Williamſburg* Family Cook Book.)

Eſcalloped

Eſcalloped Tomatoes *

MIX two and one half Cups of Tomatoes, two Slices of Bread broken in Pieces, one half Cup of finely chopped Celery, one Tableſpoon of finely minced Onion, one Teaſpoon of Salt, one fourth Teaſpoon of black Pepper and three Tableſpoons of Sugar. Pour into buttered deep Bakingdiſh and cover well with ſmall Pieces of Butter. Bake in a ſlow Oven at leaſt an Hour, ſtirring occaſionally at firſt.

(Old Recipe, adapted *Market Square Tavern* Kitchen, 1937.)

Turnip Tops *

ARE the Shoots which grow out (in the Spring) from the old Turnip Roots. Put them in cold Water an Hour before they are dreſſed; the more Water they are boiled in, the better they will look; if boiled in a ſmall Quantity of Water, they will taſte bitter; when the Water boils, put in a ſmall Handful of Salt, and then your Vegetables; they are ſtill better boiled with Bacon in the *Virginia* Style: if freſh and young, they will be done in about twenty Minutes—drain them on the Back of a Sieve, and put them under the Bacon.

(Mrs. *Mary Randolph's* Virginia Houſewife, 1831.)

Jowl and Turnip Salad *

THIS is an old *Virginia* Diſh, and much uſed in the Spring of the Year. The Jowl muſt be waſhed clean and boiled for three Hours. Put in the Salad and boil half an Hour. If you boil it too long it will turn yellow. The Jowl and Salad ſhould always be ſerved with poached Eggs.

(Old Recipe from *Toana, Virginia.*)

Salmagundi

Salmagundi *

TURN a Bowl on the Difh, and put on it in regular Rings, beginning at the Bottom, the following Ingredients, all minced: Anchovies with the Bones taken out, the white Meat of Fowls without the Skin, hard-boiled Eggs, the Yelks and Whites chopped feparately, Parfley, the Lean of old Ham fcraped, the inner Stalks of Celery; put a Row of Capers round the Bottom of the Bowl, and difpofe the others in a fanciful Manner; put a little Pyramid of Butter on the Top, and have a fmall Glafs with Egg mixed as for Sallad, to eat with the Salmagundi.

(Mrs. *Mary Randolph's* Virginia Houfewife, 1831.)

Cooking Salfify *

PREPARE it, by boiling in Milk untill the Slices are tender, adding Pepper & Salt and a good Slice Butter. When ready to ferve, ftir in two or three well beaten Eggs, taking Care not to let it boil afterwards. This is very nice poured over Slices of Toaft.

(Manufcript Cook Book, c-1839. *Morton* Family of *Charlotte* County, *Virginia*.)

To Roaſt Potatoes *

WASH and dry your Potatoes (all of a Size) and put them in a tin *Dutch* Oven, or Cheefe Toafter; take Care not to put them too near the Fire, or they will get burned on the Outfide before they are warmed through. Large Potatoes will require two Hours to roaft them. To fave Time and Trouble, fome Cooks half-boil them firft.

(Mrs. *Mary Randolph's* Virginia Houfewife, 1831.)

Potato Balls *

MIX maſhed Potatoes with the Yelk of an Egg, roll them into Balls, flour them, or cover them with Egg and Bread Crumbs, fry them in clean Dripping, or brown them in a *Dutch* Oven. They are an agreeable Vegetable Reliſh, and a Supper Diſh. (Mrs. *Mary Randolph's* Virginia Houſewife, 1831.)

To Dreſs Salad *

TO have this delicate Diſh in perfection, the Lettuce, Pepper-graſs, Chervil, Creſs, &c., ſhould be gathered early in the Morning, nicely picked, waſhed, and laid in cold Water, which will be improved by adding Ice; juſt before Dinner is ready to be ſerved, drain the Water from your Salad, cut it into a Bowl, giving the proper Proportions of each Plant; prepare the following Mixture to pour over it: boil two freſh Eggs ten Minutes, put them in Water to cool, then take the Yelks in a Soupplate, pour on them a Tableſpoonful of cold Water, rub them with a wooden Spoon until they are perfectly diſſolved; then add two Spoonfuls of Oil: when well mixed, put in a Teaſpoonful of Salt, one of powdered Sugar, and one of made Muſtard; when all theſe are united and quite ſmooth, ſtir in two Tableſpoonfuls of common, and two of Tarragon Vinegar; put it over the Salad, and garniſh the Top with the Whites of the Eggs cut into Rings and lay around the Edge of the Bowl young Scallions, they being the moſt delicate of the Onion Tribe. (Mrs. *Mary Randolph's* Recipe, 1831. Prov'd *Market Square Tavern* Kitchen, 1937.)

Salad

Salad Dreſſing (Boiled) ✳

YOLK of one Egg well beaten, add one Teaſpoonful dry Muſtard, ſmall Teaſpoonful Salt, Speck
of *Cayenne* Pepper, one Tableſpoonful Sugar, one
Tableſpoonful melted Butter, three Tableſpoonfuls
hot Vinegar, laſtly, White of Egg beaten ſtiff. Cook
on very ſlow Fire until thick as Cream.

(Old *Williamſburg* Recipe. *Barlow* Family Manuſcript.)

Sour Cream Dreſſing for Salad ✳

MIX the Yolks of four Eggs with two Tableſpoonfuls of cold Water and four of Vinegar.
Add one Teaſpoonful of dry *Engliſh* Muſtard
which has been made into a Paſte with a little
Water and one Teaſpoonful of Sugar. Cook over a
very ſlow Fire, ſtirring ſteadily until it thickens.
Cool. Add one Teaſpoonful of Salt and one Cupful
of sour Cream which has been whipped.

(Old *Morgan* Family Recipe. Prov'd, *Blair* Kitchen, 1938.)

To make a Sallad with Freſh Salmon ✳

TAKE some ſouſed Salmon, and mince it ſmall,
with Apples and Onions, put to it Oil, Vinegar
and Pepper, and ſerve it up, garniſhing your Diſh
with Slices of Lemon and Capers.

(The Lady's Companion, 1753; Cook Book
owned by Miſs *Anna Maria Dandridge*, 1756.)

Of

Of PASTRY

THE *Virginia* Housewife made Cheesecakes, Pies and Tarts from the Recipes she found in her *English* Cook Books and from favorite Family Recipes, but best of all her Recipes were those which she developed in *Virginia*. The sweet Potato, the Pecan, the Fox Grape and other native Products offered Opportunities for ingenious Adaptation. The following Recipes represent some of the *English* Favorites, but are chiefly those developed in *Virginia*.

Pastries & Cheese Cakes

Pie Crust*

SIFT together four Cups of Flour and one Teaspoon of Salt. Cut into this with Silver Knives one Cup of chilled Lard. Add just enough Ice-water to hold together, handle very lightly and roll out on a Board.

(Old Recipe. Adapted *Market Square Tavern* Kitchen, 1937.)

To

To make Puff Paſte

SIFT a Quart of Flour, leave out a Little for rolling the Paſte, make up the Remainder with cold Water into a ſtiff Paſte, knead it well, and roll it out ſeveral Times; waſh the Salt from a Pound of Butter, divide it into four Parts, put one of them on the Paſte in little Bits, fold it up, and continue to roll it till the Butter is well mixed; then put another Portion of Butter, roll it in the ſame Manner; do this till all the Butter is mingled with the Paſte; touch it very lightly with the Hands in Making—bake it in a moderate Oven, that will permit it to riſe, but will not make it brown. Good Paſte muſt look white, and as light as a Feather.

(Mrs. *Mary Randolph's* Virginia Houſewife, 1831.)

Williamſburg *Puff Paſte* *

SET aſide two Tableſpoons of Butter, and ſhape Remainder of a Pound of ſweet Butter into a circular Piece one-half Inch thick, put on floured Board. Work the two Tableſpoons Butter into one Pound of Flour. Moiſten to a Dough with Ice-water, turn on floured Board, knead five Minutes —let ſtand a few Minutes covered with a Towel. Roll lightly one-fourth Inch thick keeping Paſte a little wider than long—Corners ſhould be ſquare. Place Butter on Centre of lower Half of Paſte. Cover Butter by folding upper Half of Paſte over it. Preſs Edges firmly—so as to keep in as much Air as poſſible. Fold right Side of Paſte over encloſed Butter, the left Side under encloſed Butter.
Turn

Turn Paſte one-fourth Way round, lift, and roll one-fourth Inch thick, having Paſte longer than wide, lifting often to prevent Paſte from Sticking. Add Flour to prevent Paſte from ſticking to Board. Fold from Ends toward Centre, making three Layers. Repeat four Times turning Paſte one-fourth Way round each Time before rolling. After fourth Rolling fold from Ends to Centre and double, making four Layers. Put in Place to chill. Cut round or fancy Shapes, prick on Top with Fork. Bake in quick Oven on brown Paper.

(Recipe prov'd *Market Square Tavern* Kitchen, 1937.)

Apple Pie *

HAVING put a good Puff-paſte Cruſt round the Edge of your Diſh, pare and quarter your Apples, and take out the Cores. Then lay a thick Row of Apples, and throw in Half the Sugar you intend to put into your Pie. Mince a little Lemon-peel fine, ſpread it over the Sugar and Apples, and ſqueeze a little Lemon over them. Then ſcatter a few Cloves over it, and lay on the Reſt of your Apples and Sugar. Sweeten to your Palate, and ſqueeze a little more Lemon. Boil the Peeling of the Apples and Cores in ſome fair Water, with a Blade of Mace, till it has a pleaſing Taſte. Strain it, and boil the Syrup with a little Sugar, till there be but a ſmall Quantity left. Then pour it into your Pie, put on your upper Cruſt, and bake it. If you chooſe it, you may put a little Quince or Marmalade. In the ſame Manner you may make a *Pear Pie*; but in that you muſt omit the Quince. You
                                                    may

may butter them when they come out of the Oven, or beat up the Yolks of two Eggs, and half a Pint of Cream, with a little Nutmeg, ſweetened with Sugar. Put it over a ſlow Fire, and keep ſtirring it till it begins to boil; then take off the Lid, and pour in the Cream. Cut the Cruſt in little three-corner Pieces, and ſtick them about the Pie.

(*John Farley's* London Art of Cookery, 1787. From *Brookbury, Cheſterfield* County, *Virginia.*)

Deep Diſh Apple Pie *

PARE and ſlice five Pounds of Apples in thin Slices, place in Baking-pan, ſprinkle with Sugar and dot with Bits of Butter. Continue Layers and ſtrew with Nutmeg before covering with Pie-cruſt. Bake forty Minutes or until brown and Apples are thoroughly ſoft.

(Old Recipe. Adapted *Market Square Tavern* Kitchen, 1937.)

Bell Fritters

PUT a Piece of Butter the Size of an Egg into a Pint of Water; let it boil a few Minutes— thicken it very ſmoothly with a Pint of Flour; let it remain a ſhort Time on the Fire, ſtir it all the Time that it may not ſtick to the Pan, pour it in a wooden Bowl, add five or six Eggs, breaking one and beating it in—then another, and ſo on till they are all in, and the Dough quite light—put a Pint of Lard in a Pan, let it boil, make the Fritters ſmall and fry them to a fine amber Colour.

(Mrs. *Mary Randolph's* Virginia Houſewife, 1831.)

Caramel

Caramel Pie*

BEAT five Eggs very light, gradually beat in two Cups of brown Sugar. Then add one Cup of melted Butter and one Cup of *Damſon* Plum Pre-ſerves or of Fox-grape Preſerves. Mix well, pour into a Pie-plate lined with a good Paſtry and bake three Quarters of an Hour in a moderate Oven.

(Old Recipe from *Charlotte Court Houſe, Virginia.* Prov'd, *Market Square Tavern* Kitchen, 1937.)

To make Lemon Cheeſecakes

TAKE two large Lemons, grate off the Peel of both and ſqueeze out the Juice of one; add to it half a Pound of fine Sugar; twelve Yolks of Eggs, eight Whites well beaten; then melt half a Pound of Butter in four or five Spoonfuls of Cream; then ſtir it all together, and ſet it over the Fire, ſtirring it 'till it begins to be pretty thick; then take it off, and when 'tis cold, fill your Patty-pans little more than half full; put a fine Paſte very thin at the Bot-tom of the Patty-pans; half an Hour, with a quick Oven, will bake them.

(*E. Smith's* Compleat Houſewife, *Williamſburg,* 1742.)

Court Cheeeſcakes

BOIL a Bit of Butter in a little Water and a little Salt; thicken it with as much Flour as it will take, ſtirring it on the Fire conſtantly until it be-comes quite a Paſte; then mix the Eggs with it one

by

by one, to make it almost as liquid as a thick Batter; and mix some good Cream Cheese with it; bake it in good Puff-paste, coloured with Yolks of Eggs: serve hot or cold.

(Court and Country Confectioner. *London*, 1770. From *Tucker* House, *Williamsburg.*)

Lemon Cheesecakes

TAKE the Peel of two large Lemons, boil it very tender then pound it well in a Mortar with a Quarter of a Pound, or more of Loaf-sugar, the Yolks of six Eggs, half a Pound of fresh Butter, mix all well together and fill your Patty-pans half full, Orange Cheesecakes are done the same Way. only the Peel must be boiled in two or three Waters to take the Bitterness out.

(Manuscript Cook Book, c-1825, of Miss *Margaret Prentis* of *Williamsburg*. Owned by *Robert H. Webb*, Esq., *Charlottesville.*)

Chess Cakes*

CREAM one half Pound of Butter and one half Pound of Sugar well together. Beat the Yolks of six Eggs until light in Color and add to the Butter and Sugar. Put in a Pinch of Salt and stir in one third of a Cup of white Wine. Bake in small Pastry Shells rolled thin in Muffin Tins. Fill the Shells about three-fourths full. Bake in a moderately hot Oven. Serve cold. Will keep for several Days in a cool Place.

(Traditional *Virginia* Recipe, *Morgan* Family. Prov'd, *Market Square Tavern* Kitchen, 1937.)

Chess

Cheſs Pie*

TAKE one fourth of a Pound of Butter and mix well with one Cup of Sugar and one Tableſpoon of Flour. Beat eight Egg Yolks very light and ſlowly beat in them one Cup of Sugar. Combine. Add one Cup of Milk ſlowly, and laſt, the Juice of one Lemon. Pour into two Pie pans lined with rich Paſtry and bake in a ſlow Oven about one Hour or until firm.

(Mrs. *Frances Bland Tucker Coalter's* Recipe, c-1801
Adapted *Travis* Houſe, 1938.)

Cheeſe Pie*

SEPARATE four Eggs. Beat Yolks with one and a half Cups of Sugar. Add Juice and grated Rind of one Lemon. Beat thoroughly. Rub one Pound Cottage Cheeſe through Colander. Whip Whites of Eggs ſtiff, and fold in well. Line large, deep Pie-tin with rather thick Paſtry. Pour in the Mixture. Sprinkle with Nuts and bake in moderate Oven about thirty Minutes.

(Mrs. *E. Smith's* Recipe, 1742.
Adapted *Market Square Tavern* Kitchen, 1937.)

Crullers*

MIX ſix Tableſpoons of Sugar well with two of Butter. Add four Egg Yolks, and four Tableſpoons of thick ſour Cream. Sift in four Tableſpoons of Flour mixed with one Teaſpoon of Salt and one half Teaſpoon of Soda. Roll out on a floured Board and cut in ſmall Shapes. Fry in deep, hot Fat.

(Recipe from *Woodſtock, Virginia,* c-1829.)

Plain

Plain Custard Pie *

FOUR Eggs, one Quart Milk, four Tablespoons white Sugar; flavor with Nutmeg, or other Spice to Taste. Bake without top Crust; the same Mixture cooked in a Dish set in boiling Water makes a good boiled Custard Pudding. Bake in moderate Oven about forty-five Minutes.

(*Williamsburg* Recipe, c-1837.
From Collection of Mrs. *Elizabeth Labbé Cole.*)

Damson Pie *

TAKE the Yolks of five Eggs and beat them well, then add slowly three fourths of a Cup of Sugar, beating well. Beat another three fourths of a Cup of Sugar into a half a Cup of Butter. Combine, adding one eighth of a Teaspoon of Salt and one Tablespoon of Flour. Add one Cup of *Damson* Plum Preserves, and last the beaten Whites of the Eggs. Bake in Pastry-shells in a moderate Oven until set (about thirty-five Minutes). This makes ten small Pies.

(Traditional *Virginia* Recipe, *Morgan* Family.
Prov'd *Market Square Tavern* Kitchen, 1937.)

Lemon Chess Pie *

MIX well one Teacup of Sugar with two Tablespoons of Butter. Beat the Yolks of four Eggs very light, and beat in well. Add the grated Rind of two Lemons and the Juice of one. Beat the Whites of the Eggs stiff, and fold in lightly. Pour into lightly baked Pie Shell, and bake in moderately slow Oven until set and light golden brown.

(Old *Buckingham* County Recipe of *Gracie Mason.*)

Lemon

Lemon Pies*

TAKE three large freſh Lemons; grate off the Rind; pare off every Bit of the white Skin of the Lemon (as it toughens while cooking); then cut the Lemon into very thin Slices with a sharp Knife, and take out the Seeds; two Cupfuls of Sugar, three Tableſpoonfuls of Water, and two of ſifted Flour. Put into the Pie a Layer of Lemon, then one of Sugar, then one of the grated Rind, and, laſtly, of Flour, and so on till the Ingredients are uſed; ſprinkle the Water over all, and cover with Upper-cruſt. Be ſure to have the Under-cruſt lap over the Upper, and pinch it well, as the Syrup will cook all out if Care is not taken when finiſhing the Edge of Cruſt. Bake in moderate Oven. This Quantity makes one medium-ſize Pie.

(Mrs. *Cole's* Recipe, c-1837. Prov'd *Market Square Tavern* Kitchen, 1937.)

Maids of Honor*

BEAT four Eggs well, adding gradually a Cup of Sugar in which you have mixed well four Tableſpoons of Flour. Add five Tableſpoons of melted Butter and one Cup of ground Almonds or Almond Paſte moiſtened with a little Sherry and ſeaſon with Nutmeg. Line Patty-pans with rich Paſtry, and ſpread on the Bottom of each a Tableſpoon of Strawberry or Raſpberry Preſerves. Put the Filling on Top and bake in a moderate Oven twenty-five Minutes.

(Early *Engliſh* and *Virginia* Recipe. Adapted *Market Square Tavern* Kitchen, 1937.)

Molaſſes

Molaſſes Pie ✻

FOUR Eggs—beat the Whites ſeparate—one Teacupful of brown Sugar, half a Nutmeg, two Tableſpoonfuls of Butter; beat them well together; ſtir in one Teacupful and a half of Molaſſes, and then add the Whites of Eggs. Bake on Paſtry.

(Mrs. *Cole's* Recipe, c-1837. Prov'd *Market Square Tavern* Kitchen, 1937.)

Another Way ✻

BEAT ſix Eggs very light with two Cups of Sugar, add one fourth of a Cup of Molaſſes, three Tableſpoons of melted Butter, one Teaſpoon of Cinnamon, one of Allſpice and mix well. Add one Pint of Milk. Pour into a large Pie-tin lined with rich Paſtry and bake ſlowly.

(Recipe from *Cheſterfield, Virginia*, c-1800.)

Moonſhines ✻

MIX and ſift together into one beaten Egg and one half Cup of Milk, one third Cup of Sugar one and a third Cups of Flour, two Teaſpoons of baking Powder, one fourth Teaſpoon of Salt, one half Teaſpoon of Nutmeg, one Teaſpoon of melted Butter. Drop into boiling Fat, drain on brown Paper. Split and put Currant Jelly between. Roll in Confectioner's Sugar.

(Mrs. *Cole's* Recipe, c-1837. Adapted *Market Square Tavern* Kitchen, 1937.)

Orange

Orange Pie*

PUT two Tableſpoons of Butter in three-fourths of a Cup of Sugar and mix well. Add three well-beaten Egg Yolks, then the Juice and grated Rind of one-half of an Orange and one-half of a Lemon, Nutmeg to Taſte. Pour into Pie-pan lined with good Paſtry and bake in moderate Oven about forty-five Minutes. Beat the Egg Whites ſtiff, and ſlowly ſift in three Tableſpoons of powdered Sugar, ſpread on your Pie and bake very ſlowly until ſlightly browned.

(Old *Williamſburg* Recipe, c-1837.
Adapted *Market Square Tavern* Kitchen, 1937.)

A Bon Chretien Pear Pye
(Call'd a la Bonne Femme)

SLIT in two ſome *bon chretien* Pears, take out the Core, pare them. Put into an earthen Pot ſome of the Parings, put the Apple over them, add a Stick of Cinnamon and ſome Sugar, and a Glass of red Wine, with a little Water; and cover the Same with the Reſt of the Parings. Cover your Pot with ſome Paſte round, and let your Pears be doing ſlowly during five or ſix Hours, with Fire under and over; then put ſome Paſte in the Bottom of a Baking-pan, as large as the dainty Diſh you deſign to ſerve up, making round it a Cruſt the Breadth of a Thumb; and let the Paſte be not too thick. Put the Pan in the Oven, and when baked, glaze the Paſte. Your Pears being done, place them in the Pan, with their Liquor, which muſt be of a lively red, ſtrain it
through

through a Sieve, and pour it over them. If your Liquor is too thin, ſet it over again to thicken, then pour it over your Pears. Serve it up either hot or cold.

(Court & Country Confeðioner. *London*, 1770. From *Tucker* Houſe, *Williamſburg*.)

Pecan Pie*

BEAT three Eggs very light, then ſlowly beat in three-fourths of a Cup of Sugar, one-fourth of a Pound of melted Butter and one Cup of brown Corn Syrup. Pour into uncooked Pie-cruſt and cook very ſlowly forty Minutes until almoſt ſet, cover the Top with halves of Pecans, return to Oven and increaſe Heat and cook for another ten or fifteen Minutes in a moderate Oven.

(Traditional *Virginia* Recipe. Prov'd) *Market Square Tavern* Kitchen, 1937.)

Potato Pies*

POTATOES (Sweet) well cooked, boiled or baked. When cold, ſlice them about one fourth of an Inch thick. A Layer of Potatoes placed on the Paſtry in the Pan. Then a Layer of Sugar, finely beaten Allſpice ſprinkled over it. Conſiderable Butter over this if deſired to be rich. According to Taſte. Then Potatoes, Allſpice, Sugar and Butter again: and keep alternating thus until Pie is of deſired Thickneſs, then fill the Plate with White-wine, cover the Whole with Paſtry, cook it well and ſend me a Piece. Eat hot. For Mrs. *Cote*, with Mrs. *Peyton's* Compliments.

(Mrs. *Cole's* Recipe, c-1837. Prov'd *Market Square Tavern* Kitchen, 1937.)

Sweet

Sweet Potato Pie *

MASH five Cups of ſweet Potatoes well. Add one Cup of Milk, three well-beaten Eggs, two Cups of Sugar, and one Teaſpoon of Cinnamon. Bake in a Pie-pan lined with good Paſtry about one-half Hour in a moderate Oven. Makes two Pies.

(Traditional *Virginia* Recipe. Adapted.)

Pumpkin Pye *

TAKE one Quart of Milk, two beaten Eggs, one Teaſpoon Salt, one of Ginger, one of Cinnamon, one half Cup of Sugar, three Tableſpoons of Molaſſes and one Pint of maſhed, ſteamed Pumpkin. Beat well together. Pour into partially baked Pie-cruſts. This will make two Pies.

(Recipe from *Wicomico* Church, c-1829.
Prov'd *Market Square Tavern* Kitchen, 1937.)

Williamſburg *Snow Balls* *

PARE and core ſix large Apples, and fill the Holes with Orange Marmalade. Make a Paſte by mixing together one-fourth of a Cup of Butter, one-half Cup of brown Sugar, four Teaſpoons of Cinnamon, one Teaſpoon Allſpice and one Teaſpoon Nutmeg. Spread an Apple with the Paſte then wrap each Apple in a good Paſtry. Bake in a ſlow Oven about one Hour. Serve hot with Rum Hard-ſauce.

(Mr. *Farley's* Recipe, 1787. Adapted
Market Square Tavern Kitchen, 1937.)

Of

Of Preſerving & Pickling

PICKLES, Preſerves, Jellies, Sweetmeats, Conſerves and Reliſhes were ſuch ſtaple Table Delicacies in colonial *Virginia* that one can rarely examine the Inventory of any Perſon's Eſtate without finding Preſerving-kettles, ſtone and earthen Jars, Jelly Glaſſes, Pickle Diſhes, Corner Diſhes and an Abundance of Utenſils for making or ſerving them.

Ships coming into *Virginia's* Rivers and Harbours from *England* and the northern *Colonies* almoſt invariably brought in large Supplies of earthen and ſtone Ware. This Trade was of great Intereſt to the *Britiſh* Potteries and the Lords of Trade and Plantations obſerved carefully any Sign of colonial Manufacturing that might diminiſh it. The royal Governors were required to reply to elaborate Queſtionnaries ſent them each Year by theſe Commiſſioners.

In 1732, Governor *Gooch* reported to them, "a "poor Potter at *Yorke* makes Veſſels of Earthen-"ware, but this is of ſo little Conſequence that I "believe it hath occaſion'd little or no Diminution "in the Quantity of Earthen-ware that hath been "commonly imported." Each Year he reported deprecatingly of the poor Potter at *York;* until in the year 1743, in Reply to the Queſtion, "What Manu-"factories have you?", he anſwered "None, as the "poor old Potter is dead."

Preſerves

Preſerves & Pickles

Apricots in Brandy *

TAKE freſhly gathered Apricots not too ripe; to Half their Weight of loaf Sugar, add as much Water as will cover the Fruit; boil and ſkim it: then put in the Apricots, and let them remain five or ſix Minutes; take them up without Syrup, and lay them on Diſhes to cool; boil the Syrup till reduced one Half; when the Apricots are cold, put them in Bottles, and cover them with equal Quantities of Syrup and *French* Brandy. If the Apricots be clingſtone, they will require more ſcalding.

(Mrs. *Mary Randolph's* Virginia Houſewife, 1831.)

To Pickle Beet Root *

BOIL them till tender, take the Skins off, cut them in Slices and gimp them in the Shape of Wheels, Flowers, or what you pleaſe; put them in a Jar and take as much Vinegar as you think will cover them, boil it with a little Mace, Ginger, and Horſe-radiſh, pour it hot on the Root, it makes pretty Garniſh for Fiſh or other Things.

(Court & Country Confectioner. *London*, 1770.
Recipe prov'd *Market Square Tavern* Kitchen, 1937.)

Spiced Cantaloupe *

USE ripe Cantaloupes. Pare and ſlice in deſired Size and Shape and place in crockery Jar. Cover with Vinegar and let ſtand twelve to fifteen Hours.

Hours. Drain off Vinegar and to each Gallon of
Cantaloupe uſe five Pounds of Sugar, whole Cloves
and Cinnamon Sticks and ſmall Amount of Mace
to Taſte, add to the Vinegar which has been
drained off. Boil fifteen Minutes. Then add Cantaloupe and continue to boil about twenty Minutes
or until Cantaloupe is clear. Remove the Cantaloupe and continue to boil the Syrup ten Minutes
longer. Again add the Fruit to the Syrup and boil
five Minutes. Remove and place in Jars.

(Miſs *Margaret Prentis'* Recipe, c-1825, Adapted 1938.)

Cherries in Brandy *

GET the short ſtemmed bright red Cherries in
Bunches—make a Syrup, with equal Quantities of Sugar and Cherries; ſcald the Cherries, but
do not let the Skins crack, which they will do if the
Fruit be too ripe. Put them in Bottles, and cover
them with equal Quantities of Syrup and *French*
Brandy.   (Mrs. *Mary Randolph's* Virginia Houſewife, 1831.)

Brandy Cherries *

SELECT the niceſt Cherries, trim them, leaving
a short Stem to each Cherry that the Juice may
be retained. Waſh & wipe them gently & put them
in large-mouthed Bottles. Have ready a good
Syrup (a Pint of Water to a Pound of Sugar) &
when it is nearly cold add one Pint & a Half of
French Brandy to every Pint of Syrup mix it thoroughly & pour it cold over yr. Cherries. Seal the
Bottles well.   (Manuſcript Cook Book, *Charlotteſville*, 1836.
Owned by Mrs. *Virginia Graſty Griffin.*)

Celery

Celery Vinegar *

POUND two Gills of Celery-ſeed, put it into a
Bottle and fill it with ſtrong Vinegar; ſhake it
every Day for a Fortnight, then ſtrain it, and keep
it for Uſe. It will impart a pleaſant Flavour of Celery to anything with which it is uſed. A very delicious Flavour of THYME may be obtained, by
gathering it when in full Perfection; it muſt be
picked from the Stalks, a large Handful of it put
into a Jar, and a Quart of Vinegar or Brandy
poured on it; cover it very cloſe—next Day, take
all the Thyme out, put in as much more; do this a
third Time; then ſtrain it, bottle and ſeal it ſe-
curely. This is greatly preferable to the dried
Thyme commonly uſed, during the Seaſon when it
cannot be obtained in a freſh State. MINT may be
prepared in the ſame Way. The Flavour of both
theſe Herbs muſt be preſerved by Care in the Preparation: if permitted to ſtand more than twenty
Hours in the Liquor they are infuſed in, a coarſe
and bitter Taſte will be extracted, particularly
from Mint.

(Mrs. *Mary Randolph's* Virginia Houſewife, 1831.)

Engliſh *Chop Pickle* *

CHOP fine one large Cabbage, one half Gallon
of green Tomato, one half Gallon of firm Cucumbers. Sprinkle with Salt and let ſtand Overnight. Waſh off Salt and add ſix finely chopped red
Peppers, ſix finely chopped green Peppers, four
Tableſpoons of Celery-ſeed, eight Tableſpoons of
Muſtard-ſeed. One Teaſpoon each of Allſpice, Ginger,

ger, Turmeric, Cloves, and if defired one Pound of finely chopped Raifins. Heat four Pounds of brown Sugar until diffolved in three Quarts of good Vinegar. While warm but not hot pour over your Relifh and put it away in covered Stone Crocks.

(Old Recipe from *Toano, Virginia.*
Prov'd *Travis* Houfe, 1938.)

Pickled Figs *

BRING to a boil one Quart of Vinegar, five Sticks Cinnamon, one Tablefpoon each whole Cloves, Allfpice, and Celery-feed. Drop in Figs wafhed and dried. Cook twenty Minutes.

(Traditional *Virginia* Recipe.)

Gerkins

TAKE a large earthen Pan with Spring-water in it, and to every Gallon of Water put two Pounds of Salt. Mix them well together, and throw in five hundred Gerkins. In two Hours take them out, and put them to drain. Let them be drained very dry, and then put them into a Jar. Put into a Pot a Gallon of the beft white-wine Vinegar, half an Ounce of Cloves and Mace, an Ounce of Allfpice, the fame Quantity of Muftard-feed, a Stick of Horfe-radifh cut in Slices, fix Bay-leaves, two or three Races of Ginger, a Nutmeg cut in Pieces, and a Handful of Salt. Boil up all together in the Pot, and pour it over the Gerkins. Cover them clofe down, and let them ftand twenty-four Hours. Then put them in your Pot, and let them fimmer over the Fire till they be green; but be careful not

to

to let them boil, as that will fpoil them. Then put them into your Jar, and cover them clofe down till they be cold. Then tie them over with a Bladder and a Leather, and put them in a cold, dry Place.

(*John Farley's* London Art of Cookery, 1787. From *Brookbury, Chefterfield* County, *Virginia.*)

Green Gages

TAKE any Quantity of Green-gages, prick them with a Pin, put them in a Pan with Water, and fet them on the Fire; when you fee the Water is beginning to boil, take them off and leave them in the fame Water to cool till the next Day, when you are to fet them again on a very gentle Fire, that they may turn green. When you fee they are green enough, you put them in a Sieve to drain; then you take the firft Degree of clarified Sugar, in which you add three Parts Water, then the Plums, and fet the Whole on a flow Fire to make them throw off their Water; after which, you put them in a Pan for two Days, and then you add clarified Sugar, and proceed as for Preferves.

(Court & Country Confectioner. *London*, 1770. From *Tucker* Houfe, *Williamfburg.*)

Conferve of Lemons *

WASH and dry yᵣ Lemons, pare off the yellow Rinds clear of the White and beat them in a Marble Mortar with nearly double their Weight of white Sugar. Pack clofely in a Jar or Glafs and cover the Top with the Balance of the Sugar. One
ever

even Teaspoonful added to six Bottles Toddy gives an agreeable Flavour. This Conserve is delightful in all sweet Dishes when you have not fresh Fruit.

(Manuscript Cook Book, c-1801,
of Mrs. *Frances Bland Tucker Coalter.*
Owned by Dr. *St. George Tucker Grinnan, Richmond.*)

To make Lemon Wafers*

TO the Juice of two or three Lemons, with the Rind of one of them grated or cut very fine, put of double refined Sugar, pounded and sifted, enough to make it of a Consistency like thick Cream. Set it over a Lamp in a Silver Bason or Plate, stirring it as it heats, and when hot (but not boiling) dip in your Wafer Paper(cut in what Form and Size you please) one Bit at a Time, and when both Sides are wetted, lay them on Glasses, or glazed Plates at a Distance from the Fire to dry. N. B. It will be two or three Days before they are dry.

(Wines & Cookery. *English* Manuscript Book, c-1740
Owned by Colonial *Williamsburg.*)

To make Melon Mangoes*

TAKE small Melons, not quite ripe, cut a Slip down the Side, and take out the Inside very clean; beat Mustard-seeds, and shred Garlick, and mix with the Seeds, and put in your Mangoes; put the Pieces you cut out into their Places again, and tie them up, and put them into your Pot, and boil some Vinegar (as much as you think will cover them) with whole Pepper, and some Salt, and *Jamaica* Pepper, and pour in scalding hot over your Mangoes,

Mangoes, and cover them close to keep in the Steam; and so do every Day for nine Times together, and when they are cold cover them with Leather.

(*E. Smith's* Compleat Housewife, *Williamsburg*, 1742.)

To pickle Nasturtium Buds

GATHER your little Knobs quickly after your Blossoms are off; put them in cold Water and Salt for three Days, shifting them once a Day; then make a Pickle (but do not boil it at all) of some White-wine, some White-wine Vinegar, Eschalot, Horse-radish, Pepper, Salt, Cloves and Mace whole and Nutmeg quartered; then put in your Seeds and stop them close; they are to be eaten as Capers.

(*E. Smith's* Compleat Housewife, *London*, 1739.)

To pickle Nasturtiums

GATHER the Berries when full grown but young, put them in a Pot, pour boiling Salt and Water on, and let them stand three or four Days; then drain off the Water, and cover them with cold Vinegar; add a few Blades of Mace, and whole Grains of black Pepper.

(Mrs. *Mary Randolph's* Virginia Housewife, 1831.)

To pickle Onions*

GET white Onions that are not too large, cut the Stem close to the Root with a sharp Knife, put them in a Pot, pour on boiling Salt and Water to cover them, stop the Pot closely, let them stand a Fortnight, changing the Salt and Water every
three

three Days; they must be stirred daily, or those
that float will become soft; at the End of this Time,
take off the Skin and outer Shell, put them in plain
cold Vinegar with a little Turmeric. If the Vinegar
be not very pale, the Onion will not be of a good
Colour. (Mrs. *Mary Randolph's* Virginia Housewife, 1831.)

Orange Marmalade*

PEEL one Dozen Oranges. Throw the Peel in a
Bucket of Water, take out the Seed, cut up the
Pulp fine with a Pair of old Scissors. Then take the
Peel, cut it in thin Strips and throw it into fresh
Water. Pare and slice Pippins (or any other nice
Apples). Weigh six Pounds of them, stew with a
little Water till perfectly done, and set away. Next
Day, run this Pulp through a Colander into a Pre-
serving-kettle. Add six Pounds Sugar and boil
slowly, constantly scraping from the Bottom.

Take the Orange-peel (which should have been
left in soak all Night), boil till perfectly soft and
free from Bitterness, changing the Water three
Times while boiling. In another Preserving-kettle,
simmer this with the Orange Pulp and two Pounds
Sugar. When both are nearly done, turn the
Oranges into the Apples and cook them very thick.
Store in covered Jars.

(Traditional Recipe, *Lynchburg, Virginia.*
From a *Williamsburg* Family Cook Book.)

Candied Orange or Lemon Peel*

TAKE large Pieces of Orange-peel or Lemon-
peel and cover them well in cold Water. Bring
slowly to a Boil and boil very gently for a few Minutes

utes until ſlightly tender. Drain, and put them in cold Water. Scrape out the looſe white Pulp with a ſilver Spoon and cut the Peel in long narrow Strips. Return the Peel to cold Water, bring ſlowly to a Boil, then drain and blanch. Repeat four Times. Make a boiling Syrup of one fourth Cup Water and one half Cup Sugar for the Peeling from two Pieces of Fruit. Add the Peel and boil it ſlowly until all the Syrup is gone—do not burn. Cool the Peel, roll it in coarſe Sugar and ſpread it out to dry.

(Recipe from Wines and Cookery, c-1740.
Adapted *Blair* Kitchen, 1938.)

Peaches in Brandy *

GET yellow ſoft Peaches, perfectly free from Defect and newly gathered, but not too ripe; place them in a Pot, and cover them with cold, weak Lye; turn over thoſe that float frequently, that the Lye may act equally on them; at the End of an Hour take them out, wipe them carefully with a ſoft Cloth to get off the Down and Skin, and lay them in cold Water; make a Syrup as for the Apricots, and proceed in the ſame Manner, only ſcald the Peaches more.

(Mrs. *Mary Randolph's* Virginia Houſewife, 1831.)

Brandy Peaches—Mrs. Madiſon *

PEEL your Peaches & put them in a Stone Pot, ſet the Pot into a Veſſel of Water and let it boil until a Straw will pierce the Fruit, then make a Syrup of Brandy & Sugar, one Pound of Sugar to a
Quart

Quart of Brandy, put in your Peaches. They will be fit for uſe in a Month. Brown Sugar will do very well. (Better without peeling.)—*St. G. T.*

(Recipe found in letter written February 6 [1804], by *St. George Tucker*, of *Williamſburg*, to his Daughter, Mrs. *Frances Coalter*.)

Brandy Peaches—Mrs. Skipwith *

MAKE a rich Syrup. Have Lye boiling hot, put in a few Peaches at a Time & let them remain juſt long enough to take off the Fur. Wipe or rub them as they are taken out with a coarſe Towel, & drop them in cold Water—then put the Peaches in Syrup, & let them boil gently till a Straw will pierce the Fruit—when ſufficiently done put them in a Jar & whilſt the Syrup is hot, mix equal Quantities of Brandy with it, & pour it hot, over the Peaches.

(Manuſcript Cook·Book, *Charlotteſville*, 1836. Owned by Mrs. *Virginia Graſty Griffin*.)

Peach Chips *

SLICE them thin, and boil them till clear in a Syrup made with Half their Weight of Sugar; lay them on Diſhes in the Sun, and turn them till dry; pack them in Pots with powdered Sugar ſifted over each Layer; ſhould there be Syrup left, continue the Proceſs with other Peaches. They are very nice when done with pure Honey inſtead of Sugar.

(Mrs. *Mary Randolph's* Virginia Houſewife, 1831.)

Peach

Peach Mangoes※

TAKE large plum Peaches, sufficient Quantity to fill the Jar. Peel nicely and take out the Stones. Have ready the Stuffing in Proportion to the Peaches. Mince fine some soft Peaches, preserved Orange-peel, preserved Ginger, Coriander-seed, Celery-seed, a small Quantity of Mace, Cinnamon, candied Strawberries, if you have them, and pickled Cherries. Sew the Peaches up after stuffing them and fill the Jar. Then to every Pound of Sugar add one-half Pint of Vinegar, allowing the above Quantity to two Pounds of Fruit. Make a Syrup of the Sugar and Vinegar, and pour on the Peaches, boiling hot. Repeat this for three Mornings; the fourth Morning put them all on together, and boil a short Time; add a few Spices, Cinnamon, and Ginger to the Syrup when you make it. They will be ready for Use in a few Weeks.

(Recipe from a *Williamsburg* Family Cook Book.)

Peach Marmalade※

TAKE the ripest soft Peaches (the yellow ones make the prettiest Marmalade), pare them, and take out the Stones; put them in the Pan with one Pound of dry, light-coloured brown Sugar to two of Peaches: when they are juicy, they do not require Water; with a Silver or Wooden Spoon, chop them with the Sugar; continue to do this, and let them boil gently till they are a transparent Pulp, that will be a Jelly when cold. Puffs made of this Marmalade are very delicious.

(Mrs. *Mary Randolph's* Virginia Housewife, 1831.)

Sweet

Sweet Pickled Peaches✻

PUT four Pounds of Sugar into a Preserving-kettle with one Quart of Vinegar and Spices. Boil them for five Minutes after the Sugar is dissolved. Pare seven Pounds of Peaches and stick a Clove into each one. Place a few at a Time in the boiling Syrup and cook them until they look clear, but are not softened enough to fall apart. When all are cooked, continue to boil the Syrup until it is reduced nearly one half, and pour it over the Peaches.

(Old Recipe from *Richmond, Virginia.*)

Pear Marmalade✻

SLOWLY boil Pears until soft. Chill and put through Sieve. To each two Pounds of Pears add one Pound of Sugar. Boil this to a Jelly.

(Traditional *Virginia* Recipe. Prov'd *Market Square Tavern* Kitchen, 1937.)

To pickle Peppers

GATHER the large bell Pepper when quite young, leave the Seeds in and the Stem on, cut a Slit in one Side between the large Veins, to let the Water in; pour boiling Salt and Water on, changing it every Day for three Weeks—you must keep them closely stopped; if, at the End of this Time, they be a good green, put them in Pots, and cover them with cold Vinegar and a little Turmeric; those that are not sufficiently green, must be continued under the same Process till they are so. Be careful not to cut through the large Veins, as the Heat will instantly diffuse itself through the Pod.

(Mrs. *Mary Randolph's* Virginia Housewife, 1831.)

Pepper

Pepper Vinegar

GET one Dozen Pods of Pepper when ripe, take
out the Stems, and cut them in Two; put
them in a Kettle with three Pints of Vinegar, boil
it away to one Quart, and ſtrain it through a Sieve.
A little of this is excellent in Gravy of every Kind,
and gives a Flavour greatly ſuperior to black Pepper; it is alſo very fine when added to each of the
various Catſups for Fiſh Sauce.

(Mrs. *Mary Randolph's* Virginia Houſewife, 1831.)

Quinces*

SELECT the fineſt and moſt perfect Quinces, lay
them on Shelves, but do not let them touch
each other; keep them till they look yellow and
have a fragrant Smell; put as many in the Pre-
ſerving-pan as can lie conveniently, cover them
with Water, and ſcald them well: then take out the
Cores, and put them in Water; cover the Pan and
boil them ſome Time; ſtrain the Water, add to it
the Weight of the Quinces in pounded Loaf Sugar,
diſſolve and ſkim it, pare the Quinces, put them in
the Pan, and ſhould there not be Syrup enough to
cover them, add more Water—ſtew them till quite
tranſparent. They will be light coloured if kept
covered during the Proceſs, and red if the Cover be
taken off. Fill the Space the Cores occupied with
Quince Jelly, before they are put into the Pots—
and cover them with Syrup.

(Mrs. *Mary Randolph's* Virginia Houſewife, 1831.)

Moiſt

Moist Quinces*

TAKE any Quantity of Quinces; cut them into four Quarters; take well off the Heart and the Skin, and put them in a Pan of Water which you have on the Fire; boil them thus till a Skewer can get into them eafily. Then take them off and put them upon a Cloth to drain their Water away; while this is doing, you fet your Preferving-pan on the Fire, with the Quantity of Sugar of the firft Degree which is neceffary, and put your Quinces in it; boil the Whole well, till you fee the Sugar becomes very red. Then to know the proper Time of its being done, take a little Syrup with a Spoon in a Saucer, and let it cool; if it turns into a Jelly, you muft directly take away your Quinces from the Fire, and put them immediately quite hot into very dry Pots, for fhould you let them be cold before you pot them, they would jelly, and you could no more make them fill all the Parts of the Pots without fome Air along with them. Take Care that your Syrup fhould always well cover your Fruit, as I have faid before.

(Court & Country Confectioner. *London,* 1770.
From *Tucker* Houfe, *Williamfburg.*)

Quince Marmalade*

BOIL the Quinces in Water until foft, let them cool, and rub all the Pulp through a Sieve: put two Pounds of it to one of Sugar, pound a little Cochineal, fift it through fine Muflin, and mix it with the Quince to give a Colour; pick out the
Seeds,

Seeds, tie them in a Muslin Bag, and boil them with the Marmalade; when it is a thick Jelly, take out the Seeds, and put it in Pots.

(Mrs. *Mary Randolph's* Virginia Housewife, 1831.)

Conserve of Red Roses

BEAT one Pound of red Rose-leaves in a Mortar. Add this to two Pounds of refined Sugar. Make a Conserve.

After the same Manner are prepared the Conserves of Orange-peel, Rosemary Flowers, Seawormwood, of the Leaves of Wood Sorrel, etc.

(Old Recipe, *Wicomico* Church. *Virginia*.)

Tomato Pickle*

CUT up one-half Peck of Onions, one Peck of Tomatoes and add one and one-half Cups of Salt. Let stand for twelve Hours, boil in Vinegar and Water, drain off and boil for two Hours. Add three Pounds Sugar, two Tablespoons of Celeryseed, two Tablespoons ground Mustard, one Tablespoon black Pepper, one Ounce Mace, one and one-half Ounce Alspice, one Ounce Cloves. Cover with good Vinegar and boil slowly for two Hours.

(Old *Barlow* Family Recipe, *Williamsburg, Virginia*.)

To make Walnut Catsup

GATHER the Walnuts as for pickling, and keep them in Salt Water the same Time; then pound them in a marble Mortar—to every Dozen Walnuts, put a Quart of Vinegar; stir them well every Day for a Week, then put them in a Bag,
and

and prefs all the Liquor through; to each Quart, put a Teafpoonful of pounded Cloves, and one of Mace, with fix Cloves of Garlic—boil it fifteen or twenty Minutes, and bottle it.

(Mrs. *Mary Randolph's* Virginia Houfewife, 1831.)

To Pickle Englifh *Walnuts*

THE Walnuts fhould be gathered when the Nut is fo young that you can run a Pin into it eafily; pour boiling Salt and Water on, and let them be covered with it nine Days, changing it every third Day—take them out, and put them on Difhes in the Air for a few Minutes, taking Care to turn them over; this will make them black much fooner —put them in a Pot, ftrew over fome whole Pepper, Cloves, a little Garlic, Muftard-feed, and Horfe-radifh fcraped and dried; cover them with ftrong, cold Vinegar.

(Mrs. *Mary Randolph's* Virginia Houfewife, 1831.)

Sweet *Watermelon Pickle**

TRIM the Rinds nicely, being careful to cut off the hard Coating with the outer green. Weigh ten Pounds Rind and throw in a Kettle and cover with foft Water. Let this boil gently for half an Hour, take it off and lay it on Difhes to drain. Next Morning put one Quart of Vinegar, three Pounds brown Sugar, one Ounce Cinnamon, one Ounce Mace, the White of one Egg well beaten, and put on Top of the Liquid (to clear it as you would Jelly), three Teafpoonfuls Turmeric, all together and

and boil for a few Minutes. Skim off what riſes as Scum with the Egg. Throw in the Rind and boil for twenty Minutes. The Peel of two freſh Lemons will give a nice Flavor, though not at all neceſſary.

(Old Recipe, *Toano, Virginia.*)

*Watermelon Rind Pickle**

PARE the Rind of a Melon, cutting away all pink Meat inſide. Then place it in an earthen Crock of ſalt Water, ſalt enough to float an Egg. Let the Rind remain a Week in this, or longer if you wiſh. Make a Brine by filling the Crock with Water and placing a Lump of Alum or two Teaſpoons of powdered Alum. Let the Rind remain in this two Days, then ſoak the Rind in cold Water for a Day and Night, then cook it in cold Water until clear, ſqueeze the Water out and let it ſtand for a Night, and then make a Syrup of Vinegar and Sugar and mixed Spices, cooking the Rind awhile in it. (Old Recipe, *Norfolk, Virginia.*)

Williamſburg *Watermelon Pickle**

PARE the Rind of a Watermelon, cutting away the pink Part. Cut them in ſmall Pieces with a fluted Cutter and let ſtand over Night in equal Parts of Vinegar and Water to cover. Put it on to boil in this Vinegar, cook until tender and drain well. Make a Syrup of five Pounds of Sugar, one Quart of Vinegar and put in a Spice Bag containing ſeveral Blades of Mace, two Ounces of Cloves, and

one

one Ounce of whole Cinnamon. Boil for ten Minutes. Put Rind in and cook a few Minutes, then remove it to hot Jars. Boil the Syrup down until it is thick and pour it over the Rind and ſeal hot.

(Traditional *Virginia* Recipe. Adapted
Market Square Tavern Kitchen, 1937)

*To make Vinegar for Pickles**

TO every Peck of very ripe Gooſeberries of any Sort, put two Gallons of Water, cruſh the Fruit well with your Hands, and mix it well with the Water; let it work three Weeks, ſtirring it four or five Times a Day, then ſtrain the Liquor, put a Pound of brown Sugar, a Pound of Treacle, and a Spoonful of freſh Barm; let it work three or four Days, turn it in iron-hooped Barrels, let it ſtand a Year or more, it is the beſt Vinegar for Uſe.

(Court & Country Confe&ioner *London*, 1770.
From *Tucker* Houſe, *Williamſburg.*)

❧❦❧❦❧❦❧❦❧❦❧❦❧❦❧❦❧❦❧❦❧❦❧❦

Favorite *Williamsburg* Garden Herbs

COMMON NAME	BOTANICAL NAME	USE
Agrimony	*Agrimonia Eupatoria*	Flavoring
		Medicine
Angelica	*Archangelica officinalis*	Culinary
		Medicine
Anise	*Pimpinella Anisum*	Flavoring
		(Seeds)
		Medicine
		(Seeds)
		Culinary
		(Seeds)
		Seasoning
		Garnishing
Apple Mint	*Mentha rotunaifolia*	Flavoring
Balm of Gilead	*Cedronella triphylla*	Medicine
		Scent
Basil	*Ocimum basilicum*	Seasoning
		Scent
Bay	*Laurus nobilis*	Seasoning
Beebalm	*Monarda diayma*	Medicine
		Scent
Bergamot	*Monarao fistulosa*	Medicine
Betony	*Stachys Betonica*	Medicine
Bloodroot	*Sanguinaria canadensis*	Medicine
Borage	*Borago officinalis*	Cordials
		Salads
Calamint	*Calaminta Acinos*	Scent
		Medicine
Caraway	*Carum carvi*	Flavoring
		(Seeds)
Catnip	*Nepeta cataria*	Medicine

Celery

Rosemary　Sage　Mint　Thyme　Marjoram　Chives

*The Blair Kitchen and Herb Garden
at Williamsburg.*

PLATE III.　　　　　　　　　E. JONES.

Common Name	Botanical	Use
Celery	*Apium graveolens*	Salads
		Seasoning
Chamomile	*Anthemis nobilis*	Medicine
		Scent
Chervil	*Anthriſcus Cerefolium*	Seasoning
		Salads
Chicory	*Chichorium intybus*	Salads
		Flavoring
Chives	*Allium ſchœnopraſum*	Seasoning
Clary	*Salvia Sclarea*	Medicine
		(Salves)
		Seasoning
Common Balm	*Meliſſa officinalis*	Flavoring
Coriander	*Coriandrum ſativum*	Confectionery
		Cordials
		(Seeds)
		Seasoning
		(Seeds)
		Flavoring
		(Seeds)
Fennel	*Foeniculum vulgare*	Seasoning
		Flavoring
		Scent
Feverfew	*Chryſanthemum parthenium*	Medicine
Garden	*Valeriana officinalis*	Scent
Heliotrope		Medicine
Garlic	*Allium ſativum*	Seasoning
Hoarhound	*Marrubium vulgare*	Culinary
		Medicine
Horse Mint	*Mentha longifolia*	Scent
		Medicine
Horse-radiſh	*Raaicula Armoracia*	Relish
		Seasoning
		Medicine
Hyſſop	*Hyſſopus officinalis*	Seasoning
		Medicine
Lavendar	*Lavenaula vera*	Relish
		Scent
		Lemon

COMMON NAME	BOTANICAL NAME	USE
Lemon (Bergamot) Mint	*Mentha citrata*	Reliſh Flavoring Scent
Monkſhood	*Aconitum Napellus*	Medicine
Mandrake	*Poaophyllum peltatum*	Medicine
Muſtard	*Braſſica nigra*	Seeds Condiment Medicine
Muſtard	*Braſſica japonica*	Salads
Naſturtium	*Tropaeolum Majus*	Garniſhes Reliſh (Seeds) Salads
Parſley	*Petroſelinum hortenſe*	Seaſoning Garniſh Medicine
Pennyroyal	*Mentha Pulegium*	Medicine Seaſoning
Peppermint	*Mentha piperita*	Medicine Flavoring Scent
Peppers	*Capſicum*	Condiment Medicine Seaſoning
Periwinkle	*Vinca minor*	Medicine
Rhubarb	*Theum Rhaponticum*	Medicine (Root) Food (Stalks)
Roſemary	*Roſmarinus officinalis*	Scent Seaſoning
Rue	*Ruta graveolens*	Medicine Seaſoning Flavoring Scent
Saffron	A form of *Crocus ſativus*	Seaſoning Medicine Scent
Sage	*Salvia officinalis*	Medicine Seaſoning Scent

Savory,

COMMON NAME	BOTANICAL NAME	USE
Savory, Summer	*Satureia hortenſis*	Seaſoning
Self Heal	*Brunella vulgaris*	Medicine
Shallot	*Allium Aſcalonicum*	Seaſoning
Sorrel	*Rumex Acetoſa*	Culinary
		Medicine
		Salads
		Drinks
Spearmint	*Mentha ſpicata*	Medicine
		Flavoring
Sweet Marjoram	*Origanum Majoram*	Seaſoning
		Scent
Tanſy	*Tanacetum vulgare*	Flavoring
		Medicine
Tarragon	*Arſemiſia Dracunculus*	Seaſoning
Thyme	*Thymus citrioaous*	Seaſoning
Thyme	*Thymus Serpyllum*	Seaſoning
Thyme	*Thymus vulgaris*	Seaſoning
		Scent
Turmeric	*Curcuma longa*	Condiment
		Flavoring
		Medicine
		Dyes
Violet	*Viola oaorata*	Scent
		Confection
Winter Savory	*Satureia montana*	Seaſoning
		Scent

CONFECTIONERY

IT ſeems to have been the Fate of moſt Cookery Books to have found their Way to the Kitchen from the Library—and there to have had a Period of ſuch ſtrenuous Uſe that they ended their Days with Batter-beſpattered Pages and broken Backs. The Life of a Book might be prolonged by binding the Pages of an earlier Cookery Book with a newer one, perhaps ſewing in extra Pages for the Houſe-wife to uſe for Writing or Pinning in her own favor-ite Recipes.

However, in the Library of *St. George Tucker*, Eſquire, of *Williamſburg*, there is one neat leather-bound Volume, called the "Confectioner" which ſeems worn and uſed, but entirely unſtained by even a ſingle Drip of Syrup. One Explanation might be that in his well-managed Houſehold the Recipes went out to the Kitchen on ſmall Slips of Paper and the Cookery Book was replaced on the Library Shelf. Another Solution to this Puzzle, in *St. George Tucker's* own Hand, is a ſhort Verſe which he penned in *May*, 1781, to his Friend, Mr. *Lomax* who had failed to avail himſelf of an Invita-tion to viſit him at *Matoax:*

> Though you expected naught to eat,
> We could have given you some Meat.
> Veal that had ſucked two well-fed Cows.
> Lamb that was fattened in a Houſe.

Bacon

Bacon well-fed on *Indian* Corn.
And Chicken crammed both Night & Morn.
Sturgeon likewise adorned the Board.
Of Pears we had a monstrous Hoard.
Half ate, and half untouched remained
For scanty Messes we disdained.
Next Strawberries in View appear.
And Apple Tarts bring up the Rear.
These Dainties too were one half left,
Madeira filled each Chink & Cleft.
We ate, we drank, we went to Bed,
And slept as though we all were Dead.

Where, in such a Bill of Fare could one find Room for even a single *Savoy* Biscuit, a Coffee-cream Bomboon, a Petticoat Tail, a Wig, or a Quire of Paper Pancakes?

All Sorts of Confectionery

To fricasy Almonds *

TAKE a Pound of *Jordan* Almonds, do not blanch them, or but one Half of them; beat the White of an Egg very well, and pour it on your Almonds, and wet them all over; then take half a Pound of double-refin'd Sugar, and boil it to Sugar again; and put your Almonds in, and stir them till as much Sugar hangs on them as will; then set them on Plates, and put them into the Oven to dry after Bread is drawn, and let them stay in all Night. They will keep the Year round if you keep them dry, and are a pretty Sweetmeat.

(*E. Smith's* Compleat Housewife, *Williamsburg*, 1742.
Prov'd *Market Square Tavern* Kitchen, 1937.)

A

A Method to make All Sorts of Light, Seed, And Other Cakes*

IT may not be improper to obſerve, that before you proceed to make any Sort of Cakes, that Care ſhould firſt be taken to have all your Ingredients ready before you begin, then beat your Eggs well, and not leave them till you have finiſhed the Cakes, for by ſuch Neglect, they would go back, and your Cakes would not be light; if your Cakes are to have Butter in, take Care you beat it to a fine Cream before you put in your Sugar, for if you beat it twice the Time after it will not anſwer ſo well.

(Court & Country Confectioner. *London*, 1770. From *Tucker* Houſe, *Williamſburg*.)

Williamſburg *Almond Cakes* *

CREAM together one Cupful of Sugar and one half Pound of Butter, add three well-beaten Eggs, one Teaſpoonful of Mace or of Cinnamon and one Wine-glaſs of Brandy. Sift in enough Flour to make a Dough which will roll out very thin. Cut your Cakes, place them on unbuttered Tins, ſprinkle with chopped Almonds and bake in moderate Oven.

(Old Recipe from *Richmond, Virginia*. Adapted *Market Square Tavern* Kitchen, 1937.)

To make little hollow Biſkets

BEAT ſix Eggs very well with a Spoonful of Roſe-water, then put in a Pound and two Ounces of Loaf-ſugar beaten and ſifted; ſtir it together
gether

gether till 'tis well mixed in the Eggs; then put in as much Flour as will make it thick enough to lay out in Drops upon Sheets of white Paper; ſtir it well together till you are ready to drop it on your Paper; then beat a little very fine Sugar and put into a Lawn Sieve, and ſift ſome on them juſt as they are going into the Oven; to bake them, the Oven muſt not be too hot, and as ſoon as they are baked, whilſt they are hot, pull off the Papers from them, and put them in a Sieve, and ſet them in an Oven to dry; keep them in Boxes with Papers between.

(*E. Smith's* Compleat Houſewife, *Williamſburg*, 1742.)

Empire Biſcuits *

SIFT well ſix heaping Tableſpoons of Flour, four Tableſpoons of Sugar, one Teaſpoon of Cinnamon. Cut into this one fourth of a Pound of Butter. Knead together lightly, roll out thin. Prick all over with a Fork and cut with ſmall round Cutters. Bake in moderate Oven on greaſed Papers about twenty Minutes. Cool. Put Currant Jelly between two Biſcuits, ſpread the Top with a flavored white Icing then decorate with candied Angelica or Cherries.

(Old *Richmond* Recipe. Prov'd *Market Square Tavern* Kitchen, 1937.)

Williamſburg *Naples Biſcuits* *

BEAT the Whites of three Eggs very light adding gradually one third of a Cup of powdered Sugar, beating conſtantly. Fold in three well-beaten Egg Yolks. Sift in and mix lightly, one third Cup

Cup of Flour fifted with a Pinch of Salt. Add one half Teafpoon of Vanilla. Shape carefully into Fingers on unbuttered Paper; fprinkle with finely powdered Sugar and bake ten Minutes in a moderate Oven.   (Mrs. *Randolph's* Recipe, 1831.

Adapted *Market Square Tavern* Kitchen, 1937.)

Palais Royal *Bifcuits*

TAKE eight Eggs, break them and put the Yolks in one Pan, and the Whites in another; then weigh half a Pound of Sugar, which you put in the Pan where the Yolks are, beat well your Yolks and the Sugar together with a Spoon, till it makes a white Pafte; weigh fix Ounces of Flour which you put on a white Sheet of Paper; when your Yolks of Eggs are well-beaten with the Sugar, and your Flour weighed, and put on a Sheet of Paper, take a fmall Whifk, beat well your Whites of Eggs till they come up like a Syllabub, and they are so hard that your Whifk can ftand upright in them; then take your Yolks which are like a Pafte, and put them with the Whites, and mix them in, turning them gently with your Whifk. When both the Yolks and Whites are well mixed, take a Sieve, put your Flour in it, and fift it gently over your Mixture, and continue ftirring till you fee all is well mixed, and there is no Lump of Flour in your Pafte; when your Compofition is finifhed, have little Paper Moulds made long and fquare, fill them with that Pafte, and fift on the Top of each of them a little of fine pounded Loaf Sugar, which is called the Icing of them, then put them in the Oven.

(Court & Country Confectioner. *London*, 1770.
From *Tucker* Houfe, *Williamfburg.*)

Tavern

Tavern Biscuits *

TO two Cups of Flour, add one Cup of Sugar, one Cup of Butter, some Mace and Nutmeg powdered, and a Glass of Brandy or Wine; wet it with Milk, and when well kneaded, roll it thin, cut it in Shapes, and bake it quickly.

(Mrs. *Mary Randolph's* Recipe, 1831.
Adapted *Market Square Tavern* Kitchen, 1937.)

Coffee-Cream Bomboons

TAKE about a Pint of Coffee made with Water, put in it a Pound of loaf Sugar, set it on the Fire, and boil it to the ninth Degree, then you add a full Pint of double Cream, and let it boil again, keeping continually stirring till it comes to Caramel Height; to know when it is come to that Point, you must have a Bason of Water by you, dip your Finger in it, and put it quickly in your Sugar, then in the Water again to remove the Sugar, which will have stuck to it; take a Bit of it in your Teeth, if it is hard in its Crackling take it off, it is to the Height required; pour it upon a buttered Tin Plate, and roll it thin with a buttered Rolling-pin. When it is warm you may cut it in little Squares, or Lozenges, or any other shapen Pastiles, and draw a few Strokes over them with a Knife.

(Court & Country Confectioner, *London*, 1770.
From *Tucker* House, *Williamsburg*.)

Currant

Currant Squares*

HEAT until warm, but not hot, one Cupful of Cream on a very low Fire, ſtir in one half Cupful of melted Butter, add one Cup of Sugar, then three well beaten Eggs. Add one ſmall Yeaſt Cake diſſolved in a little Milk-warm Water. Sift in four Cups of Flour, one Tableſpoon of powdered Mace, one Teaſpoon of Salt. Beat well for at leaſt fifteen Minutes. Pour into ſhallow buttered Baking-pans and let riſe until double in Bulk. Bake in a quick Oven, ſprinkle with powdered Sugar and Cinnamon juſt before removing from Oven. Cool a little and cut into Squares.

(Old *Henrico* County Recipe.
Prov'd *Market Square Tavern* Kitchen, 1937.)

Cookies of 1812*

CREAM one Cup of Butter with two Cups of fine Sugar. Beat the Yolks of four Eggs very light, then combine with the well-beaten Whites and add to creamed Mixture. Sift in two Cups of Flour, one Teaſpoon of Cream of Tartar, one half Teaſpoon of Nutmeg. Add two Tableſpoons of ſweet Milk, one half Teaſpoon of Soda in a little warm Water, one Teaſpoon of Vanilla. Mix well, adding more Flour if neceſſary to make Dough ſtiff enough to roll out thin. Bake in moderate Oven, a delicate brown. This Dough may be made into ſmall Rolls, chilled Overnight and ſliced into ſmall Cakes for baking.

(Traditional *Virginia* Recipe.
Adapted *Market Square Tavern* Kitchen, 1937.)

Dough

Dough Nuts—*A* Yankee *Cake**

DRY half a Pound of good brown Sugar, pound
it, and mix it with two Pounds of Flour, and
ſift it; add two Spoonfuls of Yeaſt, and as much
new Milk as will make it like Bread; when well
riſen, knead in half a Pound of Butter, make it in
Cakes the Size of a half Dollar, and fry them a light
brown in boiling Lard.

(Mrs. Mary Randolph's Virginia Houſewife, 1831.)

Another Way*

SIFT together five Cups of Flour, one Teaſpoon
of Salt, one and three fourths Teaſpoons of
Soda, the ſame of Cream of Tartar, one half Tea
ſpoon of Nutmeg and one fourth Teaſpoon of Cinnamon. Cut in one Tableſpoon of Butter; beat one
Egg well with one Cup of Sugar, add one Cup of
ſour Milk. Knead ſlightly, roll out one fourth Inch
thick, cut with a Doughnut-cutter. Fry in deep
Fat, drain on brown Paper.

(Market Square Tavern Kitchen, 1937.)

To make Dutch Gingerbread*

TAKE four Pounds of Flour, and mix with it
two Ounces and half of beaten Ginger, then
rub in a quarter of a Pound of Butter, and add to
it two Ounces of Carraway-ſeeds, two Ounces of
Orange-peel dry'd and rubb'd to Powder, a few
Coriander-ſeeds, bruiſed, two Eggs, then mix all
up in a ſtiff Paſte with two Pounds and a quarter
of Treacle; beat it very well with a Rolling-pin,
and make it up into thirty Cakes; put in a candied
Citron;

Citron; prick them with a Fork; butter Papers three double, one white, and two brown; wash them over with the White of an Egg; put 'em into an Oven not too hot for three quarters of an Hour.

(*E. Smith's* Compleat Housewife, *London*, 1739.)

Soft Ginger Cakes⁕

CREAM together one Cup Sugar, one half Cup of Lard. Add one Cup black Molasses. Dissolve one Teaspoon Soda in one Cup sour Milk. Add enough Flour to make Batter stiff. Sift with Flour, one Teaspoon ground Ginger, one Teaspoon Cinnamon. Drop from Spoon. Bake in moderate Oven on greased Tins.

(Old *Richmond* Recipe. Prov'd
Market Square Tavern Kitchen, 1937.)

Gingerbread Cakes

TAKE three Pounds of Flour, a Pound of Sugar, the same Quantity of Butter rolled in very fine, two Ounces of Ginger beat fine, and a large Nutmeg grated. Then take a Pound of Treacle, a quarter of a Pint of Cream, and make them warm together. Make up the Bread stiff, roll it out, and make it up into thin Cakes. Cut them out with a Teacup or small Glass or roll them round like Nuts, and bake them in a slack Oven on tin Plates.

(*John Farley's*, London Art of Cookery, 1787.
From *Brookbury, Chesterfield* County.)

Mrs. J. Randolph Page's *Ginger Cakes*

TWO Quarts of Flour, one Teacupful of Sugar, one Pint of Molasses, half a Pound of Lard, four Tablespoonfuls of ground Ginger, one Tablespoonful

ſpoonful of ground Cloves, and one Teaſpoonful of Salt. Let any one try this Recipe who wants to be convinced that the beſt Things are not always the moſt expenſive. The Dough muſt be juſt as ſtiff as it can be to handle well, and rolled out to Wafer-like Thickneſs. Stick as you do Biſcuits, and bake quickly without burning. Cut out alſo with a plain round Biſcuit Cutter.

(Mrs. *Mary Stuart Smith's* Virginia Cookery Book, 1885.)

Williamſburg *Ginger Cakes*✻

CREAM one half Cup of Lard with two Cups of brown Sugar, ſtir in two Cups of light Molaſſes. Sift into this four Cups of Flour, two Tableſpoons of Ginger, one half Teaſpoon of Salt, one Teaſpoon of Soda. Add enough Flour to make a ſtiff Dough which can be rolled very thin. Cut with ſmall round or fancy Cutters and bake in buttered Tins in a quick Oven. They will burn eaſily.

(Adapted and prov'd *Market Square Tavern* Kitchen, 1937.)

Jumbles✻

ONE Pound of Flour, one of Sugar, half Pound of Butter, three Eggs, a little Cinnamon. Mix firſt the Flour and Sugar and let them dry a little. Beat the Eggs, then mix the Butter and Eggs together—then mix them all and knead them well, roll the Dough ſmall and long. Form them like a Hoop. Dip them in pounded Sugar, bake them on Paper.

(Manuſcript Cook Book, prior 1839.
Morton Family of *Charlotte* County *Virginia*.)

Williamſburg

Williamſburg *Jumbals* *

MIX one third of a Cup of Butter and the ſame of fine Sugar, together. Add one well beaten Egg. Sift in three fourths of a Cup of Flour with one fourth Teaſpoonful of Salt, and one Teaſpoonful of powdered Mace. Drop by Spoonfuls far apart on a buttered Tin, ſpread thin, and bake in moderate Oven about ten Minutes.

(Mrs. *E. Smith's* Recipe, 1742.
Adapted *Market Square Tavern* Kitchen, 1937.)

Macaroon Cakes

ONE Pound of blanched Almonds, one of double refined Sugar—the Whites of four Eggs—beaten to Froth, a Spoonful Brandy or Roſe-water —mix the Ingredients well together, ſift Sugar over them and bake them.

(Manuſcript Cook Book, prior 1839.
Morton Family of *Charlotte* County, *Virginia*.)

To Candy Orange Chips

PARE your Oranges and ſoak the Peelings in Water two Days, and ſhift the Water twice; but if you love them bitter ſoak them not: Tie your Peels up in a Cloth, and when your Water boils, put them in, and let them boil till they are tender; then take what double refin'd Sugar will do, and break it ſmall and wet it with a little Water, and let it boil till' tis near Candy-high, then cut your Peels of what Length you pleaſe, and put 'em into the Syrup; ſet 'em on the Fire and let 'em heat well thro', then let them ſtand a while, heat them twice

twice a Day, but not boil: Let them be ſo done till they begin to candy, then take them out and put them on Plates to dry, and when they are dry, keep them near the Fire.

(Mrs. *E. Smith's* Compleat Houſewife, *Williamſburg,* 1742.)

King's Arms *Pecan Confeſtions* *

BEAT one Egg White to a ſtiff Froth, add gradually one Cupful of brown Sugar, one Pinch of Salt, one level Tableſpoonful of Flour. Stir in one Cupful of chopped Pecans, drop on greaſed Tins by ſmall Spoonfuls far apart. Bake in very ſlow Oven for fifteen Minutes. Remove from Tin when partly cooled. Makes two Dozen.

(Old Recipe. Adapted *Travis* Houſe, *Williamſburg.*)

Petticoat Tails *

SIFT together ſeveral Times five Cups of Flour and one Cup of fine powdered Sugar. Cut and knead into this two Cups of Butter. Shape the Dough in Rolls and chill overnight. Slice thin and bake in moderate Oven.

(Old Recipe, *Sparta, Virginia.*
Prov'd *Market Square Tavern* Kitchen, 1937.)

Williamſburg *Ratafia Cakes* *

TAKE one half Pound of Almond Paſte, and three eighths of a Pound of Sugar together on a marble Slab and work them together ſlowly with a broad flat Knife until they are ſmooth. Add
ſlowly

ſlowly the Whites of three Eggs well beaten. Drop
from a Spoon on buttered Paper and bake in a ſlow
Oven about fifteen Minutes.

(Court & Country Confectioner *London*, 1770.
Adapted *Market Square Tavern* Kitchen, 1937.)

Scotch *Shortbread**

B EAT one Pound Butter to a Cream. Mix together and gradually ſift in two Pounds Flour,
one fourth Pound Cornſtarch. Then add one fourth
Pound granulated Sugar, one Ounce Almonds,
blanched and cut in ſmall Pieces. Work the Paſte
quite ſmooth. Cut ſmall Pieces off and roll into
three Inch Squares about one Inch thick. Pinch up
the Edges and prick well with a Fork. Ornament
with a Strip of Orange-peel. Bake in moderate
Oven twenty five or thirty Minutes.

(Old *Richmond* Recipe. Prov'd
Market Square Tavern Kitchen, 1937.)

Shrewſbury *Cakes*

B EAT half a Pound of Butter to a fine Cream,
and put in the ſame Weight of Flour, one Egg,
ſix Ounces of beaten and ſifted Loaf-ſugar, and
half an Ounce of Carraway-ſeeds. Mix them into a
Paſte, roll them thin, and cut them round with a
ſmall Glaſs or little Tins; prick them, lay them on
Sheets of Tin, and bake them in a ſlow Oven.

(*John Farley's* London Art of Cookery, 1787.
From *Brookbury, Cheſterfield* Co., *Virginia*.)

Shrewſbury

Shrewsbury *Cakes*

TAKE to one Pound of Sugar three Pounds of the finest Flour, a Nutmeg grated, some beaten Cinnamon, the Sugar and Spice must be sifted into the Flour, and wet it with three Eggs, and as much melted Butter as will make it of a good Thickness to roll it to a Paste. Cut it into what Shape you please, perfume them and prick them before they go into the Oven.

(Manuscript Cook Book, c-1825, of Miss *Margaret Prentis* of *Williamsburg*, Owned by *Robert H. Webb*, Esq., *Charlottesville*.)

Shrewsbury *Cakes* *

MIX a Pound of Sugar with two Pounds of Flour and a large Spoonful of pounded Coriander-seeds; sift them, add three quarters of a Pound of melted Butter, six Eggs, and a Gill of Brandy; knead it well, roll it thin, cut it in Shapes, and bake without discolouring it.

(Mrs. *Mary Randolph's* Virginia Housewife, 1831.)

All Sorts of Seed Cakes *

MIX one Cup of Sugar in three fourths of a Cup of well-creamed Butter, add three slightly beaten Eggs, one fourth of a Cup of Brandy, and two Cups of Flour. Roll out thin, sprinkle with Seeds, roll again, cut in Shapes and bake slowly a light golden Color. Pounded Cardamon-seeds, Coriander-seeds, Bene-seeds or Carraway-seeds were the old Favorites.

(The four Recipes preceding adapted *Market Square Tavern* Kitchen, 1937.)

Of

Of CAKES

FROM Chriſtenings to Funerals, Cakes were
moſt intimately aſſociated with family and ſocial Life. There was a ſpecial Cake for each happy
or ſad Occaſion—Pancakes for St. *Valentine's* Day,
Bride's Cakes for Weddings, large Fruit Cakes for
Chriſtmas Holidays, elaborately decorated Twelfth-
night Cakes, and laſt of all the Funeral Cake (uſually provided by the Eſtate of the Deceaſed).

Even the *Engliſh* Language itſelf defers to the
Cake, and the Word has become a Symbol for the
prized Things in Life: One cannot have one's
Cake and eat it. To have *Cakes and Ale* is to enjoy
Mirth and good Living—a winning Perſon *takes
the Cake*, and when one has failed his *Cake's all
Dough.*

In the Memoirs of *William Wirt* there is this
elegant Deſcription of the Bride's Cake at the beautiful Miſs P———'s Wedding in *Williamſburg* in
April, 1806:

> . . . It was paſt eleven when the Sanctum
> Sanctorum of the Supper-room was thrown open
> —although I don't know but that the Deſignation
> of the Sanctum would be better applied to an-
> other Apartment in the Houſe—and it was near
> twelve when it came to my Turn to ſee the Show.
> And a very ſuperb one it was, I aſſure you. The
> Tree in the centre Cake was more ſimply elegant
> than anything of the Kind I remember to have
> ſeen.

feen. It was near four Feet high: the Cake itfelf,
the Pedeftal, had a rich—very rich—Fringe of
white Paper furrounding it: the Leaves, Bafkets,
Garlands, &c., &c., were all very naturally done
in white Paper, not touched with the Pencil, and
the Bafkets were rarely ornamented with filver
Spangles. At the Ends of the Tables were two
lofty Pyramids of Jellies, Syllabubs, Ice-creams,
&c.—the which Pyramids were connected with
the Tree in the centre Cake by pure white Paper
Chains, very prettily cut, hanging in light and
delicate Feftoons, and ornamented with Paper
Bow-knots. Between the centre Cake and each
Pyramid was another large Cake made for Ufe:
then there was a Profufion of Meats, Cheefe-
cakes, Fruits, &c., &c.

But there were two unnatural Things at Table;
—a fmall filver Globe on each Side of the Tree,
which might have paffed—if Charlotte, to en-
hance their Value, had not told us that they were
a Fruit—whofe Name I don't recollect—between
the Size of a Shaddock and an Orange, covered
with filver Leaf;—which was rather too outlan-
difh for my Palate. All the Grandees of the Place
were there.

All Sorts of Cakes

Beeffteak Cake *

CREAM two Cups of Sugar and one half Cup
of Butter. Add three well-beaten Eggs. Sift in
three and one fourth Cups of Flour, two Teafpoons
baking Powder, one fcant Teafpoon of Salt, alternately with one Cup of fweet Milk. Add one Teafpoon of Vanilla. Greafe and flour three Layer-cake
Tins

Tins and fill two of them. To the remaining Third of the Batter add three Tablefpoons Molaſſes, one Tablefpoon of Allſpice and one Teaſpoon each of Cloves and Cinnamon and one Cup of chopped Raiſins. Bake in a moderate Oven about thirty Minutes. Ice with brown Sugar Icing.

(Recipe from *Cole* Family, *Williamſburg.*
Adapted *Market Square Tavern* Kitchen, 1937.)

Brown Sugar Icing*

BRING to Boil one Cup brown Sugar, one Cup white Sugar, one Cup rich Milk, one Tableſpoon Corn Syrup, one Tableſpoon Butter, and Pinch of Salt. Continue cooking until Syrup forms ſoft Ball in Water. Cool and beat until creamy. Add one Teaſpoon Vanilla, one fourth Teaſpoon baking Powder—beat until ready to ſpread on Cake.

(*Market Square Tavern* Kitchen, 1937.)

Black Walnut Cake*

CREAM one Pound of Butter with one Pound of Sugar, then add one Egg Yolk. Blend thoroughly, then add another, and ſo on until all nine Yolks are thoroughly mixed and creamed. Sift one Pound of Flour in gradually, and finally add ſtiffly beaten Egg Whites. Dredge one Pound of black Walnut-meats in ſmall amount Flour and add to Batter. Bake in very ſlow Oven for two and one half to three Hours, in a deep Mould.

(Recipe from *Diſputanta, Virginia,* c-1729.)

To

To make a Bride Cake Mrs. Raffald's *Way*

TAKE four Pounds of fine Flour well dried, four Pounds of freſh Butter, two Pounds of loaf Sugar, pound and ſift fine a quarter of an Ounce of Mace, the ſame of Nutmegs, to every Pound of Flour put eight Eggs, waſh four Pounds of Currants, pick them well and dry them before the Fire, blanch a Pound of ſweet Almonds (and cut them lengthway very thin) a Pound of Citron, one Pound of candied Orange, the ſame of candied Lemon, half a Pint of Brandy; firſt work the Butter with your Hand to a Cream, then beat in your Sugar a quarter of an Hour, beat the Whites of your Eggs to a very ſtrong Froth, mix them with your Sugar and Butter, beat your Yolks half an Hour at leaſt, and mix them with your Cake, then put in your Flour, Mace, and Nutmeg, keep beating it well till your Oven is ready, put in your Brandy, and beat your Currants and Almonds lightly in, tie three Sheets of Paper round the Bottom of your Hoop to keep it from running out, rub it well with Butter, put in your Cake, and lay your Sweet-meats in three Lays, with Cake betwixt every Lay, after it is riſen and coloured, cover it with Paper before your Oven is ſtopped up; it will take three Hours baking.

(Court & Country Confectioner. *London*, 1770. From *Tucker* Houſe, *Williamſburg.*)

To make Almond Iceing for the Bride Cake

BEAT the Whites of three Eggs to a ſtrong Froth, beat a Pound of *Jordan* Almonds very fine with Roſe-water, mix your Almonds with the Eggs lightly

lightly together, a Pound of common Loaf-ſugar beat fine, and put in by Degrees, when your Cake is enough, take it out and lay your Icing on, and put it in to brown.

(Court & Country Confeɛ́tioner. *London*, 1770.
From *Tucker* Houſe, *Williamſburg.*)

Buttermilk Cake*

BLEND well together three Cups of Sugar and one Cup of Butter. Beat in four Eggs, adding one at a Time and beating the Mixture well each Time. Sift in three Cups of Flour with one Teaſpoon of baking Powder alternately with one Cup of Buttermilk. The Buttermilk ſhould have one Teaſpoon of Soda diſſolved in it. Add one Teaſpoon Vanilla and bake in three well-greaſed Tins in a moderate Oven about forty Minutes. An Orange Icing is good with this Cake.

(Mrs. *Cole's* Recipe, c-1837. Prov'd
Market Square Tavern Kitchen, 1937.)

Orange Icing*

TO three Cups of Confectioner's Sugar add one third of a Cup of Butter and mix well together. Thin with Orange-juice which has ſome finely grated freſh Orange-peel in it until it is right to ſpread. A Decoration of candied Orange-peel about the Edge is nice.   (*Market Square Tavern* Kitchen, 1937.)

Glazed Cocoanut Cake*

SIFT together ſeveral Times, one and three fourths Cups of Flour, one Cup of Sugar, one fourth Teaſpoon of Salt, two and one half Teaſpoons

ſpoons of Baking-powder. Melt one third of a Cup of Butter and mix it with two thirds of a Cup of warm (not hot) Milk. Add to Flour Mixture then beat in two Eggs. Beat well, add one Teaſpoonful of Vanilla. Pour into a large Layer-cake Tin. Bake for ten Minutes in a moderately quick Oven and reduce the Heat for the next fifteen Minutes. Turn your Cake out onto a Rack, with the Top up. Glaze: Six Tableſpoonfuls of melted Butter mixed with ſix Tableſpoonfuls of brown Sugar, three Tableſpoons of Cream, and one half Cupful of grated Cocoanut. Spread on hot Cake, put under Broiler to brown. Do not burn. Serve warm.

(*Richmond* Recipe, c-1840.
Prov'd *Blair* Kitchen, 1938.)

A Faſhion Cake

MIX a Handful of Flour with a Pint of good Cream, half a Pound of Beef-ſuet, melted and ſifted, a quarter of a Pound of Sugar-powder, half a Pound of Raiſins ſtoned and chopped, dried Flowers or Orange, a Glaſs of Brandy, a little Coriander and Salt; bake it as all other Cakes, about an Hour, and glaze or garniſh it.

(Court & Country Confectioner. *London*, 1770.
From *Tucker* Houſe, *Williamſburg.*)

Mrs. *Governor* Floyd's *Good but Cheap Cake*

THREE Cups of Sugar, three Eggs, three Cups of ſifted Flour, one Cup of ſour Cream, one Teaſpoonful of Soda. Add the Cream and Soda laſt.

laft. The Batter will be uncommonly ftiff. Half fill
Cups with it, and bake in a quick Oven. Flavor
with what you like.

(Mrs. *Mary Smith's* Virginia Cookery Book, 1885.)

Another Way*

BEAT together one Tablefpoon of Butter and
one Cup of Sugar. Add three Eggs and beat
well, add one Cup of four Cream and beat flightly.
Sift in one and three fourths Cups of Flour, one
half Teafpoon of Salt, one Teafpoon of Soda and
one half Teafpoon of Mace. Mix together but do
not over mix. Pour into a well-greafed Loaf-pan
and bake in a moderately flow Oven about three
quarters of an Hour. Half a Cup of *English* Walnuts may be added at the laft if defired.

(Mrs. *Floyd's* Recipe. Adapted
Market Square Tavern Kitchen, 1937.)

Dried Prune Cake*

FIRST ftew your Prunes, then work them
through a coarfe Colander to take out the
Seeds. Take two thirds of a Cup of the Prune Pulp
and cool. Cream one half Cup of Shortening with
one and one half Cups of Sugar. Beat in two Eggs
and the Prunes. Sift in one and one half Cups of
Flour with one half Teafpoon each of Cinnamon,
Nutmeg, Allfpice alternately with two thirds of a
Cup of four Milk. One third of a Cup of broken
English Walnut Meats may be added. Bake in one
well-greafed large Pan in a moderate Oven about
twenty-five

twenty-five Minutes. This may be ſerved warm with a Syllabub of flavored, whipped Cream, or with hard Sauce ſent up in a Boat. For Icing, uſe Wine Icing (page 180).

(Mrs. *Cole's* Recipe, c-1837.
Adapted *Blair* Kitchen, 1938.)

Mrs. Garrett's *Ten-minute Cake* ❊

TAKE two Teaſpoonfuls of Cream of Tartar and mix it, by ſifting, with one Pint of dry Flour, one even Teaſpoonful of Soda, diſſolved in a Teacupful of Milk; rub a Piece of Butter the Size of an Egg into the dry Flour; then beat up one Egg and a Teacupful of Sugar; mix all well together and bake without Delay. Have your Oven ready heated before you begin mixing, and you can make and bake the Cake in ten Minutes.

(From Mrs. *Smith's* Virginia Cookery Book, 1885.
Prov'd *Market Square Tavern* Kitchen, 1937.)

Hurry-up Gingerbread ❊

BEAT together well one half Cup of Sugar, one half Cup of Butter and one Egg. Add one Cup of Molaſſes, then ſift together two Cups of Flour, one Tableſpoon of Ginger, one Teaſpoon of Cinnamon, one half Teaſpoon of Salt. Add theſe alternately with one Cup of ſour Milk to which you have added one Teaſpoon of Soda. Bake in a ſhallow greaſed Pan in moderate Oven about thirty Minutes.

(Old Recipe, *Sparta, Virginia.*)

Another

Another Way *

Inſtead of the ſour Milk you may diſſolve your
Soda in boiling Water and add it at the laſt.

(*Williamſburg* Family Recipes
in *Barlow* and *Cole* Family Cook Books.)

Robert E. Lee *Cake* *

BEAT nine Egg Yolks very light then ſlowly beat
in one Pound of Sugar. Fold in the well-beaten
Egg Whites. Sift in one half Pound of Flour with
one half Teaſpoon of Salt and mix lightly together,
ſtir in one Tableſpoonful of Lemon-juice. Bake in
a ſlow Oven in three ungreaſed Layer-pans.

FILLING: Squeeze the Juice of two Lemons and
three Oranges over two Cups of Sugar and flavour
with a little of the grated Rinds. Add a Cup of
grated Cocoanut and put between Layers and on
Top. Sprinkle with dry Cocoanut.

(*Lane* Family Recipe, c-1870, *Williamſburg.*
Prov'd *Market Square Tavern* Kitchen, 1937.)

Lemon Jelly *Cake* *

MIX well one Cup of Sugar and one half Cup
of Butter. Add five well beaten Egg Yolks
and beat until light. Sift into this two Cups of
Flour with one Teaſpoon of Soda and one and a
half Teaſpoons of Cream of Tartar, alternately
with one Cup of ſweet Milk. Flavor as you chooſe.
Add well-beaten Whites of the Eggs and bake in
two or three Layers in a moderate Oven.

JELLY: Take the Juice and Rind of two Lemons
and one Cup of Sugar. Cook until Sugar is diſſolved
and

and add three well-beaten Eggs. Cook this over
boiling Water until thick. Spread between Layers
and ſprinkle Top of Cake and Sides with powdered
Sugar.

(Old Recipe, *Bridgetown, Virginia.*)

A Liſbon *Cake*

IN order to make this Cake, get four or five
Pounds of fine Flour, and make a good Puff-
Paſte; that being done, roll it as thin as a half crown
Piece. Then put over it a Diſh of the Bigneſs of the
Cake you deſign to make, cut your Paſte round it,
and put this Piece of Paſte to cut round upon a
Sheet of Paper. Cut out in the ſame Manner ſeven
or eight Abbeſſes more, cutting one of them into
ſeveral Figures, to be placed on the Top of your
Cake. This being done, let them be baked ſeparately, then glaze the Abbeſs cut out into Figures
and make your Cake as follows: Put over one of
theſe Abbeſſes a Laying of Apricot Marmalade;
then over this another Abbeſs with a Laying of Jelly
of Currants; again, another Abbeſs over the Laſt
with Jelly of Gooſeberries. Continue after the ſame
Manner to place the Reſt of your Abbeſſes, putting
between them your ſeveral Layings of preſerved
Raſpberries, Apple Jelly, etc., placing on the Top
your figured and glazed Abbeſs, ſo that the Reſt
may not be ſeen: To which Purpoſe, your Cake
muſt be glazed with a white Glaze, a green Glaze,
and a Cochineal-colour Glaze, that it may appear
no more than one Abbeſs. Make the Glaze thus, viz.
beat together in an earthen Veſſel with a wooden
Spoon about a Pound of powder Sugar, the White

of

of two Eggs, and the Juice of half a Lemon. If this Mixture proves to be too thin, put some more Sugar in it; then divide this Composition into three Parts: in the First, put Nothing, but leave it white as it is; in the Second, put a Cochineal, to make it red; and the Third green, with some Juice of Spinage. Glaze your Cake from Top to Bottom, first, with a Streak of your white Composition, then with a Streak of the Red, and afterwards with a Streak of the Green; following the same Order till your Cake is entirely glazed. Then to dry your Icing, put your Cake for a little While, in a warm Oven, or before the Fire, turning it round now and then. Your Cake being as it should be, you lay it in its Dish, and serve it up. It may be made as small or as large as you please.

(Court & Country Confectioner. *London*, 1770.
From *Tucker* House, *Williamsburg*.)

Molasses Cake *

TAKE one Cup of Butter or Lard and mix well with one Cup of Sugar, then beat in three Eggs. Add two Cups of Molasses, one Cup of sour Milk alternately with three and one half Cups of Flour sifted with two Teaspoons of Soda, one half Teaspoon of Salt and one Tablespoon of Ginger. Bake in a slow Oven in a greased Tin about forty Minutes.

(Old Recipe, *Richmond, Virginia*
Prov'd *Market Square Tavern* Kitchen, 1937.)

Orange

Orange Cake＊

TAKE one Cup of Sugar, half a Cup of Butter, two Cups of Flour, half a Cup of ſweet Milk, a Teaſpoonful of baking Powder ſifted with the Flour. Rub the Butter and Sugar to a Cream, add two Eggs, the Whites and Yolks beaten ſeparately, then the Milk, then the Flour. Bake in Jelly-pans in moderate Oven about thirty Minutes. Squeeze the Juice from an Orange, add to it the grated Rind, make it ſtiff with powdered Sugar, and ſtir in the White of one Egg well-beaten. Spread this on the Cakes and lay one on another, like Jelly Cake.

(Mrs. *Cole's* Recipe, c-1837. Prov'd
Market Square Tavern Kitchen, 1937.)

Williamſburg *Orange Wine Cake*＊

CHOP very fine or grind, one medium-ſized, tender Orange-rind and one Cup of Raiſins. Add one half Cup of coarſely-chopped *Engliſh* Walnuts.

Cream one half Cup of Butter with one Cup of Sugar, add two beaten Eggs, one Teaſpoon of Vanilla and chopped Mixture. Sift two Cups of Flour with one Teaſpoon of Soda, one half Teaſpoon of Salt and add alternately with one Cup of ſour Milk. Pour into well-greaſed ſquare Cake-pan and bake in moderate Oven about thirty or forty Minutes. While hot this Cake may be glazed by ſpreading over it one Cup of Sugar mixed with one third of a Cup of Orange-juice and returning it to the Oven.

Oven. Others prefer this Cake ſerved warm with a Syllabub of frothed Cream and ſtill others ſerve it with

*Wine Icing**

MIX well one third of a Cup of Butter with two Cups of Confectioner's Sugar. Add Sherry to this, ſlowly beating well, add ſome finely-grated Orange-peel, and when thick enough, ſpread on the Cake. Beating the White of an Egg into this Icing much improves its Texture.

(Old *Williamſburg* Recipe. Prov'd
Market Square Tavern Kitchen, 1937.)

*Little Plumb Cakes**

CREAM one Cup of Shortening with one and one half Cups of brown Sugar, add two well-beaten Eggs. Sift together three Cups of Flour, one Teaſpoon of Soda, one Teaſpoon of Cinnamon, one half Teaſpoon each of Allſpice and Ginger. Mix well, add one Cup of Raiſins, one half Cup of Nut Meats broken, and (if deſired) two Table-ſpoonfuls of chopped, candied Orange-peel or Lemon-peel. Drop by Spoonfuls on greaſed baking Tin and bake about twenty Minutes in a moderate Oven. This makes between four and five Dozen Cakes.

(Mrs. *Randolph's* Recipe, 1831.
Adapted *Blair* Kitchen, 1938.)

Pork

Pork Cake*

CUT fine one Pound of salt Pork and pour over it two Cups of boiling Water. Add two Cups of Molasses, one Cup of brown Sugar. Sift together seven Cups of Flour, two Tablespoons each of Cinnamon and Allspice, two Teaspoons each of Cloves, Nutmeg and Soda, and beat well into the Batter. Add one Pound of well-cleaned Currants and one and one half Pounds of Raisins (which have soaked overnight in one Cup of Brandy if you choose). Bake in three large Loaf-pans in a very slow Oven about one Hour.

(Old Recipe, *Highland Springs, Virginia.*)

Pound Cake*

BEAT one Cup of Butter to a Cream, slowly beat in one and one third Cups of Sugar. Add one Teaspoonful of Mace and beat in five whole Eggs adding them one at a Time. Sift in two Cups of Flour, turn at once into a greased and floured Pan or Mould and bake slowly for one Hour.

(Recipe from *Wicomico* Church, c-1754.)

Mount Vernon *Pound Cake*

WASH all the Salt from a Pound of Butter, then put it dry between the Folds of a clean Cloth and set away in a cold Place. Sift one Pound of Pastry Flour and separate the Yolks and Whites of twelve Eggs. Cream the Butter and Flour together very thoroughly and beat the Yolks of the Eggs to a thick, almost white, Froth with one
Pound

Pound of granulated Sugar. Add one Teaſpoonful of Vanilla and a Grating of Mace. Gradually add the creamed Butter and Flour to the Sugar and Egg Mixture and whip well, then fold in the ſtiffly beaten Whites of the Eggs, pour into a well-greaſed and floured Tube-pan, ſcatter a little grated Lemon or Orange-rind over the Top and bake in a moderate Oven about one and a quarter Hours.

(Old Recipe, *Chaſe City, Virginia.*)

Williamſburg *Pound Cake*＊

CREAM one Pound of Butter and one Pound of Sugar together, add the well beaten Yolks of twelve Eggs, and the ſtiffly beaten Whites and one Pound of Flour (ſifted twice) alternately to the Sugar and Butter Mixture. Beat until *very light*. Pour into a well-greaſed and floured Mold and bake in a moderate Oven. The Secret of this Cake lies in careful Baking.

(Prov'd *Market Square Tavern* Kitchen, 1937.)

Savoy *or Spunge Cake*＊

TAKE twelve freſh Eggs, put them in the Scale, and balance them with Sugar: take out half, and balance the other half with Flour: ſeparate the Whites from the Yelks, whip them up very light, then mix them, and ſift in, firſt Sugar, then Flour, till both are exhauſted; add ſome grated Lemon-peel; bake them in Paper Caſes, or little Tin Moulds. This alſo makes an excellent Pudding, with Butter, Sugar and Wine, for Sauce.

(Mrs. *Mary Randolph's* Virginia Houſewife, 1831. Prov'd 1937.)

Williamſburg

Williamſburg *Sponge Cake**

BEAT three Egg Yolks until very light, ſlowly beat in one third of a Cup of Sugar. Add one Teaſpoonful of Lemon-juice. Stir in lightly three well-beaten Egg Whites. Sift in one third of a Cup of Flour and one fourth Teaſpoon of Salt. Bake in ſmall buttered Muffin Tins, or in a ſmall Cake-pan in a very moderate Oven about twenty-five Minutes.

(Mrs. *Randolph's Recipe.*
Adapted *Blair* Kitchen, 1938.)

*Silver Cake**

CREAM together three Cups of ſifted Sugar and one Pound of waſhed Butter. Add alternately one Pound of Flour ſifted three Times and the Whites of fourteen Eggs beaten to a ſtiff Froth. Flavor with one Teaſpoon of Almond Extract and bake in a ſlow Oven.

(*Coleman* Family Recipe, c-1840.
From *Cheſter, Virginia.*)

*Spice Cake**

TAKE one Cup of brown Sugar and beat it well with one fourth Pound of Butter. Add well beaten Yolks of two Eggs. Sift together one and one fourth Cups of Flour, one half Teaſpoon each of Cloves, Cinnamon, Nutmeg and baking Powder, add this to your Mixture alternately with one half Cup of ſour Milk in which you have mixed one half Teaſpoon of Soda. Pour your Batter in a ſmall
well-greaſed

well-greafed fquare Pan, and fpread it with a
Meringue made by beating the two Egg Whites
with one Cup of fifted brown Sugar. Sprinkle with
one third Cup of chopped *Englifh* Walnuts. Bake
in moderate Oven about thirty-five Minutes. This
may be ferved warm.

(Old *Richmond* Recipe, adapted 1937.)

Sponge Cake*

WEIGH ten Eggs, take the Weight of the Eggs
in Sugar, one half the Weight of the Eggs in
Flour, Juice and Rind of one frefh Lemon and two
Teafpoons of Vanilla. Beat Yolks well, add Sugar
gradually, Lemon-juice and Rind, then Flour, one
half Teafpoon of Salt and Flavoring. Fold in
beaten Whites and bake in a flow Oven for about
twenty-five Minutes.

(Old *Richmond* Recipe. Prov'd
Market Square Tavern Kitchen, 1937.)

Tipfy Cake*

TAKE two Layers of Sponge Cake and foak
them well in Sherry and chill well. Take a
Quart of cold boiled Cuftard and pour Part of it
over one Layer. Add the fecond Layer and ftuff
the Top with fplit blanched Almonds and pour the
remaining Cuftard over it. On the Top of the Cake
put frothed Cream and a few chopped toafted
Almonds.

(Traditional *Williamfburg* and *Virginia* Recipe.
Prov'd *Market Square Tavern* Kitchen, 1937.)

Tipfy

Tipsy Squire*

INSTEAD of making a large Cake you may cut your Sponge in square Portions and send it up in separate Sauce Dishes for each Serving.

(Traditional *Williamsburg* and *Virginia* Recipe.
Prov'd *Travis* House, 1938.)

George Washington *Cake—1780**

RUB two Cups of Butter and two Cups of Sugar to a light Cream. Beat four Egg Yolks very light with one Cup of Sugar and stir together. Sift together four Cups of Flour, one Teaspoon of Mace two Tablespoons of baking Powder, and add alternately with one Cup of Milk. Stir in one Cup of Raisins, one half Cup of Currants and one fourth Cup of finely-cut Citron. Fold in the well-beaten Whites. Bake in square shallow Pan in moderate Oven about one Hour; when cold ice with white Icing.

(Old *Williamsburg* Family Cook Book.)

✿✿✿✿✿!✿✿✿✿✿!✿✿✿✿✿!✿✿✿✿✿

Of DESSERTS

DESSERTS were made to please the Eye as well as the Palate, and sometimes, one might suspect, the Eye had the Preference. Elaborate Flummeries, molded Blanc-manges, exhuberantly decorated Puddings were important Dishes upon every well-set and compleat Table.

If the Pudding smacked strongly of the "Spinage"

age" that had been used to make it a lively Green,
or if the Flavour of the Beets was as predominant
as the Colour, it was politely overlooked by the
pleased Guest, who saw such culinary Miracles as
Solomon's Temple in Flummery rise from the Center of the Table.

It was a painstaking Age. From the yellowed
Pages of the finely-written little Cook Book of
Frances Bland Tucker Coalter, a *Williamsburg*
Bride, one can visualize the young Housekeeper
supervising the Preparation of a *Hen's Nest* for
some special Occasion. First a Blanc-mange was
prepared, laboriously, with Isinglass to congeal it;
then several Dozen Eggs were blown and filled
with it. A Nest was made by partly filling a Bowl
with Jelly, on the Top of which a Straw made of
shredded Orange and Lemon-peel was placed—
then the Eggs were laid in the Straw and Jelly was
poured over to hold them in Place. This realistic
Sculpture in Jelly was then turned out in a *China*
Dish and garnished with green Sweetmeats.

In this Matter of dressing Victuals to please the
Eye, *Beverley* said of the *Virginians* in 1705:

> . . . They have their Graziers, Seedsmen, Gar-
> diners, Brewers, Bakers, Butchers, and Cooks
> within themselves: they have a great Plenty and
> Variety of Provisions for their Table; and as for
> Spicery, and other things that the Country don't
> produce, they have constant Supplies of 'em from
> *England*. The Gentry pretend to have their
> Victuals drest, and serv'd up as Nicely, as at the
> best Tables in *London*.

That Nothing was lacking in Spicery or other
Table Delicacies to prevent the *Virginia* Cook from
attempting

attempting the moſt elegant and genteel Exploits in Cookery is evidenced by a ſmall Order for Sundries by Lord *Dunmore*, from the Governor's Palace in *Williamſburg*, to *John Norton & Sons*, Merchants of *London*, on the twelfth of June in 1773: Invoice of Sundries for the Earl of *Dunmore*.

    15 Dozen bottles of Strong Beer
    15 Do. of Ale.
     3 Hogſheads of Porter
    12 large *Cheſhire* Cheeſe
     2 Dozen *Glouceſter* do.
   100 lb. Currants
    50 lb. Jar Raiſins
     4 lb. Mace
     2 lb. Nutmegs
     1 lb. Cloves
     1 lb. Cinnamon
    24 lb. Black Pepper
     6 lb. *Jamaica* do.
     2 Boxes Hand Soap
     2 Caſks of Barley
    24 Bottles Muſtard
    20 lb. Iſinglaſs
   100 lb. Rice
   100 lb. Split Peas
    50 lb. Maccaroni
    20 Dozen Packs of Cards
     1 Barrel of good Vinegar
     1 Dozen Wine and Beer Cocks
    30 lb. Almonds
    12 Bottles of Olives
     6 Do. of Capers
     4 Dozen pint Bottles of beſt Oil
    12 Bottles ſmall pickled Onions
    12 Do. of ſmall pickled Cucumbers
    12 Dozen Wine Glaſſes
     6 Do. Tumblers
     6 Do. Quart Bottle Decanters with Handles
     3 Do. 2 Quart Decanters

To

Defferts

To make an Almond Pudding

TAKE a Pound of the beft *Jordan* Almonds
blanched in cold Water, and beat very fine
with a little Rofe-water; then take a Quart of
Cream, boiled with whole Spice, and taken out
again, and when 'tis cold, mix it with the Almonds,
and put to it three Spoonfuls of grated Bread, one
Spoonful of Flour, nine Eggs, but three Whites,
half a Pound of Sugar, a Nutmeg grated; mix and
beat thefe well together, put fome Puff-pafte at
the Bottom of a Difh; put your Stuff in, and here
and there ftick a Piece of Marrow in it. It muft
bake an Hour, and when 'tis drawn, fcrape Sugar
on it, and ferve it up.

(Mrs. *E. Smith's* Compleat Houfewife,
Williamfburg, 1742.)

Apple Dumplings＊

HAVING pared your Apples, take out the Core
with an Apple-fcraper, and fill the Hole with
Quince or Orange Marmalade, or Sugar, as may
fuit you beft. Then take a Piece of cold Pafte, and
make a Hole in it, as if you were going to make a
Pie. Lay in your Apple, and put another Piece of
Pafte in the fame Form, and clofe it up round the
Side of your Apple, which is much better than
gathering

gathering it in a Lump at one End. Tie it in a Cloth and boil it three quarters of an Hour. Serve them up, with melted Butter poured over them.

(*John Farley's* London Art of Cookery, 1787. From *Brookbury, Chesterfield* County, *Virginia*.)

To make Apple Fritters

TAKE the Yolks of eight Eggs, the Whites of four, beat them well together, and strain 'em into a Pan; then take a Quart of Cream, warm it as hot as you can endure your Finger in it; then put to it a quarter of a Pint of Sack, three quarters of a Pint of Ale, and make a Posset of it; when your Posset is cool, put to it your Eggs, beating them well together; then put in Nutmeg, Ginger, Salt and Flour to your Liking: Your Batter should be pretty thick; then put in Pippins sliced or scraped; fry them in good Store of hot Lard with a quick Fire.

(Mrs. *E. Smith's* Compleat Housewife. *Williamsburg*, 1742.)

Williamsburg *Apple Fritters* *

PEEL and core six Apples and cut them in thin Slices. Soak them for two Hours in Brandy (or Lemon Juice). Dip them in Batter and fry them in a Kettle of boiling Fat, or you may sauté them in Butter.

BATTER: Beat two Egg Yolks and add one fourth Cup of rich Milk, one fourth Cup of cold Water, one Tablespoonful of Brandy (or Lemon Juice) and one Tablespoonful of melted Butter.
Sift

Sift in one Cup of Flour, two Tablespoonfuls of Sugar, and one fourth Teaspoonful of Salt. Mix quickly, then stir in lightly two well-beaten Egg Whites.

(Mrs. *Mary Randolph's* Recipe, 1831.
Adapted *Blair* Kitchen, 1938.)

A Pupton of Apples *

PARE a Dozen and half of fine, sound, well-tasted Apples, and quartering them take out the Cores.

Put them into a Sauce-pan and pour over them three Spoonfuls of Water; dust on five Ounces of the finest Sugar powdered, and set them over a gentle Fire in a Stove; stir them about from Time to Time, and when they are tender put in half a Teaspoonful of powdered Cinnamon.

Let them keep on some Time longer, and they will grow thick and like Marmalade; then pour the Whole into a *China* Bowl, and let it cool.

Grate some Bread very fine, and beat up six Yolks of Eggs; mix with this a quarter of a Pound of fresh Butter, and some of the Crumb of Bread: When this and the Apples are both cold mix them together, and put the Whole into a Silver Dish, or Baking-pan; set it in a slow Oven, and half an Hour will very well do it; turn it upside down into the Dish, and serve it up hot: Send up with it some Slices of fresh Butter in a Saucer, with fresh Parsley.

(Mrs. *Martha Bradley's* British Housewife.)

Apple

Apple Pudding

HALF a Pound of Apples boiled, and ſqueezed through a hair Sieve half a Pound of Butter—beaten to a Cream and mixed with the Apples before they are cold, ſix Eggs well beaten, half a Pound of fine Sugar—the Rind of two Lemons—or Oranges—boiled well ſhifting the Water ſeveral Times—then beat all togather—bake them on a Cruſt. Half an Hour will bake it.

(Manuſcript Cook Book, prior 1839.
Morton Family of *Charlotte* County, *Virginia*.)

To make an Apple Tanſy*

TAKE three Pippins, ſlice them round in thin Slices, and fry them with Butter; then beat four Eggs, with ſix Spoonfuls of Cream, a little Roſe-water, Nutmeg, and Sugar, and ſtir them together, and pour it over the Apples: Let it fry a little, and turn it with a Pye-plate. Garniſh with Lemon and Sugar ſtrew'd over it.

(Mrs. *E. Smith's* Compleat Houſewife,
Williamſburg, 1742.)

Blanc Mange

TO an Ounce of Iſinglaſs pour a Pint of boiling Water to ſtand Overnight. Next Morning add three Pints of ſweet Milk, a Pound and a quarter of loaf Sugar, and a Tableſpoonful or two of Roſe-water. Put it in Braſs Kettle, boil fifteen or twenty Minutes very faſt; wet your Moulds and pour it in.

(Old *Williamſburg* Recipe, c-1837.
Mrs. *Elizabeth Labbé Cole's* Collection)

Williamſburg

Williamſburg *Blanc Mange**

SCALD two and one quarter Cups of Milk. Mix well three fourths of a Cup of cold Milk, one fourth of a Cup of Cornſtarch, two Tableſpoonfuls of Sugar and a Pinch of Salt. Add to the hot Milk and cook very ſlowly until thick and the Cornſtarch is well cooked. Then add one Egg which has been beaten well with two Tableſpoonfuls of Sugar, and finiſh cooking for a Minute or two. Flavor with Vanilla. Pour into a Mould and chill well. Unmould and ſerve with a Sauce of cruſhed freſh Fruit or a well-flavored Cuſtard Sauce.

(Mrs. *Cole's* Recipe, c-1837.
Adapted *Blair* Kitchen, 1938.)

*A baked Bread Pudding**

TAKE a Penny-loaf, cut it in thin Slices, then boil a Quart of Cream or new Milk, and put in your Bread, and break it very fine; put five Eggs to it, a Nutmeg grated, a quarter of a Pound of Sugar, and half a Pound of Butter; ſtir all theſe well together; butter a Diſh, and bake it an Hour.

(Mrs. *E. Smith's* Compleat Houſewife,
Williamſburg, 1742.)

Williamſburg *Carrot Pudding**

TAKE one Cup of grated raw Carrots, one half Pound of fine dry Bread Crumbs, one Teaſpoonful of Nutmeg, two of Cinnamon and one fourth of Salt. Over this pour one fourth Cup of Sherry.
Beat

Beat four Eggs very light with one half Cup of Sugar, add four large Tablespoonfuls of melted Butter. Bake in moderate Oven in buttered Baking-dish about forty-five Minutes. Serve hot with Pudding Sauce.

(Mrs. *E. Smith's* Recipe, 1742.
Adapted *Market Square Tavern* Kitchen, 1937.)

Clouted Cream

TAKE a Gill of new Milk, and set it on the Fire and take six Spoonfuls of Rose-water, four or five Pieces of large Mace, put the Mace on a Thread; when it boils, put to them the Yolks of two Eggs very well beaten; stir these very well together; then take a Quart of very good Cream, put it to the Rest, and stir it together, but let it not boil after the Cream is in. Pour it out of the Pan you boil it in, and let it stand all Night; the next Day take the Top off it, and serve it up.

(Mrs. *Hannah Glasse's* Art of Cookery,
London, 1774.)

Cocoanut Pudding

TAKE three quarters of a Pound of Sugar, the same of Butter—creamed together, the Whites of twelve Eggs beat them to a Froth—add them to the Butter and Sugar—add three quarters of a Pound of grated Cocoanut—half a Glass of Brandy bake on a thin Crust.

(Manuscript Cook Book, prior 1839.
Morton Family of *Charlotte* County, *Virginia.*)

To

To make baked Cuſtards*

ONE Pint of Cream boiled with Mace and Cinnamon; when cold take four Eggs, two Whites
left out, a little Roſe and Orange-flower Water and
Sack, Nutmeg and Sugar to your Palate; mix them
well together, and bake them in *China* Cups.

(Mrs. *Hannah Glaſſe's* Art of Cookery, *London*, 1774.)

Ice Cuſtard

TO one Quart of new Milk put three Eggs with
Sugar a little cold Water to the Eggs and Sugar
after it is beaten before put to the boiling Milk—
to prevent it from turning take the Kettle off the
Fire when the Eggs are ſtirred in—freeze it as you
do Ice Cream.

(Manuſcript Cook Book, prior 1839.
Morton Family of *Charlotte* County, *Virginia*.)

Cuſtard Ice Cream*

SCALD a Cup and a half of Milk, ſtir in three
fourths of a Cup of Sugar and a Pinch of Salt.
Pour ſlowly over two or three beaten Egg Yolks.
Cook very ſlowly until thick. Cool, add one Tableſpoonful of Vanilla and one Pint of rich Cream
which has been whipped to a Froth and freeze.

(Mrs. *Coalter's* Recipe, c-1801.
Adapted *Blair* Kitchen, 1938.)

Cream Puffs*

PUT one half Cup of Butter and one Cup of
boiling Water in a Sauce-pan when it comes to
a Boil ſift in one Cup of Flour, ſtirring well. Remove

move from Fire and beat in four Eggs one at a Time. Drop on buttered Tins by ſmall Spoonfuls and bake in a quick Oven about half an Hour. Theſe may be filled with thick boiled Cuſtard, or flavored whipped Cream.

(Mrs. *Cole's* Recipe, c-1837, *Williamſburg.*
Adapted *Market Square Tavern* Kitchen, 1937.)

Delicate Pudding *

BEAT one half Cup of Sugar with two Egg Yolks. Pour over this one and one half Cups of ſcalded Milk. Add one and one half Tableſpoons of Gelatine diſſolved in one half Cup of cold Water. When cool, add the ſtiffly beaten Whites of the Eggs, one half Cup of Cream which has been whipped, and one Teaſpoonful of Vanilla. Pour into Moulds and chill.

(Mrs. *Cole's* Recipe, c-1837, *Williamſburg.*
Adapted *Market Square Tavern* Kitchen, 1937.)

Dutch *Puff Pudding* *

MIX together well one half Cup of Flour, one half Cup of Sugar, one half Teaſpoon of Salt and one Quart of Milk. Add four well beaten Eggs. Pour into a buttered Pudding Diſh and bake in a moderate Oven.

Sauce *

POUR two Cups of boiling Water over one Cup of brown Sugar, half an Orange Rind dried and grated, and one Teaſpoon of Flour. Boil well for five Minutes and serve hot over the Pudding.

(Recipe, c-1700, from *Wicomico Church, Virginia.*
Prov'd *Market Square Tavern* Kitchen, 1937.)

Eve's

Eve's *Pudding*[*]

CHOP and mix one half Pound of Beef-fuet, one half Pound of Apples, with one half Pound of fine Bread Crumbs, one Cup of Flour, one grated Nutmeg, one Teaspoon of Salt. Beat five Egg Yolks well, flowly beating in one Cup of Sugar. Add one Cup of ftoned Raifins and one Ounce each of finely cut Citron and Lemon-peel which have foaked Overnight in a Glafs of Brandy. Mix all, adding laft the Whites of the Eggs beaten to a ftiff Froth. Butter a Mould well and fteam for three Hours, then bake about fifteen Minutes in a moderate Oven.

(Traditional *Virginia* Recipe. Prov'd *Market Square Tavern* Kitchen, 1937.)

The floating Ifland, a pretty Difh for the Middle of a Table at a fecond Courfe, or for Supper

YOU may take a Soop-difh, according to the Size and Quantity you would make, but a pretty deep Glafs is beft, and fet it on a *China* Difh; firft take a Quart of the thickeft Cream you can get, make it pretty fweet with fine Sugar, pour in a Gill of Sack, grate the yellow Rind of a Lemon in, and mill the Cream till it is all of a thick Froth, then as carefully as you can, pour the Thin from the Froth, into a Difh; take a *French* Roll, or as many as you want, cut it as thin as you can, lay a Layer of that as light as poffible on the Cream, then a Layer of Currant Jelly, then a very thin Layer of Roll, and then Hartfhorn Jelly, then *French* Roll, and over that whip your Froth which you faved off the Cream very well milled up, and lay

lay at Top as high as you can heap it; and as for the Rim of the Diſh, ſet it round with Fruit or Sweetmeats, according to your Fancy. This looks very pretty in the Middle of a Table with Candles round it, and you may make it of as many different Colours as you fancy, and according to what Jellies and Giams or Sweetmeats you have; or at the Bottom of your Diſh you may put the thickeſt Cream you can get; but that is as you fancy.

(Mrs. *Hannah Glaſſe's* Art of Cookery, *London*, 1774.)

Williamſburg *Floating Iſland* *

TAKE two Cupfuls of cuſtard Sauce (page 211) and place it in your Baking-diſh. Beat three egg Whites very ſtiff and ſlowly beat in three Tableſpoonfuls of Sugar and one fourth Teaſpoonful of Salt, flavor with a few Drops of Almond Extract. Drop by Spoonfuls on the Cuſtard, leaving Spaces between each Iſland. Bake in a hot Oven for about two Minutes until the Iſlands be ſlightly browned.

(Mrs. *Cole's* Recipe, c-1837.
Adapted *Blair* Kitchen, 1938.)

To make a Grateful Pudding

TAKE a Pound of fine Flour, and a Pound of white Bread grated, take eight Eggs but half the Whites, beat them up, and mix with them a Pint of new Milk, then ſtir in the Bread and Flour, a Pound of Raiſins ſtoned, a Pound of Currants, half a Pound of Sugar, a little beaten Ginger; mix all well together, and either bake or boil it. It will
take

take three quarters of an Hour's Baking. Put Cream in, inſtead of Milk, if you have it. It will be an Addition to the Pudding.

(Mrs. *Hannah Glaſſe's* Art of Cookery, *London*, 1774.)

Caramel Ice Cream *

MELT one and three fourths Pounds dark brown Sugar in an iron Skillet. Add one Pint of Water, diſſolve and ſtrain. Make Cuſtard of two Quarts of Milk and ten Eggs. Cool both Mixtures, mix, add one Quart of Cream and freeze.

(Old Recipe, *Diſputanta, Virginia.*)

Williamſburg *Lemon Cream* *

GRATE two Teaſpoonfuls of Lemon-rind onto two Cups of Sugar. Boil for five Minutes with three fourths of a Cup of Lemon-juice and one fourth Teaſpoon of Salt. Freeze until muſhy. Then add two ſtiffly beaten Egg Whites and freeze until firm.

(Mrs. *Coalter's* Recipe, c-1801
Adapted *Travis* Houſe, 1938.)

Solomon's *Temple in Flummery*

DIVIDE a Quart of ſtiff Flummery into three Parts, and make one Part a pretty thick Colour with a little Cochineal bruiſed fine, and ſteeped in *French* Brandy. Scrape an Ounce of Chocolate very fine, diſſolve it in a little ſtrong Coffee, and mix it with another Part of your Flummery, to make it a light Stone Colour. The laſt Part muſt be White. Then wet your Temple Mould, and
ſet

ſet it in a Pot to ſtand even. Fill the Top of the
Temple with red Flummery for the Steps, and the
four Points with white. Then fill it up with Choco-
late Flummery, and let it ſtand till the next Day.
Then looſen it round with a Pin, and ſhake it looſe
very gently; but do not dip your Mould in warm
Water, as that will take off the Gloſs, and ſpoil the
Colour. When you turn it out, ſtick a ſmall Sprig of
Flowers, down from the Top of every Point, which
will not only ſtrengthen it, but alſo give it a pretty
Appearance. Lay round it Rock-candy Sweetmeats.

(*John Farley's* London Art of Cookery, 1787.
From *Brookbury, Cheſterfield* County, *Virginia.*)

Indian *Meal Pudding—Mrs.* Hopkins

TAKE eight Ounces Muſh, good Weight, ſix
Ounces Butter, ſix Ounces Sugar, the Yolks of ſix
Eggs and White of one. Mix the Butter in the Muſh
while ſtill warm, beat the Eggs light, mix the Sugar
with them, and add them to the Muſh when cool.
Put Mace, Nutmeg, and Wine to your Taſte.

(Manuſcript Cook Book, c-1801,
of Mrs. *Frances Bland Tucker Coalter.*
Owned by Dr. *St. George Tucker Grinnan, Richmond.*)

Frozen Plumb Pudding✳

MAKE a Cuſtard of one Quart of Milk, two
Cups of Sugar and four Eggs. Cool. Add two
Cups of chopped Raiſins, one Cup of chopped
Nuts, one half Cup of brandied Cherries, one Cup
of

of chopped preſerved Pineapple, and two Tableſpoons of Orange Marmalade. Beat one Quart of
Cream, mix with Cuſtard and Fruits and freeze.

(Old Richmond Recipe.
Prov'd Market Square Tavern Kitchen, 1937.)

Another Way*

MAKE a Cuſtard of three Cups of Milk, Yolks
of ten Eggs, two Cups of Sugar, little Salt.
When cool add one and one half Pints Cream or
more, three fourths Cup candied Fruit, one third
Cup Raiſins, one half Cup blanched Almonds, one
half Cup pounded Macaroons, one half Cup Sherry.
Freeze. This makes about three Quarts.

(Old Richmond Recipe. Prov'd 1937.)

King's Arms *Green-gage Plum Ice Cream*

SKIN, ſeed and maſh one Pint of preſerved Green-
gage Plums, add the Juice of two Lemons, two
Cups of Sugar, one and one half Quarts of Milk
and one Quart of Cream with a Pinch of Salt.
Freeze.

Hunting Pudding

MIX eight Eggs beat up fine with a Pint of good
Cream, and a Pound of Flour. Beat them
well together, and put to them a Pound of Beef-
ſuet finely chopped, a Pound of Currants well
cleaned, half a Pound of Jar Raiſins ſtoned and
chopped ſmall, two Ounces of candied Orange cut
ſmall, the ſame of candied Citron, a quarter of a
Pound

Pound of powdered Sugar, and a large Nutmeg grated. Mix all together with half a Gill of Brandy, put it into a Cloth, tie it up cloſe, and boil it four Hours.

(*John Farley's* London Art of Cookery, 1787.
From *Brookbury, Cheſterfield* County, *Virginia.*)

Lemon Ice Cream

THE Juice of ſix Lemons to two Quarts Water, (or two Cups bottled Juice). Steep the Peels for ſometime in the Water (or ſome Lemon Conſerve if you have not freſh Peels) and ſtrain it. Mix into it two Pounds white Sugar and the Whites of twenty-four Eggs beat till they will adhere to the Bowl. The Freezer muſt be kept in Motion till yᵣ Cream is of the Conſiſtence of Snow.

(Manuſcript Cook Book, c-1801,
of Mrs. *Frances Bland Tucker Coalter.*
Owned by *St. George Tucker Grinnan, Richmond.*)

Lemon Pudding

HALF a Pound of beaten Sugar—the ſame Quantity of Flour dried and ſifted, half Pound of Butter, the Yolks of ten Eggs well beaten, add the Rine of one Lemon grated—Mix the Juice of the Lemon with half a Glaſs of Brandy beat them together bake them on a Cruſt or as Fancy may direct.

(Manuſcript Cook Book, prior 1839.
Morton Family of *Charlotte* County, *Virginia.*)

Potatoe

Potatoe Pudding—Iriſh

TAKE one half Pound Potatoes, finely maſhed, one half Pound Sugar, one half Pound Butter, ſix Eggs with the Whites—beat them. Cream the Butter mix all together and beat very light. You may add Orange or Lemon-peel or Mace and a large Wine-glaſs of Wine.

(Manuſcript Cook Book, c-1801,
of Mrs. *Frances Bland Tucker Coalter.*
Owned by Dr. *St. George Tucker Grinnan, Richmond.*)

*Clear Sauce for Puddings**

MIX Wine, Sugar and melted Butter to yᵉ Taſte. Stir them together, taking Care to ſkim off the Salt as it riſes.

(Manuſcript Cook Book, c-1801,
of Mrs. *Frances Bland Tucker Coalter*
Owned by Dr. *St. George Tucker Grinnan, Richmond.*)

*Pudding Sauce**

HEAT one half Cup Milk and one half Cup Cream on a low Fire. Beat two Egg Yolks till thick. Add two Tableſpoons Sugar. Pour Milk and Cream gradually on Egg Mixture, beating conſtantly, and cook ſlowly till thick. Add two Tableſpoons Brandy or Wine, one half Teaſpoon Vanilla and a Bit of Salt. Pour over the two Egg Whites beaten till ſtiff.

(Old Recipe, *Richmond, Virginia*
Prov'd, *Blair* Kitchen, 1938.)

Snow

Snow a nice Dressing for a boiled Custard

TAKE the Whites of four Eggs, some beaten Sugar and a little Rose-water, whip them to a Froth, have ready some boiling Milk and Water, throw in the Froth, dip it up as quick as you can, and dress the Custard on the Top and tip it about with a little red Currant Jelly.

(Manuscript Cook Book, prior 1839.
Morton Family of *Charlotte* County, *Virginia*.)

To make an Orange Pudding

TAKE the out-side Rind of three *Sevil* Oranges, boil them in several Waters till they are tender; then pound them in a Mortar with three quarters of a Pound of Sugar; then blanch and beat half a Pound of Almonds very fine, with Rose-water to keep them from oiling; then beat sixteen Eggs, but six Whites, and a Pound of fresh Butter; beat all these together very well till 'tis light and hollow; then put it in a Dish, with a Sheet of Puff-paste at the Bottom, and bake it with Tarts; scrape Sugar on it, and serve it up hot.

(Mrs. *E. Smith's* Compleat Housewife,
Williamsburg, 1742.)

A Quire of Paper

TAKE three Spoonfuls of fine Flour, a Pint of Cream, six Eggs, three Spoonfuls of Sack, one of Orange-flower Water, a little Sugar, half a Nutmeg grated, and half a Pound of melted Butter almost cold. Mix all well together, and butter the
Pan

Pan for the firſt Pancake. Let them run as thin as poſſible, and when they be juſt coloured, they will be enough. In this Manner all the fine Pancakes ſhould be fried.

(*John Farley's* London Art of Cookery, 1787.
From *Brookbury, Cheſterfield* County, *Virginia.*)

Quire of Paper-pancakes

TAKE the Yolks of four Eggs well beat, mix in one half Pint of Milk, three Spoonfuls Flour, three Ounces Sugar, four Ounces freſh Butter, melted & cooled, (this muſt not be put in until the others are well mixed) and three Spoonfuls white Wine. Greaſe your Pan once with freſh Butter which will be ſufficient for all.

(Recipe in the Handwriting of *Lelia Tucker* in a
Letter written by *St. George Tucker* from
Williamſburg, 6th February [1804],
to his Daughter *Frances Coalter.*)

Another Way*

BEAT the Yolks of four Eggs well, add one Cup of rich Milk, ſift in three Tableſpoons of Flour, one fourth Cup of Sugar, one half Cup of melted Butter, three Spoonfuls white Wine. Butter a Griddle once, and do not cook too faſt. Serve at once.

(Mrs. *Coalter's* Recipe [1804],
Adapted *Market Square Tavern* Kitchen, 1937.)

Pink coloured Pancakes

BOIL a large Beet tender—beat it fine in a marble Mortar add the Yolks of four Eggs three Spoonfulls of Cream—two Pounds of Flour; ſweeten

ſweeten to Taſte, half a Nutmeg, Glaſs of Brandy
—beat all togather half an Hour, fry them with
Butter, garniſh with Sweetmeats.

(Manuſcript Cook Book, prior 1839.
Morton Family of *Charlotte* County, *Virginia*.)

To make a Quaking Pudding

TAKE a Pint of Cream, and boil it with Nutmeg
and Cinnamon and Mace; take out the Spice
when 'tis boiled; then take the Yolks of eight Eggs,
and four of the Whites; beat them very well with
ſome Sack, and mix your Eggs with your Cream,
with a little Salt and Sugar, and a ſtale Half-penny
white Loaf, and one Spoonful of Flour, and a
quarter of a Pound of Almonds blanch'd and beat
fine, with ſome Roſe-water; beat all theſe well together, and wet a thick Cloth, and flour it, and put
it in when the Pot boils. It muſt boil an Hour at
leaſt. Melt Butter, Sack, and Sugar, for the Sauce;
ſtick blanch'd Almonds and candied Orange-peel
on the Top.

(*E. Smith's* Compleat Houſewife, *Williamſburg*, 1742.)

Quaking Pudding

TAKE one Pint of Cream out of which take two
or three Spoonfuls and mix quite ſmooth with
a Spoonfull of fine Flour. Set the Reſt to boil—
when it has boiled take it off and ſtir in the cold
Cream and Flour very well. When it is cool beat
five Yolks and two Whites of Eggs—ſtir in Nutmeg or Mace and a little Salt—Sweeten to your
Taſte—butter a wooden Bowl or other Veſſel and
put

put it in—tie a Cloth over and boil it half an Hour.
It muft be put into boiling Water and turned about
a few Minutes to prevent the Egg going to one Side
—when done turn it into a Difh and pour over it a
Sauce of melted Butter, Wine and Sugar. You may
drefs it with Citron or other Sweetmeats.

(Manufcript Cook Book, c-1801, of Frances Bland
Tucker Coalter</i>. Owned by Dr. <i>St. George
Tucker Grinnan, Richmond.</i>)</div>

Queen of Puddings *

POUR one Quart of Milk over two Cups of fine
dry Bread-crumbs. Beat four Egg Yolks add one
half Cup of Sugar, then combine them with one
half Cup of Butter creamed with one Cup of Sugar.
Add a Spoonful of Flavoring and pour into a fhal-
low buttered Baking-difh and bake until fet in a
moderate Oven. Spread the Top with a thick Layer
of frefh or preferved Strawberries or Rafpberries.
If frefh Berries are ufed, ftrew well with Sugar, if
Preferves, ufe no Sweetening. Spread over the Top
a light Meringue made by whipping the four Egg
Whites to a Froth with two Tablefpoonfuls of
powdered Sugar. Return to moderate Oven and
cook until the Meringue is fet and flightly browned.

(Old James City County, Virginia, Recipe.
Adapted <i>Market Square Tavern</i> Kitchen, 1937.)</div>

Rice Blanc Mange *

BOIL a Teacupfull of Rice in a very fmall Quantity of Water, till it is near burfting—then add
half a Pint of Milk, boil it to a Mufh, ftirring all
the

the Time; ſeaſon it with Sugar, Wine and Nutmeg; dip the Mould in Water, and fill it; when cold, turn it in a Diſh, and ſurround it with boiled Cuſtard ſeaſoned, or Syllabub—garniſh it with Marmalade.

(Mrs. *Mary Randolph's* Virginia Houſewife, 1831.)

Williamſburg *Rice Blanc Mange* ❉

BOIL one Cup of Rice in four Cups of Water with one fourth Teaſpoon of Salt until well done. Add one Pint of Milk and boil it to a Muſh, ſtirring all the Time. Seaſon with one fourth Cup of Sugar, one fourth Cup of Wine or Brandy, one Teaſpoon of Nutmeg. Dip a Mould in Water, fill it and chill. Turn out on a Diſh, cover with Cuſtard Sauce or Syllabub (Page 211).

(Mrs. *Randolph's* Recipe, 1831.
Adapted *Market Square Tavern* Kitchen, 1937.)

A Carolina *Rice Pudding*

TAKE half a Pound of Rice, waſh it clean, put it into a Saucepan, with a Quart of Milk, keep it ſtirring till it is very thick; take great Care it don't burn; then turn it into a Pan, and grate ſome Nutmeg into it, and two Teaſpoonfuls of beaten Cinnamon, a little Lemon-peel ſhred fine, ſix Apples, pared and chopped ſmall: mix all together with the Yolks of three Eggs, and ſweetened to your Palate; then tie it up cloſe in a Cloth; put it into boiling Water, and be ſure to keep it boiling all the Time; an Hour and a quarter will boil it. Melt Butter

Butter and pour over it, and throw some fine Sugar all over it; and a little Wine in the Sauce will be a great Addition to it.

(Mrs. *Glasse's* Recipe, 1774.
Manuscript Copy in Cook Book of Miss
Margaret Prentis, Williamsburg, c-1828.)

Sippet Pudding*

CUT a Loaf of Bread as thin as possible, put a Layer of it in the Bottom of a deep Dish, strew on some Slices of Marrow or Butter, with a Handful of Currants or stoned Raisins; do this till the Dish is full; let the Currants or Raisins be at the Top; beat four Eggs, mix with them a Quart of Milk that has been boiled a little and become cold, a quarter of a Pound of Sugar, and a grated Nutmeg—pour it in, and bake it in a moderate Oven—eat it with Wine Sauce.

(Mrs. *Mary Randolph's* Virginia Housewife, 1831.
Prov'd *Market Square Tavern* Kitchen, 1937.)

To make Steeple Cream

TAKE five Ounces of Hart's-horn, and two Ounces of Ivory, and put them into a Stone-bottle, and fill it up with fair Water to the Neck, and put in a small Quantity of Gum-arabick, and Gum-dragant; then tie up the Bottle very close, and let it into a Pot of Water with Hay at the Bottom, let it boil six Hours; then take it out and let it stand an Hour before you open it, lest it fly in your Face; then strain it in, and it will be a strong Jelly; then take a Pound of blanch'd Almonds, and beat them very fine, and mix it with a Pint of thick Cream, and let it stand a little; then strain it
out

out and mix it with a Pound of Jelly; set it over the Fire till 'tis scalding hot, sweeten it to your Taste with double-refin'd Sugar; then take it off, and put in a little Amber, and pour it out into small high Gallipots like a Sugar-loaf at Top; when 'tis cold turn it out, and lay whipt Cream about them in Heaps. (Mrs. *E. Smith's* Compleat Housewife, *Williamsburg*, 1742.)

A Sweetmeat Pudding

MAKE a Quart of Flour into Puff-paste; when done, divide into three Parts of unequal Size; roll the largest out square and moderately thin, spread over it a thin Layer of Marmalade, leaving a Margin; then roll the smallest, and put it on the other two, spreading Marmalade; fold it up, one Fold over the other, the Width of your Hand—press the Ends together, tie it in a Cloth securely, and place it in a Kettle of boiling Water, where it can lie at Length without doubling; boil it quickly, and when done, pour melted Butter with Sugar and Wine in the Dish.

(Mrs. *Mary Randolph's* Virginia Housewife, 1831.)

Sweet Potato Pudding*

BOIL one Pound of sweet Potatos very tender, rub them while hot through a Colander; add six Eggs well beaten, three quarters of a Pound of powdered Sugar, three quarters of Butter, and some grated Nutmeg and Lemon-peel, with a Glass of Brandy; put a Paste in the Dish, and when the Pudding

Pudding is done, ſprinkle the Top with Sugar, and cover it with Bits of Citron. *Iriſh* Potato Pudding is made in the ſame Manner, but is not ſo good.

(Mrs. *Mary Randolph's* Virginia Houſewife, 1831.
Prov'd *Market Square Tavern* Kitchen, 1937.)

Grated Potato Pudding*

BEAT four Eggs very light, add gradually two Cups of Sugar, two Cups of grated ſweet Potato, two Cups of ſcalded Milk, one fourth Pound of melted Butter, two Teaſpoonfuls of Ginger and one Tableſpoon of Corn Starch diſſolved in cold Water. Cook ſlowly, ſtirring conſtantly, on Top of Stove for about half an Hour until Mixture thickens. Bake in buttered Baking-diſh in moderate Oven fifteen or twenty Minutes. Serve warm with whipped Cream.

(Old *Williamſburg* Recipe.)

Tanſey Pudding

BEAT ſeven Eggs very light, mix with them a Pint of Cream and nearly as much Spinach Juice, with a little Juice of Tanſey; add a quarter of a Pound of powdered Crackers or pounded Rice made fine, a Glaſs of Wine, ſome grated Nutmeg and Sugar; ſtir it over the Fire to thicken, pour it into a Paſte and bake it, or fry it like an Omelette.

(Mrs. *Mary Randolph's* Virginia Houſewife, 1831.)

Tipſy Cake*

CUT a Loaf of Sponge Cake in two-inch Squares. Split Squares in half. Saturate each Piece with Sherry. Cover each Piece with a rich Cuſtard and top with whipped Cream and whole Almonds.

Cuſtard

Custard Sauce*

BEAT three Egg Yolks lightly with one fourth of a Cup of Sugar. Pour flowly over thefe one Pint of fcalded Milk. Return to Fire and cook very flowly, ftirring continually until thick. Flavor as you choofe with Vanilla or Rum, and Nutmeg.

(Market Square Tavern Kitchen, 1937.)

To make a Trifle*

COVER the Bottom of your Difh with *Naples* Bifcuits broke in Pieces, Mackaroons, and Ratafia Cakes, juft wet them all with Sack, pour on a good boiled Cuftard when cold, then a whipt Syllabub over that.

(Court & Country Confectioner, London, 1770.
From Tucker Houfe, Williamfburg. Prov'd
Market Square Tavern Ktchen, 1937.)

Boiled Cuftard*

SCALD one Quart of Milk in a Double-boiler, beat fix Eggs flightly and add to the Milk; add one-half Cup of Sugar and one-eighth Teafpoon of Salt, combined. Cook until Cuftard thickens. It will form a Coat on a clean filver Spoon when done.

(Market Square Tavern Kitchen, 1937.)

A

A MORAL AND PHYSICAL THERMOMETER: or, A Scale of the Progress of Temperance and Intemperance.—Liquors, with their Effects in their usual Order.

WATER TEMPERANCE.

Scale	Liquor	Effects
70	WATER	Health, Wealth,
60	Milk and Water	Serenity of mind,
		Reputation, long Life, and
50	Small Beer	Happiness
40	Cider and Perry	Cheerfulness
		Strength and
30	Wine	Nourishment, when taken only
		at meals, and in moderate
20	Porter	quantities.
16	Strong Beer	

INTEMPERANCE.

Scale	Liquor	VICES.	DISEASES.	PUNISHMENTS.
10	Punch	Idleness	Sickness	
			Puking, and	
		Peevishness	Tremors of the Hands in the Morning	Debt
20	Toddy and Crank	Quarrelling	Bloatedness	Black Eyes
		Fighting	Inflamed Eyes	Rags
30	Grog		Red Nose and Face	Hunger
		Lying	Sore and swelled Legs	
		Swearing	Jaundice	Hospital
40	Flip Shrub	Obscenity	Pains in the Limbs, and burning in the Palms of the Hands, and Soles of the Feet	Poor-house
50	Bitters infus'd in Spirits Usquebaugh Hysteric water	Swindling	Dropsy	Jail
		Perjury	Epilepsy	Whipping
60	Gin, Anniseed, Brandy, Rum, and Whisky in the *Morning*	Burglary	Melancholy Madness	The Hulks
		Murder	Palsy Apoplexy	Botany Bay
70	Do. during the *Day and Night.*	Suicide	DEATH.	GALLOWS

—*The Gentleman's Magazine* for May, 1789.

Of HEALTH DRINKING

IT was a Matter of ſome Concern to the early *Virginia* Lawmakers that no one ſhould be ſuffered "to drink more than was neceſſary." To this End they paſſed many Acts for the Suppreſſion of notorious Drunkenneſs, and for the Reſtraint of Ordinaries and Tippling Houſes, that theſe Latter might not cheriſh Idleneſs and encourage looſe and careleſs Perſons to neglect their Callings and miſſpend their Times in Drunkenneſs. Ordinary Keepers were not permitted to extend Credit to their Patrons, (a Prohibition which they were careful not to apply in the Capital while the Courts and General Aſſembly were ſitting).

There was an early Rule in the Houſe of Burgeſſes fining any of its Members who ſhould, by the major Part of the Houſe, be adjudged "to be diſ-"guiſed with overmuch Drinke."

Students at the College of *William and Mary* were enjoined from Drinking to Exceſs or in a Way contrary to good Manners. A Letter from *John Alliſon* to *St. George Tucker*, Profeſſor of Law at the College, written on *March* 2, 1816, ſhows clearly the Problems that confronted the Parents of the Students who overſtepped theſe Bounds. The Diſ-
cuſſion

cuſſion of *William's* unbecoming Conduct con-
cludes:

> P.S. I hope *William* did not get drunk by himſelf,
> becauſe that would evince a total Diſregard of
> Decency and Decorum.

The Gentlemen who made the Laws for the
Colony provided alſo for the Drinking they conſidered neceſſary and polite. Ordinary Keepers
were not permitted to charge extraordinary Rates
for their Wines and Spirits—the County Courts
regulating the Price for Liquors, Diet, Lodging,
Stableage, &c. Diſtinctions were made between
domeſtic and imported Liquors, and in ſome Coun-
ties, ſuch as *Iſle of Wight*, the Court made ſome
Judgment of Quality, rating "good *Barbaaoes*
"Rum" at 10 Shillings, and "*New England* and other
"bad Rum" at 5 Shillings per Gallon.

Neceſſary Drinking included the "ſmall Drink"
uſed at the Table, which conſiſted of a Variety of
Wines, Beer and Ale. Their ſtrong Wine was
chiefly *Madeira*, a noble Wine which the
Reverend *Hugh Jones* ſaid was fitteſt to cheer the
fainting Spirits in the Heat of Summer, and to
warm the chilled Blood in the bitter Colds of Winter. There was alſo Punch, made of Rum from the
Caribbee Iſlands, or of Brandy diſtilled from *Virginia* Apples and Peaches; beſides *French* Brandy
and all Kinds of *French* and *European* Wine, eſpe-
cially Claret and Port.

Chriſtenings, Birthnight Feſtivities, *Eaſter*, *Chriſtmas*, and all other Occaſions for ſocial Gatherings,
were Occaſions alſo for Health-drinking or Toaſt-
ing. One Writer has obſerved that Rum and Funeral
Wines

Wines were as neceſſary a Part of the Funeral as the Corpſe.

When Governor *Alexander Spotſwood* led a Company of Gentlemen, Rangers, and *Indians* beyond the *Blue Ridge* Mountains, the Expedition was well-prepared to obſerve the neceſſary Niceties. One of the higheſt Peaks of the Ridge was named Mount *George* for his Majeſty, and the Journal of *John Fontaine* records:

> 6th September [1716]. We had a good Dinner, and after it we got the Men together and loaded all their Arms, and we drank the King's Health in Champagne and fired a Volley, the Princeſs's Health in Burgundy and fired a Volley, and all the Reſt of the royal Family in Claret and a Volley. We drank the Governor's Health and fired another Volley. We had ſeveral Sorts of Liquors, viz., *Virginia* red Wine and white Wine, *Iriſh* Uſquebaugh, Brandy, Shrub, two Sorts of Rum, Champagne, *Canary* Cherry, Punch, Water, Cider, etc.

From ſuch a Beginning was inſtituted the *Order of the Golden Horſeſhoe* to which any Gentleman who had drunk his Majeſty's Health on Mount *George* was admitted.

The Cellars which ſupplied the neceſſary Refreſhment for ſuch Occaſions were ample—and among the largeſt and beſt-ſtocked in the Colony were thoſe in the Governor's Palace in *Williamsburg*.

After Lord *Botetourt's* Death in 1770, the Appraiſers made an Inventory of the Palace Cellars, which had been depleted, of courſe, by the Demands of the ſtate Funeral and had not been repleniſhed.

pleniſhed. At that Time the Cellars contained Hogſheads, Caſks, and Bottles holding more than 2,566 Gallons of a choice Aſſortment of Beer, Ale, Cider, Arrack, Brandy, Porter, Burgundy, Champagne, Claret, Hock, *Madeira* (almoſt one thouſand Gallons of this Favorite), Port, Rum, old Spirits and white Wine.

It was natural that one of the moſt noted and well-accuſtomed Taverns in *Virginia*, the *Raleigh*, ſhould have been known for the Excellence of its Bar. Travellers ſpoke of "the exceeding good *Ma-* "*deira*" for which the *Raleigh* was famous, and two hundred Acres of *Goochland* County Land bear Teſtimony to the Excellence of Keeper *Henry Wetherburn's* Punch. In the Year 1738, *William Randolph* of *Tuckahoe* deeded the Land to *Thomas Jefferſon's* Father, *Peter*, for "*Henry Wetherburn's* "biggeſt Bowl of Arrack Punch."

The beſt Summary of the *Virginian's* Attitude toward Conviviality is to be found carved and gilded above the Mantel in the *Raleigh's* hiſtoric *Apollo* Room, "*Hilaritas Sapientiae et Bonae Vitae* "*Proles*"—"Jollity—the Offspring of Wiſdom and "good Living."

Caudles, Punches, &c.

Apple Toddy*

TO one Gallon of Apple Brandy or Whiſkey, add one and a half Gallons of hot Water, well ſweetened, one Dozen large Apples, well roaſted,

two

two grated Nutmegs, one Gill of Allspice, one Gill of Cloves, a Pinch of Mace. Season with half a Pint of good Rum. Let it stand three or four Days before using. (Old Recipe, *Pittsylvania* County, *Virginia*.)

An Arrack Punch*

MELT one half Pound Sugar in enough hot Water to dissolve it well, pour it over the grated Rind, of two Lemons. Add the Juice of four Lemons; one Pineapple peeled, sliced and pounded, six Cloves, twenty Coriander-seeds, one small Stick of Cinnamon, one Pint of Brandy, one Pint *Jamaica* Rum, one Cup of Arrack, one Cup of strong green Tea, one Quart boiling Water. Strain well into a clean Bottle, cork well and steep it overnight. Add one Quart of hot Milk and the Juice of two more Lemons. When cool, ice and serve.

Arrack Punch*

MIX two Quarts of Arrack, one Gallon of Spirits, one Gallon of plain Syrup (made with one Pound of Sugar and one Gallon of Water), one third of a Cup of Tincture of Lemon-peel. This Punch may be iced and served immediately or will keep well if bottled.

Another Way*

POUR the strained Juice of two large Oranges over three-fourths of a Pound of Loaf-sugar. Add a little of the outside Peel cut in very thin Slices. Pour over it one Quart of boiling Water, one
Pint

Pint of Arrack and a Pint of hot red *French* Wine.
Stir together. This may be ſerved when cold and
will improve with Age.

(As Mr. *Wetherburn* might have made it.)

For Bitters (*very fine*)

TO a Gallon of Brandy put four Ounces *Sevil*
Orange-peel, four Ounces Gentian cut fine,
two Ounces Cardimun-ſeed and one Ounce Coche-
neill, the Orange-peel, the Gentian and Cardemun
to be bruiſed—the Cochen[eal] powdered.

(Manuſcript Cook Book, c-1825, of Miſs *Margaret
Prentis* of *Williamſburg.* Owned by *Robert H.
Webb*, Eſq., *Charlotteſville.*)

Blackberry Cordial*

TO two Quarts Blackberry Juice add one Pound
Loaf-ſugar, four grated Nutmegs, one-quarter
Ounce ground Cloves, one-quarter Ounce ground
Allſpice, one-quarter Ounce ground Cinnamon.
Simmer all together, for thirty Minutes, in a Stew-
pan cloſely covered. Strain through a Cloth when
cold and add a Pint of the beſt *French* Brandy.

(Old *Virginia* Recipe.)

A fine Caudle

TAKE a Pint of Milk, turn it with Sack; then
ſtrain it, and when 'tis cold, put it in a Skillet,
with Mace, Nutmeg, and ſome white Bread ſliced;
let all theſe boil, and then beat the Yolks of four
or five Eggs, the Whites of two, and thicken your
Caudle,

Caudle, ſtirring it all one Way for fear it curdle;
let it warm together, then take it off, and ſweeten
it to your Taſte. (Mrs. *E. Smith's* Compleat Houſewife,
Williamſburg, 1742.)

Caudle *

PUT a Handfull of Allſpice in a Quart of Water,
& put it on the Fire to boil, beat well three or
four Eggs with as much Sugar as will make it ſweet
enough; pour the boiling Water to the Sugar, and
Eggs, very ſlowly, to prevent them curdling, rake
the Fire from under the Stew-pan, then pour the
Caudle back in it, ſtir it untill it is done, add a little
Wine or Rum when cool.

(Manuſcript Cook Book, prior 1839.
Morton Family of *Charlotte* County, *Virginia*.)

Cherry Shrub

GATHER ripe *Morello* Cherries, pick them from
the Stalk, and put them in an earthen Pot,
which muſt be ſet into an iron Pot of Water; make
the Water boil, but take Care that none of it gets
into the Cherries; when the Juice is extracted, pour
it into a Bag made of tolerably thick Cloth, which
will permit the Juice to paſs, but not the Pulp of
your Cherries; ſweeten it to your Taſte, and when
it becomes perfectly clear, bottle it—put a Gill of
Brandy into each Bottle, before you pour in the
Juice—cover the Corks with Roſin. It will keep all
Summer, in a dry cool Place, and is delicious mixed
with Water.

(Mrs. *Mary Randolph's* Virginia Houſewife, 1831.)

Morello

Morello *Cherry Bounce*

GATHER and pick your Cherries when perfectly ripe, put them into a Tub and maſh
them with a Rolling-pin, Stones and all, and to
every five Pints of Cherries put a Quart of Rum,
let it ſtand a Week; ſtrain it through a Flannel
Bag, to every Gallon of Bounce put three fourths
of a Pound of brown Sugar. Cheap Rum at 75
Cents or 50 Cents a Gallon anſwers equally as well
as the beſt Spirit for Bounce.

(Manuſcript Cook Book, *Charlotteſville*, 1836.
Owned by Mrs. *Virginia Graſty Griffin*.)

Cordial Water

TWO Gallons of Brandy add of Water one
fourth of the Quantity of Brandy. Two Dozen
Lemons ſliced and ſweetened and ſix of the Peel-
ings, eight Tableſpoons white Sugar, and two
Tableſpoons of good brown Sugar candied—from
Mrs. *Dunbar*.

(Manuſcript Cook Book, c-1825, of Miſs *Margaret
Prentis* of *Williamſburg*. Owned by *Robert H.
Webb*, Eſq., *Charlotteſville*.)

To make Whipt Cream

TAKE a Quart of thick Cream, and the Whites
of eight Eggs beaten with half a Pint of Sack;
mix it together, and ſweeten it to your Taſte with
double-refin'd Sugar: You may perfume it if you
pleaſe with ſome Muſk or Ambergreaſe tied in a
Rag, and ſteeped a little in the Cream; whip it up
with

with a Whisk, and a bit of Lemon-peel tied in the
Middle of the Whisk; take the Froth with a Spoon,
and lay it in your Glasses or Bason.

(Mrs. *E. Smith's* Compleat Housewife,
Williamsburg, 1742.)

Currant Shrub*

GATHER your Currants when full ripe, on a
dry Day. Mash them; then put them into a
flannel (or cotton) Bag and when the Juice has all
run out, to every Pint put twelve Ounces of Loaf-
sugar and half a Pint of Rum. Bottle and seal it
and let it away for Use. This Receipt answers
equally well for Cherries. The Shrub is indifferent
unless the Rum is good.

(Manuscript Cook Book, *Charlottesville,* 1836.
Owned by Mrs. *Virginia Grasty Griffin.*)

To make a Custard Posset

TAKE fourteen Eggs, beat them very well, and
put to them twelve Spoonfuls of Sack, nine of
Ale, and half a Pound of Sugar.

Set them upon some Coals and warm them, then
strain them, and set them on again, and heat them
till they begin to thicken; and if you please, you
may add a little Nutmeg.

Take one Quart of Cream and boil it, pour it
into the Eggs, cover it up, and let it stand half an
Hour; then serve it up.

(Mrs. *Martha Bradley's* British Housewife.)

Damson

Damſon Cordial

GET the Juice from the Fruit, ſee Jelly—ſtrain it and put a Pound of Sugar to a Pint of Juice, and boil it—throw in a Few of the Kernels, & ſome Orange-peel, one Quart of Peach Brandy to two of Syrup.

(Manuſcript Cook Book, prior 1839.
Morton Family of *Charlotte* County, *Virginia*.)

A good Dram ❋

TO a Gallon of Brandy put a Quart of Water, one Pound of Sugar, three Spoonfuls of beaten Orange-peel and a Gill of Milk.

(Manuſcript Cook Book, *Charlotteſville*, 1836
Owned by Mrs. *Virginia Graſty Griffin*.)

Eggnog ❋

BEAT well the Yolks of three Dozen Eggs, then ſlowly beat in two and one half Pounds of fine Sugar. Add ſlowly, Drop by Drop, one Pint of choice *French* Brandy, and let it ſtand while you beat the Whites of the Eggs very light with one half Pound of Sugar. Add to the Yolks two Quarts of Milk, two Quarts of Cream and one Gallon of Brandy. Add the Egg Whites and grate in a freſh Nutmeg.

(Old Recipe, *Lynchburg, Virginia*.)

Weſtmoreland *Club Eggnog* ❋

SEPARATE the Yolks and Whites of two Dozen Eggs. Beat the Yolks well, then beat in one Pound of finely pulverized Sugar. Pour over this very ſlowly one half Gallon of Brandy and one half Pint

Pint of Rum, ſtirring ſlowly and ſteadily. Pour in one Quart of rich Cream, add the well-beaten Whites, and ſtir until they diſappear. Serve very cold with grated Nutmeg.

[Eggnog is better if it is made ſome Days before it is to be uſed and is kept in a very cold Place. It muſt be well ſhaken and mixed before ſerving.]

Fiſh Houſe Punch ✽

MAKE a Syrup of three Quarts of Water, one Pound of brown Sugar, pour hot over the Rinds and Juice of a Dozen or a Dozen and a half Lemons. Cool. Add two Quarts *Jamaica* Rum, one Quart of Brandy, daſh well with Peach Brandy to make it mellow and extra fine. Serve in a Bowl of cruſhed Ice. (By uſing three Pounds of brown Sugar this Punch may be prepared for Bottling and will improve with Age.) To ſerve immediately, ſome add one Quart of Pineapple-juice inſtead of one of the three Quarts of Water.

[Note: This Recipe is an old one in the *Taylor* Family of *Norfolk*. This Copy was given by Mrs. *Taylor*, Wife of Colonel *Walter Herron Taylor*, Adjutant General of the Army of Northern *Virginia*, C. S. A. (on General *Lee's* Staff), to Mrs. *Philip Alexander Bruce*. At the Bottom of the Recipe is written "*Walter* ſays 'look out for ſwell "Head next Morning'."]

(*Taylor* Family Recipe, prior 1862, *Norfolk, Virginia*.)

To make fine Milk-punch*

TAKE two Quarts of Water, one Quart of Milk, half a Pint of Lemon Juice, and one Quart of Brandy, Sugar to your Taste; put the Milk and Water together a little warm, then the Sugar, then the Lemon Juice, stir it well together; then the Brandy; stir it again, and run it through a Flannel Bag till 'tis very fine; then bottle it; it will keep a Fortnight or more.

(Mrs. *E. Smith's* Compleat Housewife,
Williamsburg, 1742.)

Punch*

THE Juice of three good Lemons—two small Coffee-cups Rum sweetened as for Toddy (one Pound brown Sugar to each Gallon of Spirit), one do. of F. [*French*] Brandy and white Sugar—to your Taste, will make three Quarts Punch—or one small Coffee-cup of bottled Juice in place of fresh Lemons. Five good Limes equal to three Lemons.

(Manuscript Cook Book, c-1801,
of Mrs. *Frances Bland Tucker Coalter.*
Owned by *St. George Tucker Grinnan, Richmond.*)

King's Arms *Frosted Fruit Shrub**

MIX the Juice of four Lemons and six Oranges with one Cup of Pineapple Juice, one Cup of Juice from pickled Fruit and one half Cup of Spice Syrup. Chill. Serve in small Glasses topped with Orange Sherbet.

Spice Syrup: To one Cup of granulated Sugar, add one Cup of Water, one Tablespoon of clear
Corn

Corn Syrup, one Tableſpoon of whole Cloves, two Pieces of Cinnamon Bark. Stir over hot Water until Sugar is diſſolved, then ſimmer fifteen Minutes. Strain and cool.

To make a true Mint Julep*

THERE is only one approved and authentic Method of making a *Virginia* Mint Julep—and to this Truth every good *Virginian* will agree. After many Years of Study and patient Inveſtigation the Author is able to report that on this preciſe Method, few *Virginians* are able to agree. A Sympoſium held with ſome of the better Julep-makers finds them in Agreement with the following:

A Julep Glaſs or Goblet is not the proper Container in which to ſerve Salads compoſed of Oranges, Pineapples, Lemons, Cherries and other outlandiſh Fruits, ſuch as are commonly found in ſome Eſtabliſhments which pretend to ſerve Juleps.

Two Things will inevitably ruin any Julep, the firſt of which is too much Sugar, and the ſecond, too little Whiſky. Having obſerved carefully the foregoing, take a long, thin, glaſs Tumbler or a Silver Goblet and place it on a Tray. In the Bottom place the Leaves from a Sprig of Mint and add one half Tableſpoonful of powdered Sugar. Cruſh the Mint well with the Sugar, and diſſolve in a Tableſpoonful of Water. Pack the Glaſs full with very finely-cruſhed Ice, trying not to wet the Outſide of the Glaſs. Pour into this a Glaſs of Whiſky (Whiſky diſtilled from Corn is traditional but that made from Rye or other Grain is permiſſible). Some Authorities, having packed the Glaſs well with Ice, pour in the
Whiſky

Whisky until the Glass is full. Stir gently until the Glass is well-frosted on the Outside. Decorate on Top with three Sprigs of Mint and serve.

(A *Williamsburg* Sympofium 1699-1938.)

A Negus *

RUB a small Lump of Sugar over a Lemon until it is well-flavored. Put it in a heavy Glass and add two Teaspoons of Lemon Juice. Pour into this a large Wine Glassful of Port or Sherry. Fill the Glass with fresh boiling Water and serve up with grated Nutmeg on Top.

(Recipe derived from one first popularized
by Colonel *Francis Negus*, who died in 1732.
This popular Drink was known in *England* and
her Colonies by this Name.)

Panada *

PUT the Crumbs of Bread in a Bowl, add a Glass of Wine or a Spoonfull of Rum—or Vinegar, as may suit best—some grated Nutmeg, Butter, and Sugar, Spice as Fancy may direct—pour the Water on boiling hot.

(Manuscript Cook Book, prior 1839.
Morton Family of *Charlotte* County, *Virginia*.)

To make Orange Wine

TO every Gallon of Water put two Pounds & half of Sugar, beat the Whites of two Eggs well & put them to the Water & Sugar, let it boil one Hour & scum it well; to a Gallon of this Water put the Juice and Inside of eight Oranges, pare them very thin; when the Water is almost cold put it all
together

together with a little Yeast, let it stand two or three
Days, stirring it twice a Day, then strain it & put
it into the Vessell; if you please you may add a Pint
of Brandy to each Gallon. If it is ten or twelve
Gallons let it stand five or six Months & in proportion according to the Quantity you make.

(Wines & Cookery. *English* Manuscript Book, c-1740.
Owned by *Colonial Williamsburg*.)

Orgeat

A Necessary Refreshment at all Parties

BOIL two Quarts of Milk with a Stick of Cinnamon, and let it stand to be quite cold, first
taking out the Cinnamon, blanch four Ounces of
the best sweet Almonds, pound them in a Marble
Mortar with a little Rose-water; mix them well
with the Milk, sweeten it to your Taste, and let it
boil a few Minutes only, left the Almonds should
be oily; strain it through a very fine Sieve till quite
smooth, and free from the Almonds, serve it up
either cold or lukewarm, in Glasses with Handles.

(Mrs. *Randolph's* Virginia Housewife, 1831.)

Peach Cordial

GATHER ripe cling-stone Peaches, wipe off the
Down, cut them to the Stone in several Places
and put them in a Cask; when filled with Peaches,
pour on as much Peach Brandy as the Cask will
hold; let it stand six or eight Weeks, then draw it
off, put in Water until reduced to the Strength of
Wine; to each Gallon of this, add one Pound of
good

good brown Sugar—diffolve it, and pour the Cordial into a Cafk juft large enough to hold it—when perfectly clear, it is fit for Ufe.

(Mrs. *Randolph's* Virginia Houfewife, 1831.)

To make a Poffet with Ale, King William's *Poffet*

TAKE a Quart of Cream and mix with it a Pint of Ale, then beat the Yolks of ten Eggs, and the Whites of four; when they are well beaten, put them to your Cream and Ale; fweeten it to your Tafte, and flice fome Nutmeg in it; fet it over the Fire, and keep it ftirring all the While, and when 'tis thick, and before it boils, take it off, and pour it into the Bafon you ferve it in to the Table.

(Mrs. *E. Smith's* Compleat Houfewife, *Williamfburg*, 1742.)

*Mulled Wine**

GRATE one half a Nutmeg into a Pint of Wine and fweeten to your Tafte with Loaf-fugar. Set it over the Fire and when it boils take it off the Fire to cool. Beat the Yolks of four Eggs very well, ftrain them and add to them a little cold Wine, then mix them with yᵗ hot Wine gradually. Pour it backward and forward feveral Times till it looks fine and light, then fet it on the Fire and heat it very gradually till it is quite hot and pretty thick, and pour it up and down feveral Times. Put it in Chocolate Cups and ferve it with long, narrow Toaft.

(Manufcript Cook Book, c-1801,
of Mrs. *Frances Bland Tucker Coalter*.
Owned by Dr *St. George Tucker Grinnan, Richmond.*)

Quince

Quince Wine

TAKE twenty large Quinces, gathered when they be dry and full ripe. Wipe them clean with a coarse Cloth, and grate them with a large Grate or Rasp as near the Cores as you can; but do not touch the Cores. Boil a Gallon of Spring-water, throw in your Quinces, and let them boil softly about a quarter of an Hour. Then strain them well into an earthen Pan on two Pounds of double-refined Sugar. Pare the Peel off two large Lemons, throw them in, and squeeze the Juice through a Sieve. Stir it about till it be very cool, and then toast a thin bit of Bread very brown, rub a little Yest on it, and let the Whole stand close-covered twenty-four Hours. Then take out the Toast and Lemon, put the Wine in a Cask, keep it three Months, and then bottle it. If you make a twenty-gallon Cask, let it stand six Months before you bottle it; and remember, when you strain your Quinces, to wring them hard in a coarse Cloth.

(*John Farley's London* Art of Cookery, 1787. From *Brookbury, Chesterfield County, Virginia.*)

Raspberry Vinegar

MEASURE your Raspberries into a Bowl, and pour over them an equal Quantity of Vinegar. The next Day take out the Fruit and add as much more to the same Vinegar. The Day following, re-move the Raspberries as before and again replace them with Fresh and on the fourth Day put to each Pint of Liquid Pound a of Loaf-sugar—place it in a

Skillet

Skillet on a gentle Fire, ſimmer and ſkim it for a
ſhort Time when it will be ready to bottle for Uſe
—Seal it down well.

(Manuſcript Cook Book, *Charlotteſville*, 1836.
Owned by Mrs. *Virginia Graſty Griffin*.)

Regent Punch*

TO one Pint of ſtrong black Tea (in which put
the Rind of four Lemons cut very thin). Two
Pounds of Sugar, Juice of ſix Lemons, Juice of ſix
Oranges, one Pint of *French* Brandy, one Pint of
Rum, two Quarts of Champagne. Serve in a Bowl
with plenty of Ice.

(Early nineteenth Century Recipe, *Charlotte* County, *Virginia*.)

Roman *Punch**

TO make a Gallon take one and a half Pints of
Lemon Juice, Rinds of two Lemons grated on
Sugar, one Pint of Rum, half a Pint of Brandy,
two Quarts of Water, three Pounds of Loaf-ſugar,
a Pint-bottle of Champagne. Mix all together, and
chill.   (Old *Richmond* Recipe.)

To make Rum or Brandy Shrub*

TO a Gallon of Rum put a Quart of Orange Juice,
one Pound & half of double-refined Sugar &
the Ryne of two Oranges cut very thin. Let ſtand
in a Caſk ſix or ſeven Days, or till 'tis fine, then
bottle it off for Uſe.

(Wines & Cookery. *Engliſh* Manuſcript Book, c-1740.
Owned by Colonial *Williamſburg*.)

To make Shrub *

TAKE two Quarts of Brandy, and put it in a large Bottle, and put into it the Juice of five Lemons and Peels of two, half a Nutmeg, ſtop it up, and let it ſtand three Days, and add to it three Pints of White-wine, a Pound and half of Sugar; mix it, and ſtrain it twice thro' a Flannel, and bottle it up; 'tis a pretty Wine and a Cordial.

(Mrs. *E. Smith's* Compleat Houſewife, *Williamſburg,* 1742.)

Shrub

TAKE one Pint Juice, two Pounds brown Sugar, three Pints Spirit, of this Mixture put one Wine-glaſs in yᵣ Toddy Meaſure which then fill up with yᵣ ſweetened Toddy Spirit, and add two more Meaſures of the ſame Spirit and about one third of a Wine-glaſs of powdered Sugar. Theſe will make three Quarts of excellent Toddy. Note. When you mix your Fruit do it in a Stone Pot taking out the Seed of the Fruit which will give a Bitterneſs. Stir the Mixture well—tie it up very cloſe and let it ſtand two Days. It will then have a curdled Appearance and the Clear will be very pure. Strain thro' a Flannel, and bottle for Uſe.

(Manuſcript Cook Book, c-1801, of Mrs. *Frances Bland Tucker Coalter.* Owned by Dr. *St. George Tucker Grinnan, Richmond.*)

Tea Punch *

TO three Cups of ſtrong green Tea put the Rind of ſix Lemons, pared very thin, one and one-half Pounds of Sugar, Juice of ſix Lemons. Stir together

gether a few Minutes, then strain, and lastly add one Quart of good Rum. Fill the Glasses with crushed Ice when used. It will keep bottled.

(Old Williamsburg Recipe.)

To make very fine Syllabubs

TAKE a Quart and half a Pint of Cream, a Pint of *Rhenish*, half a Pint of Sack, three Lemons, near a Pound of double-refin'd Sugar; beat and sift the Sugar and put it to your Cream, grate off the yellow Rind of your three Lemons and put that in; squeeze the Juice of the three Lemons into your Wine, and put that to your Cream; then beat all together with a Whisk just half an Hour; then take it up all together with a Spoon, and fill your Glasses. It will keep good nine or ten Days, and is best three or four Days old. These are called *The everlasting Syllabubs*.

(Mrs. E. Smith's Compleat Housewife, Williamsburg, 1742.)

To make whipt Syllabubs

TAKE a Quart of Cream, not too thick, and a Pint of Sack, and the Juice of two Lemons; sweeten it to your Palate, and put it into a broad earthen Pan, and with a Whisk whip it, and as the Froth rises, take it off with a Spoon, and lay it in your Syllabub Glasses; but first you must sweeten some Claret, or Sack, or White-wine and strain it, and put seven or eight Spoonfuls of the Wine into your Glasses, and then gently lay in your Froth. Set them by. Do not make them long before you use them.

(Mrs. E. Smith's Compleat Housewife,
Williamsburg, 1742.)

To

PLATE IV.

The King's Arms in the Duke of Gloucester Street at Williamsburg.

E. JONES.

To make Toddy—Mrs. Tucker*

TAKE one Gallon of Rum and one Pound of Sugar, brown, well mixed in a Pot, kept cloſely stopped till clear—ſay two Days—and then carefully racked off in a Jug.

(Manuſcript Cook Book, c-1801,
of Mrs. *Frances Bland Tucker Coalter.*
Owned by Dr. *St. George Tucker Grinnan, Richmond.*)

Of Chriſtmas in VIRGINIA

Now *Chriſtmas* comes, 'tis fit that we
  Should feaſt and ſing, and merry be
Keep open Houſe, let Fiddlers play
  A Fig for Cold, ſing Care away
And may they who thereat repine
  On brown Bread and on ſmall Beer dine

(*Virginia* Almanack, 1766.)

IN this Manner the old Almanack-maker heralded the Advent of that Holiday of all Holidays in *Virginia—Chriſtmas*—a Holiday not obſerved with juſt one Day of Feſtivity, but with a Round of Church-going, Feaſting, Drinking, Dancing, Hunting and Celebration, which began a full Week before *Chriſtmas* and extended until the Sixth of January, or *Twelfth Night.*

    Scholars at the College of *William and Mary* contrived to lengthen their *Chriſtmas* Holidays by barring-out their Preſident and Maſters until
pledged

pledged an early Releaſe from Claſſes. After ſub-
mitting meekly to the Barring-out, the Faculty
entered the College Buildings to partake of Food
and other Entertainment; and often provided
Funds for Ammunition for *Chriſtmas* Guns.

Houſeholds always noted for their generous Hoſ-
pitality, at this Seaſon extended an even fuller
Meaſure of Diverſion to Travellers and Others.
Monſieur *Durand*, a *Frenchman* journeying through
Virginia in the *Chriſtmas* holiday Seaſon in 1686,
wrote:

> We were now approaching the *Chriſtmas* Feſti-
> val. Milor *Parker* was, as I have ſaid, a *Roman
> Catholic* . . . He wiſhed now to paſs *Chriſtmas*
> Day in *Maryland*, and as we were only five or ſix
> Leagues diſtant and had no Deſire to leave him,
> it was agreed that all ſhould go to ſpend the
> Night with Colonel *Fitzhugh*, whoſe Houſe is on
> the Shore of the great River *Potomac* . . .
>
> Mr. *Wormeley* is ſo beloved and eſteemed in
> theſe Parts that all Gentlemen of Conſideration
> of the Countryſide we traverſed came to meet
> him, and, as they rode with us, it reſulted that by
> the Time we reached Col. *Fitzhugh's* we made up
> a Troop of 20 Horſe. The Colonel's Accommoda-
> tions were, however, ſo ample that this Company
> gave him no Trouble at all; we were all ſupplied
> with Beds, though we had, indeed, to double up.
> Col. *Fitzhugh* ſhowed us the largeſt Hoſpitality.
> He had Store of good Wine and other Things to
> drink, and a Frolic enſued. He called in three
> Fiddlers, a Clown, a tight rope Dancer and an
> acrobatic Tumbler, and gave us all the Diver-
> tiſement one would wiſh. It was very cold but no
> one thought of going near the Fire becauſe they
> never put leſs than the Trunk of a Tree upon it
> and ſo the entire Room was kept warm.

From

From Plantation to Plantation the Scene was one of Excitement and Feſtivity. *Philip Vickers Fithian*, a young Tutor from *Princeton*, who was in charge of the little School at *Nomini* Hall, the *Carter* Plantation, ſaid that for a Week or more nothing had been heard in Converſation but the Balls, Fox-hunts, fine Entertainments and good Fellowſhip which were to be exhibited at the approaching *Chriſtmas*. His Fellow-tutor, Mr. *Goodlet*, had been barred-out of his School for the Holidays.

In his Diary on December 18, 1773, young *Fithian* wrote:

> . . . When the Candles were lighted, we all repaired, for the laſt Time, into the Dancing Room; firſt each Couple danced a Minuet; then all joined as before in the Country Dances, theſe continued till half after ſeven when at the Propoſal of ſeveral, we played Button, to get Pawns for Redemption; here I could join with them, and indeed it was carried on with Sprightlineſs, and Decency; in the Courſe of redeeming my Pawns I had ſeveral Kiſſes of the Ladies! Half after eight we were rung into Supper. The Room looked luminous and ſplendid; four very large Candles burning on the Table where we ſupped; three others in different Parts of the Room; a gay, ſociable Aſſembly, and four well inſtructed Waiters! So ſoon as we roſe from Supper, the Company formed into a Semicircle round the Fire, and Mr. *Lee*, by the Voice of the Company was choſen Pope, and the Reſt of the Company were appointed Friars, in the Play called "Break the "Pope's Neck." Here we had great Diverſion in the reſpective Judgments upon Offenders, but we were all diſmiſſed by ten, and retired to our ſeveral Rooms.

Fithian

Fithian related excitîng Events that were held that *Chriſtmas*. Mrs. *Carter* gave a Ball for her Friends and on *Chriſtmas* Eve when Guns were fired throughout the Neighbourhood "the Negroes "ſeemed inſpired with new Life." Early *Chriſtmas* Morning, Guns were fired all round the Houſe.

The Negroes, excuſed from all but houſehold Duties, were given new Clothes and Shoes, they appeared at the great Houſe to wiſh each Perſon "Joyful *Chriſtmas*" and to collect ſmall Sums of Money for their *Chriſtmas* Boxes. The Coachman, the Barber, the Laundreſs, the waiting Boys, the Poſtillions came—a conſtant Proceſſion.

The Fire-crackers which ſtill pop loudly in *Virginia* at this Seaſon are remindful of the old Cuſtom of *Chriſtmas* Guns. In December, 1804, *Robert Mitchell*, Eſq., the Mayor of *Richmond*, wrote, aſſuring the Governor of *Virginia* that he would do his beſt to follow the Governor's Advice to prevent the Evil of unlawful Gaming, then added:

> . . . but it does appear to me to be impoſſible to prevent firing what is called *Chriſtmas* Guns, being an old eſtabliſhed Cuſtom, although there is an Ordinance of the City Police fixing a Fine of 5s. for every Offence of firing Guns within this City.

The Church was decked with Cedar, Holly, Miſtletoe, and Evergreens and became the Orbit about which Life in Town and Country revolved—but in the Houſehold the real Center of Activity was the Kitchen. Here the buſy Houſewife and all the Houſehold Servants entered into a ritualiſtic Preparation of Plum Puddings, Fruit Cakes, Egg Nogs, and Mincemeat Pies, bringing

out

out for the Purpoſe ancient Recipes that were as valued a Part of the Family Inheritance as Great-grandfather's Sword, or Great-grandmama's beſt ſilver Spoon.

William Byrd, writing to his Friend, Sir *John Randolph*, in 1736, of the *Randolphs*' Impatience to return to *Williamſburg* after a Holiday Viſit at *Weſtover*, ſeems to attribute their haſty Departure over the wintry Roads to Lady *Randolph's* impatient Deſire to preſide over the Holiday Cookery of her own Houſehold:

> In hopes you may be ſafe at *Williamſburg* by this Time and my Lady up to the Elbow in Saſſages & Black Puddings, I can't forbear Greeting you well, and ſignifying our Joy at your Arrival in your own Chimney Corner. We have had the good Nature to be in Pain for you ever ſince you left us, 'tho in good Truth your Obſtinacy in expoſing your Wife and Children to be ſtarved with Cold and buried in the Mire, hardly deſerved it. No doubt you were obliged to have Pioneers to clean the Way before you as far as Mr. *Cuſtis'* Plantation, and you needed four Yokes of Oxen, as they do in the deep Roads of *Suſſex* to drag you thro' the Dirt. I dare ſay notwithſtanding your fine Horſes you were not able to go along faſter than Mr. *Attorney* walks.

The *Williamſburg* to which the *Randolphs* returned has always made much of the Holiday of Holidays. It was a Tradition that carried unchanged through even the genteely-decaying Years of the early nineteenth Century. The *Chriſtmas* Spirit which pervaded the old City is beſt told in the Story of the firſt *Chriſtmas* Tree in *Williamſburg*.

In

In 1842, before the Cuſtom of decorating a *Chriſtmas* Tree had found its Way from the old World to this Region of the new, a young political Exile from *Germany* was a Gueſt in the *Tucker* Houſe. He had been releaſed from a long Priſon Confinement and had fled to this Country with ſixty cheap Volumes of the Claſſics his only worldly Goods. He taught for a While in *Philadelphia* and then came to the College of *William and Mary* as Profeſſor of Ancient Languages.

The ſympathetic Friendſhip of the Family and its Friends made young *Charles Frederick Erneſt Minnigerode* welcome in the *Tucker* Houſehold, but as the Holiday Seaſon approached, he talked longingly of *Chriſtmas* in his native *Germany*, of Carols, and of Fir Trees decorated with Tinſel and Stars and Candles.

The young *Tucker* Children aſked that ſuch a *Chriſtmas* Tree be brought to their Houſe, and eagerly improviſed Ornaments from Twiſts of col-ored Paper, Fruit and a gilded Paper Star. When *Chriſtmas* came, other Children of the Neighbor-hood gathered and thrilled to the Innovation— there were Hymns and Carols and *Chriſtmas* Spirit enough to link young *Minnigerode* forever to his adopted Country.

* * *

To return again to the old *Virginia* Almanack Makers, we can find in their Pages of Penny Wiſ-dom the warmeſt of *Chriſtmas* Wiſhes, the moſt ex-preſſive

preffive of Greetings for the Season, with which we
here conclude:

> We wish you Health, and good Fires; Victuals,
> Drink and good Stomachs, innocent Diversion,
> and good Company; honest Trading, and good
> Success; loving Courtship, and good Wives, and
> lastly a merry CHRISTMAS and a happy NEW
> YEAR.

For Christmas

Roast Turkey *

AFTER washing the Fowl and putting it in Salt
Water to stand for some Hours, pour some
hot Water into the Body of the Turkey to heat it
well. Wipe it dry inside and out, then fill the Body
and Breast of the Turkey with Dressing which has
already been made. For Dressing, prepare Bread in
Quantity proportioned to the Size of the Fowl. A
twelve-pound Turkey will require a Quart Loaf to
stuff it properly; a small Hen only half as much.
Break up the Bread between your Hands, mixing
well with it a Tablespoonful of Butter and Seasoning of black Pepper, Salt and a Tablespoonful of
Butter and Seasoning of black Pepper, Salt and a
Teaspoonful of bruised Celery-feed; make the
Dressing hold together with a little hot Water, or
Yolk of an Egg and Water. After filling with the
Dressing, sew it up, rub it all over with fine Salt, tie
the Legs and Wings close down and put it to roast
with a moderate Fire. In about half an Hour baste

it

it all over with Butter and duſt on the Flour. Do this three or four Times while roaſting; it will make it look nice and brown. Pour the Gravy each Time into a Bowl to keep it from burning. For a Turkey of about ten Pounds, roaſt about three Hours.

(Recipe uſed by *Dorothea Dandridge Henry*, Wife
of *Patrick Henry*, at *Red Hill*,
Charlotte County, *Virginia*.)

Old Virginia *Roaſt Pig*✻

A FAT Pig about three Weeks old is beſt for a Roaſt. Waſh it out thoroughly inſide and out. Chop the Liver fine with Bread-crumbs, Onions, Parſley, Pepper, Salt, and Potatoes boiled and maſhed. Make into a Paſte with Butter and Egg. Put the Stuffing into the Pig and ſew it up. Put in a Baking-pan with a little Water and roaſt over a bright Fire, baſting well with Butter; rub frequently, alſo, with a Piece of Lard tied in a clean Rag. When thoroughly done, lay the Pig Back up in a Diſh, and put a red Apple or pickled Mango in the Mouth. Make a Sauce with ſome of the Stuffing, a Glaſs of Wine, and ſome of the Dripping. Serve with the roaſt Pig, and alſo in a Gravy Boat.

(Old Recipe from *Highland Springs*.)

Pork Pot Pie

A Favorite Chriſtmas *Diſh with* Virginia *Negroes*

CHINES and Spare-ribs are generally uſed for this Diſh, but any Part of lean Pork will anſwer. Crack the Bones and cut into Pieces two Inches long. Line the Pot with Paſtry. Put in the Meat,

Meat, ſprinkle with Salt and Pepper, then a Layer of parboiled *Iriſh* Potatoes, ſliced, and ſo continue until the Pot is nearly full. Then pour in a Quart of cold Water and put on the upper Cruſt, cutting a ſmall round Hole out of the Middle of the Cruſt, through which you can pour hot Water ſhould the Gravy boil away too faſt. Put on the Cover of the Pot and boil about two Hours. When done, remove the upper Cruſt carefully, turn out the Meat and Gravy into a Bowl, and take out the lower Cruſt. Put this upon a hot Diſh, put the Meat and Potatoes upon it, pour the Gravy over it, and cover with the top Cruſt. This can be browned by holding over it a red-hot Oven Lid or Stove Plate.

(Old Recipe, *Richmond, Virginia.*)

Cheſs Cakes*

CREAM one Pound of Butter and one Pound of Sugar well together. Beat the Yolks of twelve Eggs light in Color and add to the Butter and Sugar. Put in one-eighth Teaſpoon of Salt and ſtir in three-fourths of a Cup of good white Wine. Bake in ſmall Paſtry Shells rolled thin in Muffin Tins. Fill the Shells about three-fourths full. Bake in a moderately hot Oven. Serve cold. Will keep for ſeveral Days in a cool Place.

(Old *Morgan* Family Recipe.
Prov'd *Market Square Tavern* Kitchen, 1937.)

Egg Nog*

BEAT Yolks of twelve Eggs well. Add two and a fourth Cups of Sugar and continue to beat well. Add one Quart of good Brandy, one Pint of
Jamaica

Jamaica Rum alternately and flowly. To this add
three Quarts of heavy Cream and fold in half of the
beaten Egg Whites. Beat remaining fix Egg Whites
very ftiff and add one Cup powdered Sugar. Then
ftir lightly into this one Quart of Cream and fold
this Mixture into the other Ingredients. Let ftand
from fix to twelve Hours in a cold Place before
ferving.   (Old *Virginia* Recipe.
                              Adapted *Blair* Kitchen, 1938.)

*Fruit Cake**

CREAM one and a half Pounds of unfalted Butter, and fift in one and a half Pounds of Flour.
Beat the Yolks of eighteen Eggs very light, then
beat into them flowly a Pound and a half of Sugar,
then mix with them the ftiffly beaten Whites. Combine. Add one-fourth Pound each of finely cut
candied Orange-peel and Lemon-peel, candied
Cherries; three fourths of a Pound of finely cut
Citron and three Pounds of well-cleaned Currants
which have foaked Overnight in one Cup of Brandy.
Add the Fruits to the Batter and bake flowly in
Pans lined with well-greafed brown Paper for feveral Hours.

(Recipe prior to 1776, *Graves* and *Hatcher* Families.)

*Fruit Cake**

CREAM one Pound of Butter with one Pound
of Sugar, add the beaten Yolks of twelve
Eggs, and one Cup of Molaffes. Clean two Pounds
of Currants and two of Raifins and cut fine one
Pound of Citron, one-half Pound of blanched Almonds, one-fourth Pound of Orange-peel, one-
fourth

fourth Pound of Lemon-peel, one-half Pound of candied Cherries, one-half Pound of Figs, and ſift over them one Pound of Flour in which there are two Teaſpoons of Allſpice, two grated Nutmegs, two Teaſpoons of Cinnamon, one of Cloves, one ſcant Teaſpoon of Soda and three of baking Powder. Work the Fruits, Almonds, Flour and Spice well together before adding to Butter Mixture. Thin with one Cup of Sherry and laſtly add the beaten Egg Whites. If the Batter is too firm, add more Sherry. Fill the well-greaſed tube Pans (which have been lined with greaſed brown Paper) two-thirds full. Bake very ſlowly four or five Hours.

(Old Recipe, c-1829, *Sparta, Virginia.*)

Another Way*

FOLLOWING the above Directions make your Cake of the following Materials: one Dozen Eggs, two Pounds of Sugar, one Pound of Butter, four Pounds of Raiſins, two Pounds of Currants, one-half Pound of Citron, one-half Pound of Dates, one Teaſpoon each of Cinnamon, Cloves, Allſpice, Ginger, Nutmeg and one Pint of Sherry.

(Recipe, c-1737, *Courtland, Virginia.*)

Williamſburg *Fruit Cake*

TAKE two Pounds of ſeeded Raiſins, two Pounds of ſeedleſs Raiſins, two Pounds of Currants (white Raiſins are not so gritty and may be uſed), three fourths of a Pound of Dates, one Pound of Citron, one fourth Pound each of Lemon-peel and Orange-peel, one fourth Pound of blanched Almonds cut in long Strips, one fourth Pound of
Engliſh

English Walnuts cut fine, one half Pound of candied Cherries, one Glass of Currant Jelly. Clean and prepare these the Day before you bake your Cake. Cut Cherries and Dates in Quarters, shred Citron and other Peel. Blanch Almonds and soak in hot Water before cutting in long Slips. Mix together with the Jelly, pour over this a Pint of Peach or Apple Brandy and store in a covered Crock or Bowl Overnight.

To make the Cake: Cream one Pound of Butter with one half Pound of Sugar. Beat the Yolks of one Dozen Eggs well, and beat into them one half Pound of Sugar. Combine. Add the well-beaten Whites and mix with the Fruits. Sift together one Pound of Flour, two Teaspoons of Allspice, two Teaspoons of Cinnamon, one Teaspoon each of Nutmeg, Cloves, Mace and Salt and stir in with one Cup of Sherry. Enough Flour will be needed to make a stiff Batter. Pack firmly into tube Cake-Pans lined with greased brown Paper and steam about three Hours. Bake in a moderate Oven and test with a Straw, twenty-five Minutes should be enough. Store in covered Tins or Crocks and moisten occasionally with a little Sherry and the Cakes will keep indefinitely.

(The Author's own Recipe.
Adapted from a *Virginia* Recipe, c-1723.)

A rich Fruit Cake*

HAVE the following Articles prepared, before you begin the Cake: four Pounds of Flour dried and sifted, four Pounds of Butter, washed to free it from Salt, two Pounds of Loaf-sugar, pounded,

pounded, a quarter of a Pound of Mace, the ſame of Nutmegs powdered; waſh four Pounds of Currants clean, pick and dry them; blanch one Pound of ſweet Almonds, and cut them in very thin Slices; ſtone two Pounds of Raiſins, cut them in two, and ſtrew a little Flour over to prevent their ſticking together, and two Pounds of Citron ſliced thin; break thirty Eggs, ſeparating the Yelks and Whites; work the Butter to a Cream with your Hand—put in alternately, Flour, Sugar, and the Froth from both Whites and Yelks, which muſt be beaten ſeparately, and only the Froth put in. When all are mixed and the Cake looks very light, add the Spice, with half a Pint of Brandy, the Currants and Almonds: butter the Mould well, pour in Part of the Cake, ſtrew over it ſome Raiſins and Citron —do this until all is in: ſet it in a well-heated Oven: when it has riſen, and the Top is coloured, cover it with Paper; it will require three Hours' baking— it muſt be iced.

(Mrs. *Randolph's* Virginia Houſewife, 1831.)

White Fruit Cake*

CREAM one half Pound of Butter with one Pound of Sugar, add four well-beaten Egg Yolks. Cut one Pound of blanched Almonds in fine Strips and the following Fruits in ſmall Pieces: one fourth Pound of candied Cherries, one half Pound of candied Pineapple, one half Pound of Citron, one Pound of white Raiſins. Dredge Fruit well with Part of one Pound of Flour, add remaining Flour and one ſmall Cup of Sherry alternately.

Stir

Stir in one half Pound of grated Cocoanut and the floured Fruit. Fold in the well-beaten Egg Whites. Bake in a flow Oven about four Hours.

(Recipe, c-1830, from *Richmond, Virginia.*)

Another Way*

SIFT one Pound of Flour with one Teafpoonful of Soda, two Teafpoonfuls Cream of Tartar. Cream one-half Pound of Butter, add one Pound white Sugar, and beat it awhile; then add the well-beaten Whites of twelve Eggs and the Flour. After beating the Batter fufficiently, add about one third of the Fruit, referving the Reft to add in Layers, as you put the Batter in the Cake-moulds. For the Fruit ufe two Pounds Citron, cut in thin, long Strips; two Pounds Almonds, blanched and cut in Strips and one large Cocoanut, grated. Bake flowly and carefully, as you do other Fruit Cake.

(Traditional *Virginia* Recipe.)

To make Mince Pies the beft Way*

TAKE three Pounds of Suet, fhred very fine, and chopped as fmall as poffible, two Pounds of Raifins, ftoned and chopped as fine as poffible, two Pounds of Currants, nicely picked, wafhed, rubbed and dried at the Fire, half a hundred of fine Pippins, pared, cored and chopped fmall, half a Pound of fine Sugar, pounded fine, a quarter of an Ounce of Mace, a quarter of an Ounce of Cloves, two large Nutmegs; all beat fine, put all together into a great Pan, and mix it well together with half a Pint of Brandy, and half a Pint of Sack; put
it

it down close in a Stone-pot, and it will keep good
four Months. When you make your Pies, take a
little Dish, something bigger than a Soup-plate, lay
a very thin Crust all over it, lay a thin Layer of
Meat, and then a thin Layer of Citron cut very
thin, then a Layer of Mince-meat, and a thin Layer
of Orange-peel cut thin, over that a little Meat,
squeeze half the Juice of a fine *Seville* Orange or
Lemon, and pour in three Spoonfuls of red Wine;
lay on your Crust, and bake it nicely. These Pies
eat finely cold. If you make them in little Patties,
mix your Meat and Sweetmeats accordingly. If you
chuse Meat in your Pies, parboil a Neat's Tongue,
peel it, and chop the Meat as fine as possible, and
mix with the Rest; or two Pounds of the Inside of
a Sirloin of Beef boiled.

(Mrs. *Hannah Glasse's* Art of Cookery, *London*, 1774.)

To make Mincemeat for Pies*

BOIL either Calves' or Hogs' Feet till perfectly
tender, rub them through a Colander; when
cold, pass them through again, and it will come out
like pearl Barley; take one Quart of this, one of
chopped Apples, the same of Currants, washed and
picked, Raisins stoned and cut, of good brown
Sugar, Suet nicely chopped, and Cider, with a Pint
of Brandy; add a Teaspoonful of pounded Mace,
one of Cloves and of Nutmegs; mix all these together intimately. When the Pies are to be made,
take out as much of this Mixture as may be neces-
sary: to each Quart of it, add a Teaspoonful of
pounded black Pepper, and one of Salt; this
greatly improves the Flavour, and can be better
mixed

mixed with a ſmall Portion than with the whole
Maſs. Cover the Moulds with Paſte, put in a Suffi-
ciency of Mincemeat, cover the Top with Citron,
ſliced thin, and lay on it a Lid garniſhed around
with Paſte cut in fanciful Shapes. They may be
eaten either hot or cold, but are beſt when hot.

(Mrs. *Randolph's* Virginia Houſewife, 1831.)

Mince Pies*

TAKE two Pounds of Beef, two and a half of
Beef-ſuet, twelve large Apples, two Pounds of
Raiſins ſtoned and chopped, two Pounds of Currants, half an Ounce of Cinnamon, one Nutmeg,
half a Pound of brown Sugar; half an Ounce of
Cloves, a ſmall Quantity of Mace, one Pound of
Citron not cut up very fine, one Quart of Brandy,
one of Wine—the half of theſe Ingredients, that is
the half of each of them, will do for a ſmall Family—if the Weather is cool they will keep ſome
Time. (Manuſcript Cook Book prior to 1839, *Morton* Family
of *Charlotte* County, *Virginia*.)

Mince Pies*

TAKE three Pounds of Suet ſhred very fine &
chopped as ſmall as poſſible, two Pounds of
Raiſins ſtoned & well chopped, two Pounds of Currants nicely picked, waſhed & rubbed & dried at
the Fire, half a Hundred of fine Pippins pared,
cored & chopped ſmall, half a Pound of fine Sugar,
a quarter of an Ounce of Mace, a quarter of an
Ounce of Cloves, two large Nutmegs all beat fine.
Put all together into a great Pan & mix it well with
half

half a Pint of Brandy, half a Pint of Sack, put it down close in a Stone Pot & it will keep good four Months. When you bake your Pies take a little Dish something bigger than a Soup-plate & lay a thin Crust all over it, lay a thin Layer of Meat & then a thin Layer of Citron cut very thin, then a Layer of Mincemeat, & then a thin Layer of Orange-peel cut thin, over that a little Meat, & pour in three Spoonfuls of red Wine, lay on your Crust, & bake it nicely. These Pies eat finely cold. If you chuse Meat in your Pies chop in two or three Pounds of a Sirloin of Beef boiled.

(Manuscript Cook Book. *Charlottesville,* 1836.
Owned by Mrs. *Virginia Grasty Griffin.*)

Mince Meat for Pies*

SIMMER two Pounds of Beef slowly until tender; cool and chop fine. Mix with it two Pounds of stoned Raisins; two Pounds of seedless Raisins; two Pounds of cleaned Currants; one Pound of finely cut Citron; one and a half Pounds of finely cut candied Lemon-peel; four Pounds of Apples which have been peeled, cored and cut fine; two Pounds of finely chopped Beef-suet; two Pounds of light brown Sugar; one Tablespoon each of Cloves and Mace; two Tablespoons of Cinnamon; two grated Nutmegs and one Teaspoon of Salt. Mix all together well, add one Pint of Brandy. Store in a covered stone Jar in a cool Place.

(*Custis & Lee* Family Recipe, c-1760.
From *Chester, Virginia.*)

Plumb

Plumb Cake—Mrs. Cary*—or Pudding**

TAKE one and a fourth Pounds Flour, one
Pound Sugar, one Pound Butter, twelve Eggs.
Cream the Butter and Flour together till quite
light. Beat the Yolks and Whites of Eggs feparately,
beat the Sugar into the Yolks and when light add
the Whites, then mix them with the Butter and
Flour. Put in one and a fourth Pounds ftoned Raifins, cut up, or the fame of Currants with three
Spoonfuls beaten Mace and two Wine-glaffes
French Brandy. It muft be baked in a quick Oven
and the Top muft be hot enough to turn it unlefs
covered with Paper. It is very nice as a Pudding
but too large for a moderate Company.

(Manufcript Cook Book, c-1801,
of Mrs. *Frances Bland Tucker Coalter.*
Owned by Dr. *St. George Tucker Grinnan, Richmond.*)

Plumb Porridge

THIS is a famous old *Englifh* Difh, and though
at prefent difufed in *London*, yet as there are
many Families in the Country who ftill keep up the
Cuftom of Hofpitality, and admit this among the
Entertainments of the Seafon, we fhall not leave
the Cook at a Lofs how to make it.

Chufe a fine and flefhy Leg of Beef with the
Shin, crack the Bone in feveral Places, and put it
into a clean Copper with eight Gallons of Water:
Let there be a moderate Fire; add nothing to the
Meat and Water, but let them boil together till the
Meat is ready to fall from the Bones, and the Broth

is

is very ſtrong; then ſtrain it out, preſſing the Meat hard to get out the laſt of the Gravy.

Wipe the Copper, and pour in the Broth.

Cut off the Tops and the Bottoms of Half a Dozen Penny-loaves, ſlice them, and put them into a Pot with as much of the Broth out of the Copper as will cover them; let them ſtand half an Hour to ſoak, and then ſet them over the Fire to boil.

When the Bread is thoroughly ſoft pour the Whole into the Copper to the Reſt.

Let this boil up a quarter of an Hour.

While this is doing waſh and pick five Pounds of Currants, put them in, and make it boil up again.

While the Currants are boiling in the Broth, ſtone ſix Pounds of Raiſins, and a Pound and half of Prunes, put theſe in, and let them boil till they are plumped up and perfectly tender.

Then put in ten Blades of Mace, a Dozen and a half of Cloves, and half an Ounce of Nutmegs, all bruiſed together in a Mortar.

When the Spices have boiled up two or three Times take away the Fire, and let the Whole cool: When it is ſo cool that it can be taſted put in three Pounds of double-refined Sugar powdered, ſome Baſket Salt, and a Quart of Sack.

Stir it all about, and then taſte it. The Salt is the nice Article; take Care that it be neither briny nor inſipid; when it is rightly ſeaſoned put in a Quart of red Port Wine, and ſqueeze in three Lemons.

Stir all up very well together, and taſte it once again to ſee if it be rightly ſeaſoned: The Palate muſt judge of this; if there want more Wine, more Sugar, or more Lemon Juice, add theſe till it is right;

right; if it be too ſharp a little Sugar takes that off, and if too ſweet the Juice of Lemon is a Remedy for that: When it is thus well ſuited to the Palate, ladle it out into earthen Pans, and ſet it by: A proper Quantity is to be heated occaſionally, and ſent up to Table.

The *French* laugh outrageouſly at this old *Engliſh* Diſh, and to be ſure it is an odd Medley: It puts one in Mind of thoſe famous Medicines of Antiquity, the *Mithridate* and *Venice* Treacle, into which the Inventors ſtrove to put every Thing that was good, without conſulting how the ſeveral Things would agree with one another; there are, however, yet many good old *Engliſh* Palates which are well affected to the cordial Broth.

(Mrs. *Bradley's* Britiſh Houſewife, *London.*)

Plumb Pudding✽

PUT in a ſtone Crock or large Bowl one Pound of Currants, one Pound of *Sultana* Raiſins, one half Pound of Orange-peel, one half Pound of Lemon-peel, one half Pound of Citron and one quarter of a Pound of Walnuts all chopped fine. Pour over this one Cupful of good Brandy and cover well. Soak Overnight. Mix one Pound of ground Suet, one half Pound of ſifted Bread-crumbs, one Teaſpoon Salt, one Pound of brown Sugar, one half Pound of Flour with one Teaſpoon Cinnamon, and one fourth Teaſpoon each of Nut-meg, Mace, Ginger and Cloves. Beat eight Eggs well. Stir all your Pudding very well together. Pour into buttered Molds, tie down with a clean ſcalded Cloth

Cloth and boil gently for ten Hours but do not let
the Water boil over it.

This Pudding will keep indefinitely, especially
if moistened with Brandy. It should be reheated
for three Hours in boiling Water and served with
Hard Sauce. (The Author's own Recipe.
Adapted from a *Virginia* Recipe, c-1725.)

Christmas *Pudding*⁕

THIS Pudding is made like the Preceding but
with the following Ingredients: One Pound of
Beef-suet; one Pound of seeded Raisins; one Pound
of *Sultana* Raisins; one Pound of Currants; one
Pound of brown Sugar; one half Pound blanched
and chopped *Jordan* Almonds; one half Pound
each of candied Lemon-peel and Orange-peel; one
half Pound of Citron; three fourths of a Pound of
fine Bread-crumbs; one fourth of a Pound of Flour;
two Teaspoons each of Cinnamon, Cloves and Nutmeg, twelve Eggs and one Pint of Brandy.

(Old Recipe, *Richmond, Virginia.* Prov'd.)

Plumb *Pudding*⁕

ONE Pound of Flour—half a Pound of Butter,
half a Pound of Sugar, two Whites and eight
Yolks of Eggs, half Pound of Raisins stoned and
cut up. The Flour and Butter rubbed well together, the Eggs and Sugar beaten tite together,
one Pint of Milk, the Flour, Butter and Sugar
mixed all and beat them well together dip a Cloth
in boiling Water flour it thickly; pour it in, tie it
up

up—put in a Pot that boils quickly; it muſt not ceaſe boiling a Moment—keep turning the Bag—leſt the Fruit ſettle—Two and a half Hours will boil it. Uſe Butter, Sugar and Wine Sauce.

(Manuſcript Cook Book, prior 1839, *Morton* Family
of *Charlotte* County, *Virginia*.)

Plumb Pudding

TAKE a Pound of beſt Flour, ſift it and make it up before Sunriſe—with ſix Eggs beaten light—a large Spoonfull of good Yeaſt and as much Milk as will make it the Conſiſtance of Bread—let it riſe well, knead into it half a Pound of Butter, a grated Nutmeg, one Pound of Raiſins, ſtoned and chopped up, mix all togather, wet the Cloth, flower it, tie looſly, ſo the Pudding may have Room to riſe. The Raiſins ſhould be rubbed in Flower.

(Manuſcript Cook Book, prior 1839, *Morton* Family
of *Charlotte* County, *Virginia*.)

Cold Sauſe*

MIX an equal Quantity of freſh Butter and pounded Sugar—Cream together—Nutmeg or Lemmon Drop if you like, colour it with the Sirrup of Strawberries or Damſons Preſerves. Set it in the Icehouſe untill cold enough to cut with a Knife.

(Manuſcript Cook Book, prior 1839, *Morton* Family
of *Charlotte* County, *Virginia*.)

Fine Plumb Pudding*

TAKE a Pound of Flour, one half Pound Butter, one half Pound Sugar, eight Yolks and two Whites of Eggs, one Pint of Milk, one half Pound
Currants

Currants or Raifins, ftoned (tho three-fourths will make it better), one half a Nutmeg. The Flour and Butter muft be rubbed together. The Milk, Flour and Butter then mixed together and beat light. The Eggs and Sugar beat together and then the other Ingredients all mingled and beat till quite light. Flour the Bag and put them in. The Pot muft boil briſkly and muft not be ſuffered to ceaſe for a Moment. Keep turning the Bag leaſt the Fruit ſettle to one Side. Two and half Hours will boil it. Butter and Wine with a Part of the Sugar weighed for the Pudding for Sauce, a Tea-kettle of Water ſhould be kept boiling to repleniſh the Pot if neceſſary.

(Manuſcript Cook Book, c-1801,
of Mrs. *Frances Bland Tucker Coalter.*
Owned by Dr. *St. George Tucker Grinnan, Richmond.*)

Plumb Pudding—Mrs. C. Jones*

TAKE one Pound grated Bread, one Pound Suet, two Pounds Plums, eight Eggs, Flour and Milk enough to make it of a proper Conſiſtence. Add a ſmall Quantity of Mace and Citron, a Glaſs of F. [*French*] Brandy and one of Wine. It will require four or five Hours to boil.

(Manuſcript Cook Book, c-1801,
of Mrs. *Frances Bland Tucker Coalter.*
Owned by Dr. *St. George Tucker Grinnan, Richmond.*)

Williamſburg *Plum Pudding**

MIX together one Pound of ground Beef-ſuet; one Pound of Currants; two Pounds ſeeded and cut Raiſins; one Pound of Figs cut fine; one Pound of finely-cut blanched Almonds; and one Pound

Pound of fine dry Bread-crumbs. Dredge over the Fruits ʃome Flour mixed with one Teaʃpoon of All-ʃpice, one half Teaʃpoon of Salt, two Teaʃpoons of Ginger and two grated Nutmegs. Beat the Yolks of twelve Eggs very light and ʃlowly beat in one Pound of brown Sugar, mix with well-beaten Whites of Eggs. Combine both, then thin with two Cups of ʃweet Milk, one and one half Cup of Wine. Pack into ʃmall tin Molds which are well greaʃed and floured. Fill to one Inch of Top and put on a tight Cover. Stand in boiling Water for ʃix Hours. Will keep any Length of Time. Reheat in boiling Water to ʃerve.

(Old *Virginia* Recipe. Prov'd *Blair* Kitchen, 1938.)

To make a Yorkʃhire Chriʃtmas *Pie*

FIRST make a good ʃtanding Cruʃt, let the Wall and Bottom be very thick; bone a Turkey, a Gooʃe, a Fowl, a Partridge, and a Pigeon. Seaʃon them all very well, take half an Ounce of Mace, half an Ounce of Nutmegs, a quarter of an Ounce of Cloves, and half an Ounce of black Pepper, all beat fine together, two large Spoonfuls of Salt, and then mix them together. Open the Fowls all down the Back, and bone them; firʃt the Pigeon, then the Partridge, cover them; then the Fowl, then the Gooʃe, and then the Turkey, which muʃt be large; ʃeaʃon them all well firʃt, and lay them in the Cruʃt, ʃo as it will look only like a whole Turkey; then have a Hare ready caʃed, and wiped with a clean Cloth. Cut it to Pieces; that is joint it; ʃeaʃon it, and lay it as cloʃe as you can on one Side; on the

other

other Side Woodcocks, Moor Game, and what Sort of wild Fowl you can get. Seaſon them well, and lay them cloſe; put at leaſt four Pounds of Butter into the Pie, then lay on your Lid, which muſt be a very thick one, and let it be well baked. It muſt have a very hot Oven, and will take at leaſt four Hours.

This Cruſt will take a Buſhel of Flour. In this Chapter you will ſee how to make it. Theſe Pies are often ſent to *London* in a Box as Preſents; therefore the Walls muſt be well built.

(Mrs. *Hannah Glaſſe's* Art of Cookery, *London*, 1774.)

An

An Account of the BOOKS consulted in this WORK:

The Art of COOKERY made plain and eafy, by a Lady. [Mrs. *Hannah Glaffe*]. *London*, 1774. (Owned by *Harvard* Univerfity, *Cambridge, Maffachufetts*.)

The *Britifh* HOUSEWIFE: or, The Cook, Houfekeeper's and Gardiner's Companion . . . by Mrs. *Martha Bradley*. *London*, printed for *S. Crowder* and *H. Woodgate* . . . [n. d.]. (Owned by Inftitute for Refearch in Social Science, *Chapel Hill, North Carolina*.)

A Collection of above three hundred Receipts in COOKERY, PHYSICK and SURGERY for the Ufe of all good Wives, tender Mothers, and careful Nurfes, by feveral Hands. *London*, printed for *Henry Lintot*, 1749. (Owned by *Harvard* Univerfity, *Cambridge, Maffachufetts*.)

The compleat City and Country COOK: or accomplifh'd Houfewife, by *Charles Carter*. *London*, printed for *A. Betteſworth* and *C. Hitch*, 1732. (Owned by *Harvard* Univerfity, *Cambridge, Maffachufetts*.)

The compleat HOUSEWIFE: or, accomplifh'd Gentlewoman's Companion: being a Collection of upwards of fix Hundred of the moft approved Receipts, by *E. Smith*. Ninth Edition. *London*, printed for *J. and J. Pemberton*, 1739. (Owned by *Harvard* Univerfity, *Cambridge, Maffachufetts*.)

The Compleat HOUSEWIFE: or, accomplifh'd Gentlewoman's Companion: being a Collection of feveral Hundred of the moft approved Receipts . . . by *E. Smith*. Collected from the fifth Edition. *Williamſburg*, printed and fold by *William Parks*, 1742. (Firft *American* Book on Cookery. Copy —one of four extant—owned by *Colonial Williamſburg*, Incorporated.)

The court and country CONFECTIONER: or, The Houfe-Keeper's Guide; to a more fpeedy, plain, and familiar Method of of underftanding the whole Art of Confectionary, Paftry, Diftilling, and the Making of fine flavoured *Englifh* Wines from all Kinds of Fruits, Herbs and Flowers . . . by an ingenious Foreigner, now head Confectioner to the *Spanifh* Ambaffador in *England. London*, printed for *G. Riley* and *A. Cooke* . . . 1770. (Owned by Mr. and Mrs. *George P. Coleman, Tucker* Houfe, *Williamfburg.*)

Directions for COOKERY in its various Branches, by Mifs *Leflie.* [*Philadelphia, E. L. Carey & A. Hart,* 1838]. (Owned by Mrs. *H. D. Cole, Williamfburg.*)

HOUSEKEEPING in old *Virginia.* Containing Contributions from two hundred and fifty of *Virginia's* noted Housewives, diftinguifhed for their Skill in the culinary Art and other Branches of domeftic Economy. Edited by *Marion Cabell Tyree* . . . *Louisville, Kentucky, John P. Morton & Company,* 1890. (Owned by Mifs *Emma Lou Barlow, Williamfburg.* With manufcript notes added.)

THE LADY'S COMPANION. Containing upwards of three thoufand different Receipts in every Kind of Cookery: and thofe the beft and moft fafhionable; being four Times the Quantity of any Book of this Sort . . . The fixth Edition, with large Additions. *London,* printed for *J. Hodges* . . . and *R. Baldwin,* 1753. (This Copy, owned by Mifs *Anna Maria Dandridge* in 1756, now owned by Mrs. *Neville Mitchell Smith* of *York, Pennfylvania.*)

The *London* Art of COOKERY, and Houfekeeper's complete Affiftant, on a new Plan . . . by *John Farley.* Fourth Edition. *London,* printed for *J. Scatcherd* and *J. Whitaker,* 1787. (Owned by Mrs. *E. L. Bemifs, Brookbury, Chefterfield* County, *Virginia.*)

Virginia COOKERY-BOOK. Compiled by *Mary Stuart Smith. New York, Harper,* 1885. (Owned by Univerfity of *Virginia.*)

Virginia COOKERY BOOK: traditional Recipes. *Richmond Virginia* League of Women Voters, *Richmond,* 1922. (Owned by Mrs. *W. P. Clements, Richmond, Virginia.*)

The *Virginia* HOUSEWIFE: or, methodical Cook, by Mrs. *Mary Randolph* . . . Stereotype Edition, with Amendments and Additions. *Baltimore, Plafkitt & Cugle,* [1831]. (Owned by Univerfity of *Virginia.*) The

The *Virginia* HOUSEWIFE: or, the methodical Cook. *Philadelphia*, published by *E. H. Butler & Company*, 1855. (Owned by *Colonial Williamsburg*, Incorporated.)

The whole DUTY OF A WOMAN: or, an infallible Guide to the fair Sex. Containing Rules, Directions, and Obfervations, for their Conduct and Behaviour through all Ages and Circumftances of Life, as Virgins, Wives, or Widows. With Directions, how to obtain all ufeful and fafhionable Accomplifhments fuitable to the Sex. In which are comprifed all Parts of good HOUSEWIFERY, particularly Rules and Receipts in every Kind of Cookery. *London*, printed for *T. Read*, 1737. (Owned by *Harvard* Univerfity, *Cambridge, Maffachufetts.*)

Manufcript Cook Book of *Englifh* WINES AND COOKERY. c. 1740. (Owned by *Colonial Williamfburg*, Incorporated.)

Manufcript COOK BOOK. c. 1801, of Mrs. *Frances Tucker Coalter*, of *Williamfburg*. (Owned by Dr. *St. George Tucker Grinnan, Richmond, Virginia.*)

Manufcript COOK BOOK. c. 1836, *Charlottefville, Virginia.* (Owned by Mrs. *Virginia Grafty Griffin, Richmond, Virginia.*)

Manufcript RECIPES. c. 1837, of Mrs. *Elizabeth Labbé Cole.* (Owned by Mrs. *H. D. Cole, Williamfburg, Virginia.*)

Manufcript COOK BOOK, prior to 1839, of the *Morton* Family of *Charlotte* County, *Virginia.* (Depofited at the College of *William and Mary, Williamfburg.*)

Manufcript COOK BOOK. c. 1825 of Mifs *Margaret* [*Margaretta*] *Prentis* of *Williamfburg.* (Owned by *Robert H. Webb*, Efq., Univerfity of *Virginia.*)

Recipes contributed by Mrs. *Doris Morgan Macomber* (who conducted the experimental Kitchen in the *Market Square Tavern*, under the Direction of *John Green*, Efq., and Mifs *Alice Carter*), Mrs. *Archibald Bolling Shepperfon*, Mifs *Jeane Lee*, Mrs. *Frank Armiftead*, Mrs. *H. B. Stryker*, Mrs. *L. W. Lane*, Jr., Mrs. *Philip Nelfon*, Mifs *Tony Bracher*, Mifs *Genevieve Yoft*, Mrs. *H. Norton Mafon*, Mrs. *Sarah E. Sumner*, Mrs. *Sybil Tripp*, Mifs *Mildred Mofs*, Mrs. *Gracie Mafon* and *Robert A. Lancafter*, Efq.

THE

THE
INDEX.

Chestnut

Peel

Quail.

A

A Note to the READER.

EVEN as many of the Recipes which it contains are taken or adapted from the firſt *American* Cook Book, which was printed at *Williamſburg* in 1742 by *William Parks*, ſo is this Volume a typographical Adaptation from *Parks'* "*The Compleat Houſewife, or Accompliſh'd Gentle-*"*woman's Companion.*" Even as many Additions and Elaborations have been made in the Text, ſo have typographic Adjuſtments been made; yet the typographic Style and Spirit is that of *Parks*, the firſt *Virginia* Printer.

The Body of the Text is ſet in old-ſtyle *Caſlon* Types, eleven Point on twelve Point Body—the cloſeſt available Approach to the *Long Primer* uſed by *Parks*. The Ornaments are, for the moſt Part, Reproductions of thoſe employed by *Parks*. Though the Text is ſet on the *Monotype*, it has been hand-ſpaced and compoſed by *Curtis Woodcock*, of the *Dietz Printing Company*, who alſo ſet the diſplay Types.

The quoted Material, from many varying printed and manuſcript Sources, has been capitalized and *italicized* by the uniform Syſtem or Style which *Parks* would have adhered to under ſimilar Circumſtances. It is believed that this
Volume

Volume will average no more Errors and Mifcalculations than Authenticity demands.

The Book is printed on an efpecially made Paper. It reprefents a frank and careful Reconftruction of the Paper manufactured by *William Parks* at his Mill near *Williamfburg* and carries both his own Mark and the Arms of the *Virginia* Colony.

The Illuftrations, by *Elmo Jones*, of *Richmond*, *Virginia*, are newly drawn in fimulation of the Technique of eighteenth Century Engravers and are reproduced with Line Cuts.

❁❁❁❁❁

❁❁❁

❁